SCOTT FORESMAN · ADDISON WESLEY

Mathematics

Authors

Randall I. Charles

Janet H. Caldwell
Mary Cavanagh
Dinah Chancellor
Alma B. Ramirez

Warren Crown

Jeanne F. Ramos
Kay Sammons
Jane F. Schielack

Francis (Skip) Fennell

William Tate
Mary Thompson
John A. Van de Walle

Consulting Mathematicians

Edward J. Barbeau
Professor of Mathematics
University of Toronto
Toronto, Ontario, Canada

David M. Bressoud
DeWitt Wallace Professor of
    Mathematics
Macalester College
Saint Paul, Minnesota

Gary Lippman
Professor of Mathematics and
    Computer Science
California State University
    Hayward
Hayward, California

Editorial Offices: Glenview, Illinois • Parsippany, New Jersey • New York, New York

Sales Offices: Needham, Massachusetts • Duluth, Georgia • Glenview, Illinois
Coppell, Texas • Ontario, California • Mesa, Arizona

Reading Consultants

Peter Afflerbach
Professor and Director of
  The Reading Center
University of Maryland
College Park, Maryland

Donald J. Leu
John and Maria Neag
  Endowed Chair in Literacy and Technology
University of Connecticut
Storrs, Connecticut

Reviewers

Donna McCollum Derby
Teacher
Kernersville Elementary School
Kernersville, North Carolina

Terri Geaudreau
Title I Math Facilitator
Bemiss Elementary
Spokane, Washington

Sister Helen Lucille Habig, RSM
Assistant Superintendent of
  Catholic Schools
Archdiocese of Cincinnati
Cincinnati, Ohio

Kim Hill
Teacher
Hayes Grade Center
Ada, Oklahoma

Martha Knight
Teacher
Oak Mountain Elementary
Birmingham, Alabama

Catherine Kuhns
Teacher
Country Hills Elementary
Coral Springs, Florida

Susan Mayberger
Supervisor of English as a Second
  Language/Director of Migrant Education
Omaha Public Schools
Omaha, Nebraska

Judy Peede
Elementary Lead Math Teacher
Wake County Schools
Raleigh, North Carolina

Lynda M. Penry
Teacher
Wright Elementary
Ft. Walton Beach, Florida

Jolyn D. Raleigh
District Math Curriculum Specialist K–2
Granite School District
Salt Lake City, Utah

Vickie H. Smith
Assistant Principal
Phoenix Academic Magnet
  Elementary School
Alexandria, Louisiana

Ann Watts
Mathematics Specialist
East Baton Rouge Parish School System
Baton Rouge, Louisiana

ISBN: 0-328-03016-3

7 8 9 10 V064 09 08 07 06 05

Instant Check System
- Check, daily
- Think About It, daily
- Diagnostic Checkpoint, 9, 23, 35

 Test Prep
- Test Talk, 39
- Cumulative Review and Test Prep, 10, 24, 36

Reading For Math Success
- Math Story, 1A
- Reading for Math Success, 19

Writing in Math
- Writing in Math exercises, 22, 34

 Problem-Solving Applications, 33

Discovery CHANNEL SCHOOL Discover Math in Your World, 40

Additional Resources
- Home-School Connection, 1
- Practice Game, 2
- Enrichment, 37
- Learning with Technology, 38
- Chapter 1 Test, 41

Understanding Addition and Subtraction

Strategies for Addition Facts to 12

Strategies for Subtraction Facts to 12

Instant Check System

- Check, daily
- Think About It, daily
- Diagnostic Checkpoint, 135, 147

Test Prep

- Test Talk, 151
- Cumulative Review and Test Prep, 136, 148, 154A

Reading For Math Success

- Math Story, 4A
- Reading for Math Success, 131

Writing in Math

- Writing in Math exercises, 138, 146, 149

DK Problem-Solving Applications, 145

Discovery Discover Math in
CHANNEL Your World, 152
SCHOOL

Additional Resources

- Home-School Connection, 123
- Practice Game, 124
- Enrichment, 149
- Learning with Technology, 150
- Chapter 4 Test, 153

Instant Check System
- Check, daily
- Think About It, daily
- Diagnostic Checkpoint, 163, 179, 195

Test Prep
- Test Talk, 199
- Cumulative Review and Test Prep, 164, 180, 196

Reading For Math Success
- Math Story, 5A
- Reading for Math Success, 175

Writing in Math
- Writing in Math exercises, 178, 188, 194

Problem-Solving Applications, 193

Discovery CHANNEL SCHOOL Discover Math in Your World, 200

Additional Resources
- Home-School Connection, 155
- Practice Game, 156
- Enrichment, 197
- Learning with Technology, 198
- Chapter 5 Test, 201

CHAPTER 6

Time

CHAPTER 7

Counting to 100

Place Value, Data, and Graphs

CHAPTER 11

Addition and Subtraction Facts to 18

Two-Digit Addition and Subtraction

Instant Check System

- Check, daily
- Think About It, daily
- Diagnostic Checkpoint, 469, 485

Test Prep

- Test Talk, 489
- Cumulative Review and Test Prep, 470, 486, 492A

Reading For Math Success

- Math Story, 12A
- Reading for Math Success, 479

Writing in Math

- Writing in Math exercises, 470, 482, 484, 489, 492B

Problem-Solving Applications, 483

Discovery CHANNEL SCHOOL Discover Math in Your World, 490

Additional Resources

- Home-School Connection, 457
- Practice Game, 458
- Enrichment, 487
- Learning with Technology, 488
- Chapter 12 Test, 491

Name_____

Numbers

1 Write the missing numbers in order.

1			4				8		10
	12			15				18	

---

2 Write the number that tells how many.

      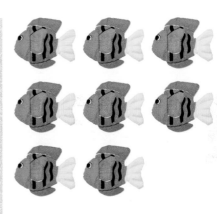

_____   _____   _____

---

3 Circle the number word that tells how many.

three   six   ten

eight   two   nine

zero   five   four

Draw pictures to show how many.

4 | | |7   5

---

5   ten   seven   one

---

6 Count backward.

Write the missing numbers.

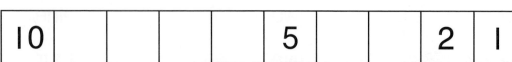

| 10 | | | | 5 | | 2 | 1 |

Name_____

Shapes and Position Words

1 Color each shape below.

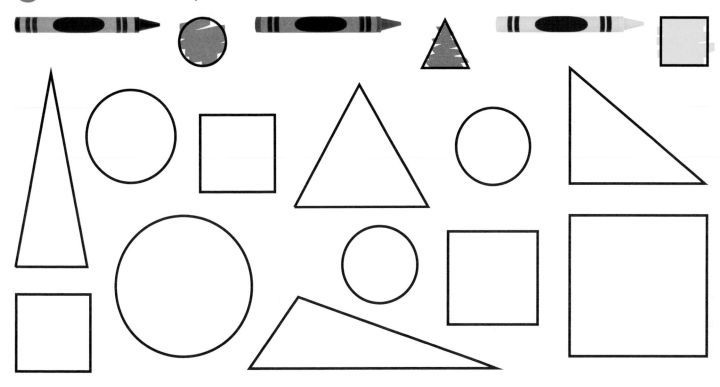

2 Listen to your teacher.
Follow the directions.

3 Listen to your teacher.
Follow the directions.

 Home Connection Your child reviewed his or her math skills to prepare for learning new skills. **Home Activity** Discuss with your child how he or she completed each of the exercises.

CHAPTER 1

Patterns and Readiness for Addition and Subtraction

Read Together

One, Two, the Cows Say, "Moo!"

A New Adaptation of an Old Rhyme, Illustrated by Carly Castillon

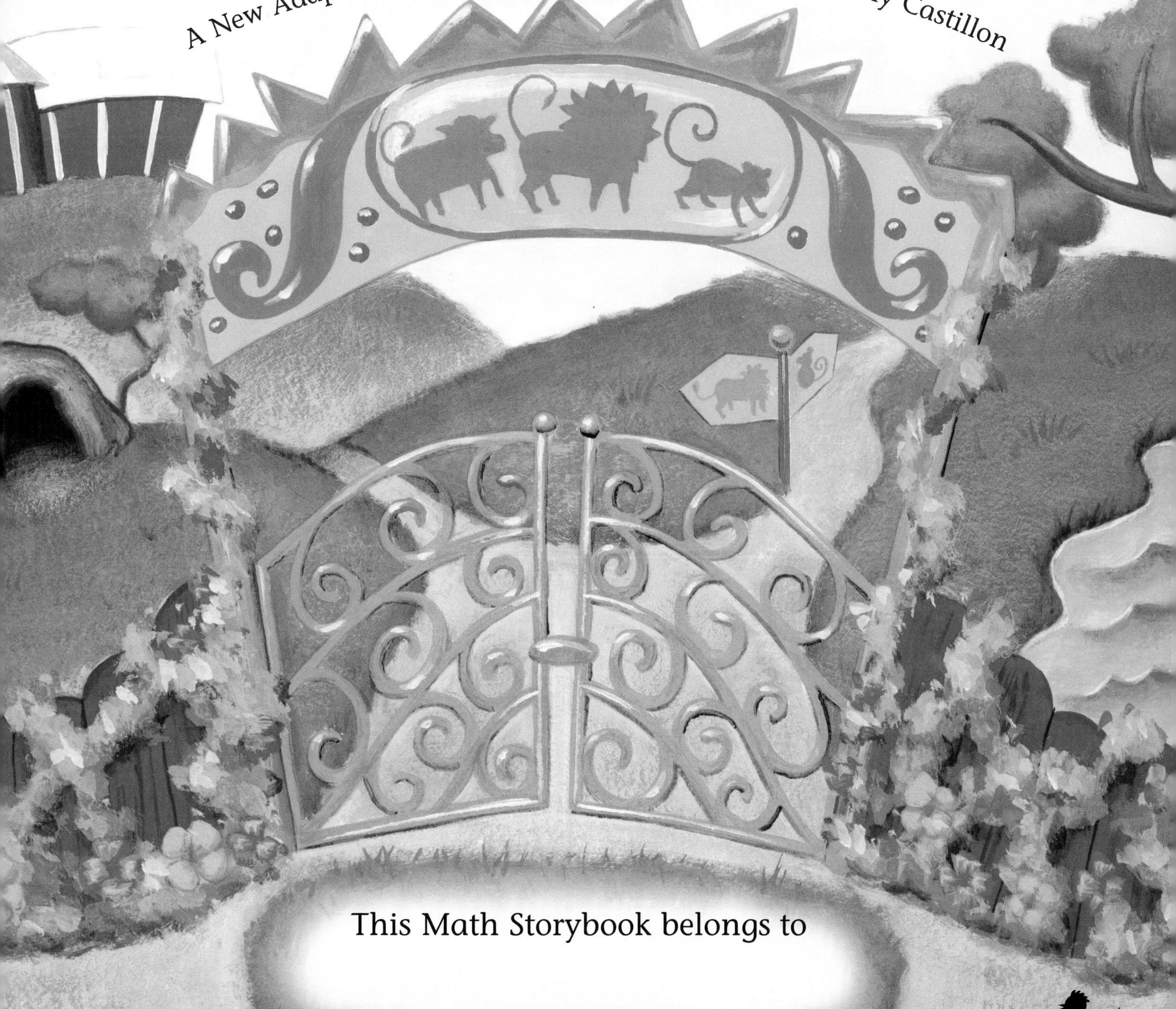

This Math Storybook belongs to

____

1A

Three, four, the lions roar.

Five, six, the monkeys do tricks.

Seven, eight, who's sitting on the gate?

Nine, ten, a big fat hen.
Now go back and count again!

Home-School Connection

Dear Family,

Today my class started Chapter 1, **Patterns and Readiness for Addition and Subtraction.** I will learn about patterns. I will also work with the numbers 6 through 12 and compare pairs of numbers. Here are some of the math words I will be learning and some things we can do to help me with my math.

Love,

_____

Math Activity to Do at Home

Help your child recognize and create simple patterns like this:

Give your child small objects with which to create patterns.

Books to Read Together

Reading math stories reinforces concepts. Look for these titles in your local library:

A Pair of Socks
By Stuart J. Murphy
(HarperCollins, 1996)

Fun with Patterns
By Peter Patilla
(The Millbrook Press, 1998)

My New Math Words

pattern A pattern has a part (a string of elements) that repeats over and over.

more than 6 is 2 more than 4.

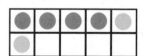

fewer than 4 is 2 fewer than 6.

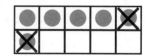

less 4 is less than 6.

greater 8 is greater than 6.

Take It to the NET
More Activities
www.scottforesman.com

one 1

Name _____

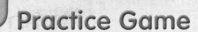
9, 10 Find the Hen!

How to Play

1. Take turns. Toss the cube. Count the dots.
2. Move your marker. If you land on a yellow space, follow the directions.
3. Keep playing until both of you find the big fat hen!

START

Go back 2

Go back 6

Go back 4

FINISH

Lose a turn ☹

Toss again ☺

Learn! Algebra

My gift shows a **pattern**. Sun, star, moon repeats over and over.

My gift does not show a pattern.

Word Bank

pattern

Check ✓

Circle the part that repeats.
Then circle the picture that comes next.

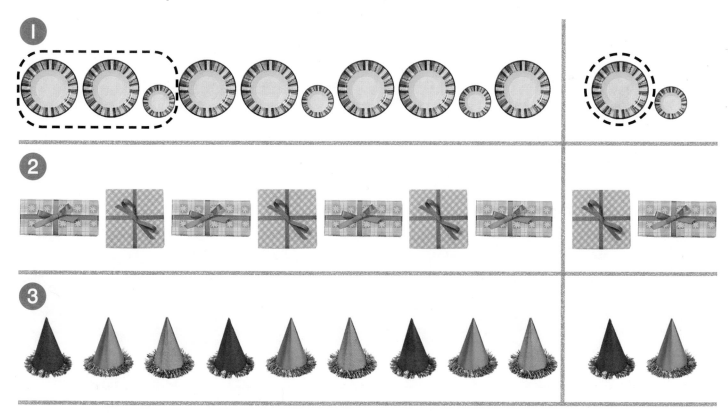

Think About It   Reasoning

How do you know what comes next in the pattern?

Chapter 1 ★ Lesson 1

three   **3**

Circle the part that repeats.

Then circle the picture that comes next.

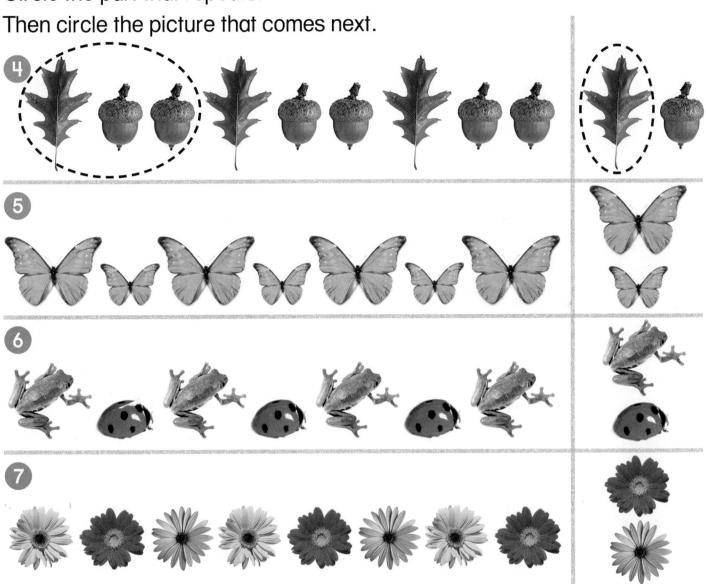

Problem Solving Algebra

8 Find the pattern. Color the white flower.

Home Connection Your child identified a pattern and then continued it.
Home Activity Make a sound pattern for your child, such as *clap hands, stomp feet, clap hands, stomp feet, clap hands, stomp feet,* and so on. Ask your child to tell what part you are repeating to make the pattern.

Name ______________________

Creating and Translating Patterns

Learn! Algebra

How is the shape pattern like the letter pattern?

How are the patterns different?

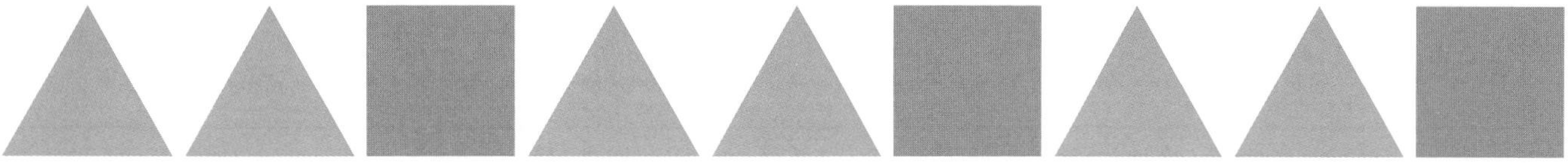

A A B A A B A A B

Check

Use pattern blocks. Make a pattern. Draw the pattern.

Then make the same pattern using letters.

1

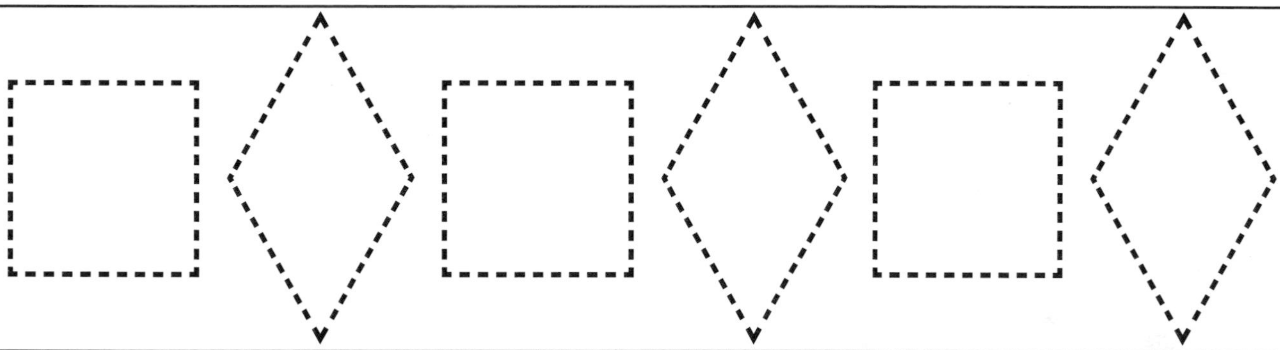

X Z X Z X Z

2

Think About It Reasoning

How did you decide which letters to use?

Use pattern blocks. Make a pattern. Draw the pattern.
Then make the same pattern using letters.

 3

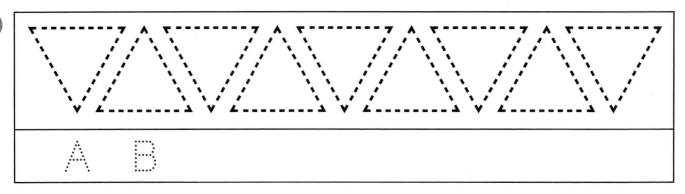

A B

4

Problem Solving Reasoning

 5 This is a growing pattern.
Draw what comes next.

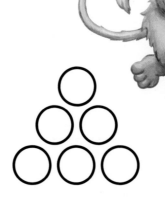

Name_____

Learn! Algebra

Lydia is placing floor tiles in a pattern.
Predict: Will she need more
blue tiles or more orange tiles?   more _____ tiles

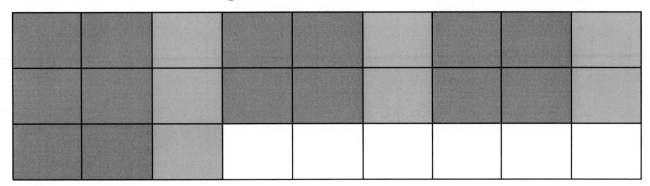

Color the rest of the floor.

How many blue tiles does it have?   18 blue tiles

How many orange tiles does it have?   9 orange tiles

Check ✓

1 Predict: Will the scarf have more
red stripes or more yellow stripes?   more _____ stripes

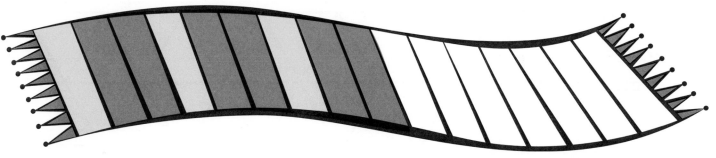

Color the rest of the scarf.

How many red stripes does it have?   _____ red stripes

How many yellow stripes does it have?   _____ yellow stripes

Think About It   Reasoning

Was your prediction correct?

2 Predict: Will the fence have more yellow boards or more purple boards?

more _____ boards

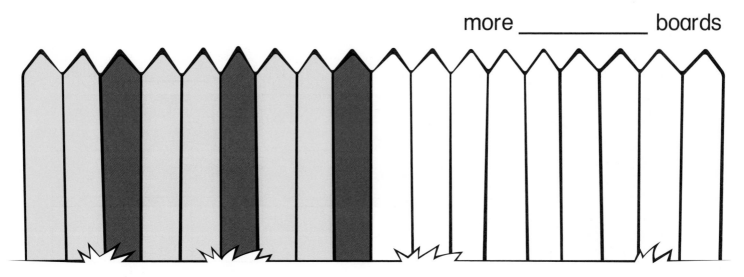

Color the rest of the fence.

How many yellow boards does it have? _____ yellow boards

How many purple boards does it have? _____ purple boards

Problem Solving   Visual Thinking

3 Color the rug to show a pattern.
Make most of the triangles green.

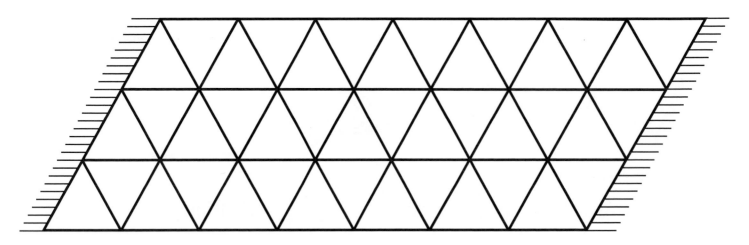

4 How many triangles are green? _____

Home Connection Your child looked at part of a pattern and made a prediction about the rest of it. **Home Activity** Draw a row of squares and color some of them in a pattern. Have your child predict which color will be used the most.

8   eight

Name_____

Circle the part that repeats.
Then circle the picture that comes next.

1
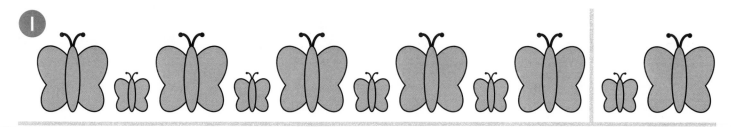

Use pattern blocks. Make a pattern. Draw the pattern.
Then make the same pattern using letters.

2

3 Predict: Will the mat have more
yellow shapes or green shapes?   more _____ shapes

Color the rest of the mat.

How many yellow shapes does it have? _____ yellow shapes

How many green shapes does it have? _____ green shapes

Name _____

1 Which part of this pattern repeats over and over?

Ⓐ 　　　Ⓒ

Ⓑ 　　　Ⓓ

2 Which letters show the same pattern as the shoes?

Ⓐ A B C D A B C D A

Ⓑ A B A B A B A B A

Ⓒ A A B A A B A A B

Ⓓ A B B A B B A B B

3 Which color will be used most in the bug?

blue	green	yellow	red
Ⓐ	Ⓑ	Ⓒ	Ⓓ

Name_____

We can show 6 in different ways.

6 is __4__ and __2__. 6 is __5__ and __1__. 6 is __6__ and __0__.

 Check ✓

Use counters and Workmat 1 to show 6 and 7.
Draw the counters. Write the numbers.

1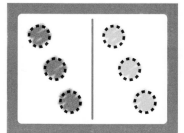

6 is __3__ and __3__.

6 is ____ and ____.

2

7 is ____ and ____.

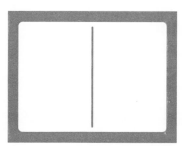

7 is ____ and ____.

Think About It   Reasoning

Did you find all of the ways to show 6?
How do you know?

Use counters and Workmat 1 to show 6 and 7.
Draw the missing counters. Write the numbers.

3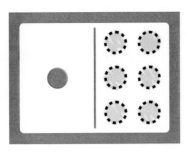

7 is __1__ and __6__.

4

6 is _____ and _____.

5

6 is _____ and _____.

6

7 is _____ and _____.

7

7 is _____ and _____.

8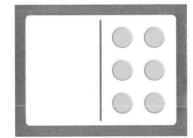

6 is _____ and _____.

Problem Solving Mental Math

Use counters. Draw the counters.
Circle **yes** or **no**.

9 Jess has 7 pennies.
Can he put the same
number in each bank?

Yes   **No**

© Pearson Education, Inc.

Name_____

Here are some different ways to show 8.

8 is 6 and 2.   8 is 7 and 1.   8 is 8 and 0.

Check ✔

Use counters and Workmat 1 to show 8 and 9.
Draw the counters. Write the numbers.

1

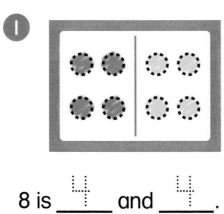

8 is __4__ and __4__.

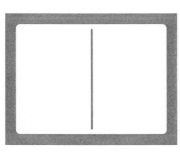

8 is ____ and ____.

2

9 is ____ and ____.

9 is ____ and ____.

Think About It   Number Sense

Is 4 and 4 the same as 3 and 5? Explain.

Use counters and Workmat 1 to show 8 and 9.
Draw the missing counters. Write the numbers.

3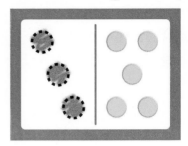

8 is __3__ and __5__.

4

9 is ____ and ____.

5

9 is ____ and ____.

6

8 is ____ and ____.

7

8 is ____ and ____.

8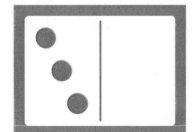

9 is ____ and ____.

Problem Solving   Visual Thinking

Write the numbers to match the picture.

9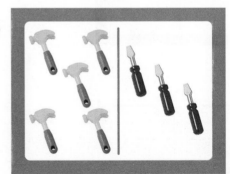

____ and ____ is ____.

14   fourteen

Name_____

Learn!

In what different ways can we show 10?

10 is 9 and 1.

10 is 8 and 2.

Check ✓

Use counters and Workmat 2 to show 10.
Draw the counters. Write the numbers.

 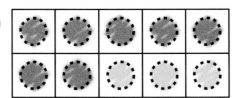

10 is __7__ and __3__.

10 is ____ and ____.

10 is ____ and ____.

 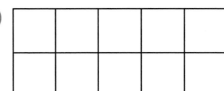

10 is ____ and ____.

Think About It Number Sense

How are these alike?
How are they different?

Use counters and Workmat 2 to show 10.
Draw the missing counters. Write the numbers.

5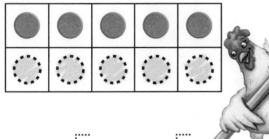

10 is __5__ and __5__.

6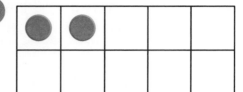

10 is ____ and ____.

7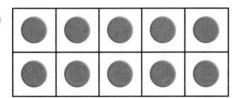

10 is ____ and ____.

8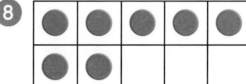

10 is ____ and ____.

9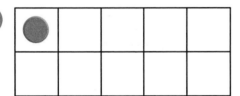

10 is ____ and ____.

10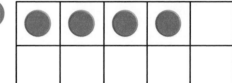

10 is ____ and ____.

Problem Solving Number Sense

11 Circle all the ways that make 10.

| 5 and 3 | 6 and 4 | 1 and 9 |

| 8 and 0 | 7 and 3 | 2 and 6 |

Home Connection Your child used a ten-frame and counters to find different ways of showing the number 10 in two parts. **Home Activity** Ask your child to draw a picture of some of the ways he or she found.

Name_____

Learn!

We can show 11 and 12 in different ways.

11 is 10 and 1.
11 is 9 and 2.

12 is 10 and 2.
12 is 9 and 3.

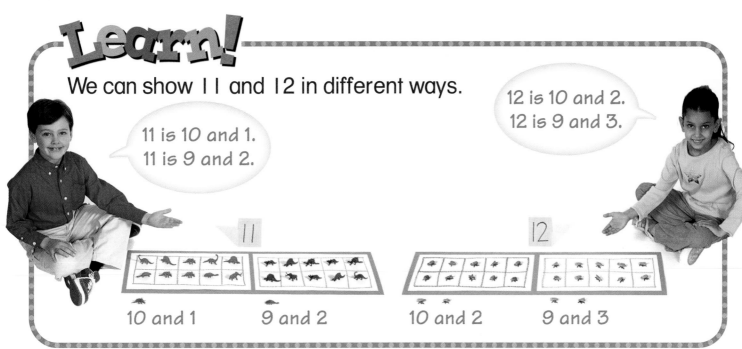

10 and 1   9 and 2   10 and 2   9 and 3

Check ✓

Use counters and Workmat 2 to show 11 and 12.
Draw the missing counters. Write the numbers.

1
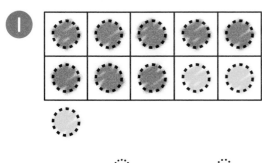

11 is __8__ and __3__.

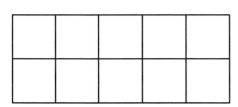

11 is ____ and ____.

2

12 is ____ and ____.

12 is ____ and ____.

Think About It   Number Sense

In what other ways can you show 12?

Use counters and Workmat 2 to show 11 and 12.
Draw the missing counters. Write the numbers.

3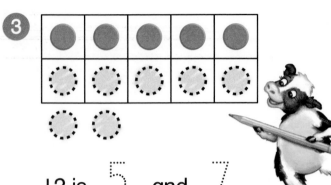

12 is __5__ and __7__.

4

11 is ____ and ____.

5

11 is ____ and ____.

6

12 is ____ and ____.

7

12 is ____ and ____.

8

11 is ____ and ____.

Problem Solving   Reasonableness

9 Glen has 5 crayons.
He says that he needs 7 more crayons
to have 11 crayons.
Does Glen's answer make sense? Explain.

18   eighteen

© Pearson Education, Inc.

Home Connection Your child used a ten-frame and counters to find
different ways of showing 11 and 12 in two parts. **Home Activity** Draw
fewer than 10 circles. Have your child draw more circles to make 11.

Name _____

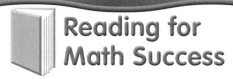

Visualize

Listen as your teacher reads this story.
Picture in your mind what is happening.

Three rabbits hopped into a garden.
They saw six big carrots.
"There are plenty for all of us," the baby said.
"How many do we each get?" asked Daddy Rabbit.
"Hmm," said Mommy, "I have an idea."

Answer these questions. Use the picture.

1 How many rabbits are there? _____

2 How many carrots are there? _____

3 Here is Mommy's idea. Did she use all of the carrots? _____

Think About It   Number Sense

What is another way that you could put
some carrots in each basket?

Listen to another story.
Picture in your mind what is happening.

Nine birds flew over the garden.
It started to rain.
Then the birds saw three houses.
"Let's fly into those houses," said one
of the birds.

4 How many birds are there? _____

5 How many houses are there? _____

6 Use counters. Show how many birds could fly
into each house.

7 Count the birds. Did all of the birds get into a house? _____

8 Use counters. Show another way that each bird
can find a house.

Home Connection Your child listened to a story and used pictures to help solve a problem. **Home Activity** Find pictures in magazines and use them to make up simple stories. Ask your child to use the pictures to show how a number of things can be separated into three groups.

Name_____

How can you put 12 eggs into 3 cartons?

Read and Understand

You need to put all 12 eggs into the cartons.
You need to put some eggs into each carton.

Plan and Solve

Use paper for cartons. Use counters for eggs.
Put some counters on each piece of paper.
Write the numbers to show one way you find.

12 is ___2___ and ___4___ and ___6___.

Look Back and Check

How do you know your answer is correct?

Check ✓

What other ways can you find?

1 12 is _____ and _____ and _____.

2 12 is _____ and _____ and _____.

Think About It   Reasoning

Is there a way to put the same number of eggs
into each carton?

Use counters.

In what different ways can you put 10 eggs into 3 cartons?

  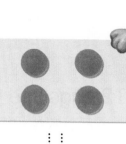 

3 10 is ___3___ and ___3___ and ___4___.

4 10 is _____ and _____ and _____.

5 10 is _____ and _____ and _____.

6 10 is _____ and _____ and _____.

Writing in Math

7 Write your own question about putting some eggs into 3 cartons. Then find ways to answer it.

_____

_____

8 _____ is _____ and _____ and _____.

9 _____ is _____ and _____ and _____.

10 _____ is _____ and _____ and _____.

 Home Connection Your child used objects to act out problems.
Home Activity Give your child 12 pennies or other items, and ask him or her to show how they can be separated into three groups.

Name _____

Use counters and Workmat 1.
Draw the missing counters. Write the numbers.

 1

8 is _____ and _____.

2
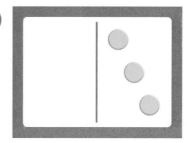

7 is _____ and _____.

Use counters and Workmat 2.
Draw the missing counters. Write the numbers.

3
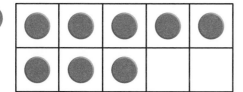

10 is _____ and _____.

4
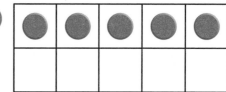

10 is _____ and _____.

5
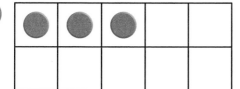

12 is _____ and _____.

6
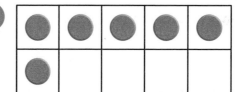

11 is _____ and _____.

Use counters. Write two ways you can
put 11 apples into 3 baskets.

7 11 is _____ and _____ and _____.

8 11 is _____ and _____ and _____.

1 Which letters show the same pattern as the presents?

Ⓐ A B C A B C A B C

Ⓑ A B A B A B A B A

Ⓒ A A B A A B A A B

Ⓓ A B C C A B C C A

---

2 What is one way you can put 10 eggs into 3 cartons?

10 is ____ and ____ and ____.

3 and 2 and 4   5 and 1 and 4   2 and 4 and 1   3 and 5 and 1
        Ⓐ   Ⓑ   Ⓒ   Ⓓ

What is the missing number?

3

9 is ____ and 5.

   2   3   4   5

   Ⓐ   Ⓑ   Ⓒ   Ⓓ

4

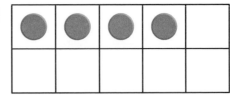

12 is 4 and ____.

 10   9   8   7

 Ⓐ   Ⓑ   Ⓒ   Ⓓ

Name_____

Learn!

We can find 1 and 2 more than a number.

●	●	●		

3

| ● | ● | ● | ○ | |
| | | | | |

3 and 1 more is 4.

| ● | ● | ● | ○ | ○ |
| | | | | |

3 and 2 more is 5.

Word Bank

more than

Check ✓

Use counters and Workmat 2.

Draw the counters. Write the numbers.

①

| ● | ● | ◌ | | |
| | | | | |

2 and 1 more is __3__.

| ● | ● | ◌ | ◌ | |
| | | | | |

2 and 2 more is __4__.

②

| ● | ● | ● | ● | ● |
| | | | | |

5 and 1 more is ____.

| ● | ● | ● | ● | ● |
| | | | | |

5 and 2 more is ____.

③

| ● | ● | ● | ● | ● |
| ● | ● | ● | | |

8 and 1 more is _____.

| ● | ● | ● | ● | ● |
| ● | ● | ● | | |

8 and 2 more is _____.

Think About It   Number Sense

What number is 1 more than 10?

What number is 2 more than 10?

Use counters and Workmat 2.
Write the numbers.

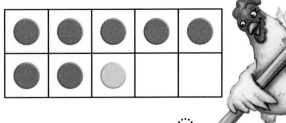 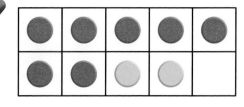

④ 7 and 1 more is _8_.   7 and 2 more is _9_.

⑤ 6 and 1 more is ____.   6 and 2 more is ____.

⑥ 9 and 1 more is ____.   9 and 2 more is ____.

⑦ 4 and 1 more is ____.   4 and 2 more is ____.

⑧ 0 and 1 more is ____.   0 and 2 more is ____.

⑨ 10 and 1 more is ____.   10 and 2 more is ____.

Problem Solving   Algebra

Use counters and Workmat 2. Write the numbers.

⑩ 7 is ____ more than 5.   ⑪ 7 is ____ more than 6.

⑫ 9 is ____ more than 8.   ⑬ 11 is ____ more than 9.

⑭ 6 is ____ more than 4.   ⑮ 10 is ____ more than 8.

Home Connection Your child used a ten-frame and counters to find numbers that are one or two more than a given number. **Home Activity** Tell your child a number less than 10, and ask him or her to say the number that is one more and then two more. Play this game on car rides.

© Pearson Education, Inc.

Name_____

We can find 1 and 2 **fewer than** a number.

●	●	●	●	●

5

●	●	●	●	✗

I fewer than 5 is 4.

●	●	●	✗	✗

2 fewer than 5 is 3.

Word Bank

fewer than

Check ✓

Use counters and Workmat 2.

Cross out the counters. Write the numbers.

❶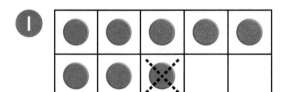

I fewer than 8 is __7__.

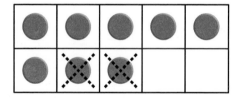

2 fewer than 8 is __6__.

❷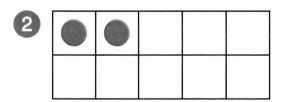

I fewer than 2 is _____.

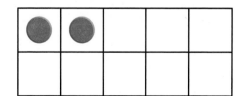

2 fewer than 2 is _____.

Think About It   Number Sense

How can you find the number that is 2 fewer
than 9 without using counters and Workmat 2?

Use counters and Workmat 2 .
Write the numbers.

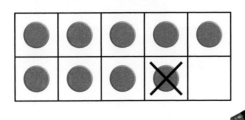 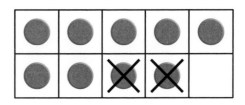

3 I fewer than 9 is _8_ .   2 fewer than 9 is _7_ .

4 I fewer than 6 is ____ .   2 fewer than 6 is ____ .

5 I fewer than 4 is ____ .   2 fewer than 4 is ____ .

6 I fewer than 7 is ____ .   2 fewer than 7 is ____ .

7 I fewer than I I is ____ .   2 fewer than I I is ____ .

8 I fewer than 3 is ____ .   2 fewer than 3 is ____ .

9 I fewer than I2 is ____ .   2 fewer than I2 is ____ .

Problem Solving   Reasoning

Circle **more than** or **fewer than**.

10 6 is I _____ 7.   **more than**   **fewer than**

11 7 is 2 _____ 5.   **more than**   **fewer than**

12 I0 is 2 _____ I2.   **more than**   **fewer than**

Home Connection Your child used a ten-frame and counters to find numbers that are one or two fewer than a given number.
Home Activity Give your child 12 or fewer paper clips or other objects. Have your child show one fewer and two fewer, and then say the numbers.

Name_____

Learn!

7 is greater than 5.
7 is less than 10.

5

7

10

Word Bank

less

greater

Check ✓

Use cubes. Circle **less** or **greater**.

1 6 is _____ than 10. (less) greater

2 12 is _____ than 5. less greater

3 3 is _____ than 5. less greater

4 11 is _____ than 10. less greater

Think About It   Reasoning

Can you find a number that is less than 5 and also
greater than 10? Explain.

Use cubes. Circle **less** or **greater**.

5 9 is _____ than 10.   (less)   greater

6 9 is _____ than 5.   less   greater

7 12 is _____ than 10.   less   greater

8 8 is _____ than 5.   less   greater

9 4 is _____ than 5.   less   greater

10 7 is _____ than 5.   less   greater

11 5 is _____ than 10.   less   greater

Problem Solving Number Sense

Use cubes. Draw lines to match.

12 | 11 | less than 10 and less than 5

| 9 | greater than 5 and less than 10

| 4 | greater than 5 and greater than 10

Home Connection Your child compared numbers to 5 and 10. **Home Activity** Name a number less than 12. Ask your child if the number is greater than or less than 10 *and* if the number is greater than or less than 5.

Name_____

We can put numbers in order.

3 is the **least** .

5 is **between** 3 and 8.

8 is the **greatest** .

Word Bank

least

between

greatest

Check ✓

Use cubes. Write the numbers in order
from least to greatest.

1

7　　　　　　4　　　　　　6

$\underline{4}$, $\underline{6}$, $\underline{7}$
least　between　greatest

2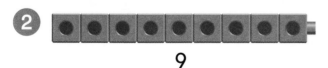

9　　　　　　2　　　　　　7

_____ , _____ , _____
least　between　greatest

Think About It Number Sense

How can you find the numbers
that are between 5 and 9?

Use cubes. Write the numbers in order
from least to greatest.

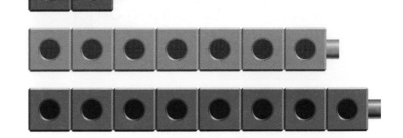

3

| 8 | 2 | 7 |

_2_ , _7_ , _8_
least between greatest

4

| 6 | 3 | 10 |

_____ , _____ , _____
least between greatest

5

| 8 | 1 | 5 |

_____ , _____ , _____
least between greatest

6

| 12 | 9 | 5 |

_____ , _____ , _____
least between greatest

7

| 10 | 7 | 3 |

_____ , _____ , _____
least between greatest

8

| 4 | 11 | 9 |

_____ , _____ , _____
least between greatest

9

| 6 | 2 | 12 |

_____ , _____ , _____
least between greatest

Problem Solving Reasoning

10 Sara, Ray, and Jackson played a game.
Sara tossed a 6.
Ray tossed a 1.
Jackson tossed a 4.

Who moved the most spaces? _____

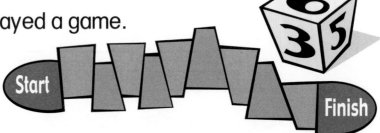

Home Connection Your child put three numbers in order from least to
greatest. **Home Activity** Tell your child three numbers, each less than 13,
and ask him or her to put the numbers in order from least to greatest. He or
she may want to use objects or draw pictures to help.

Name_____

 Dorling Kindersley

Do You Know...
that people from all over the world have been decorating with patterns for thousands of years?

Mia and Joel made patterns with party hats.
Draw the hat that should come next in each pattern.

1    _____

2   _____

3 There are 8 links in the chain. How many links will there be if 1 more is added?

_____ links

Fun Fact!
Zebras have stripes to confuse their enemies.

4 What color should the next link in the pattern be?

green   red   yellow

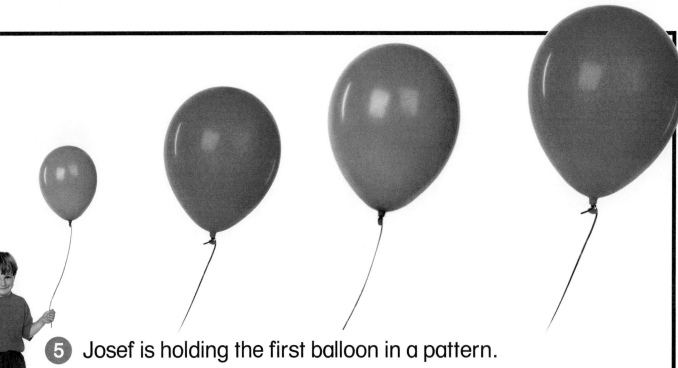

5 Josef is holding the first balloon in a pattern. If another balloon is added at the end of the pattern, what color should it be?

red   green

6 There will be 12 children at Josef's party. How many more balloons does Josef need?

_____ more balloons

7 What should be the color of the next present on this pile?

blue   yellow

8 **Writing in Math**

Draw 10 presents.
Make some of them red
and some of them blue.
Then finish the sentence.

10 is _____ and _____.

© Pearson Education, Inc.

Home Connection Your child learned to solve problems by applying his or her math skills. **Home Activity** Talk to your child about how he or she solved the problems on these two pages.

Name_____

Use counters and Workmat 2.
Draw the counters. Write the numbers.

1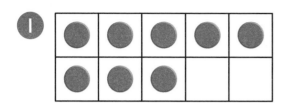

8 and 1 more is _____.

2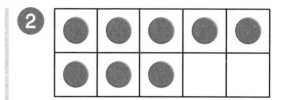

8 and 2 more is _____.

Use counters and Workmat 2.
Cross out the counters. Write the numbers.

3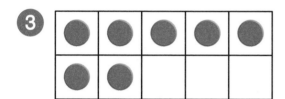

1 fewer than 7 is _____.

4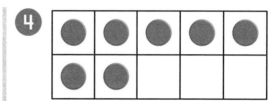

2 fewer than 7 is _____.

Use cubes. Circle **less** or **greater**.

5 7 is _____ than 10.   **less**   **greater**

6 8 is _____ than 5.   **less**   **greater**

Use cubes. Write the numbers in order from least to greatest.

7

10	3	7

_____, _____, _____

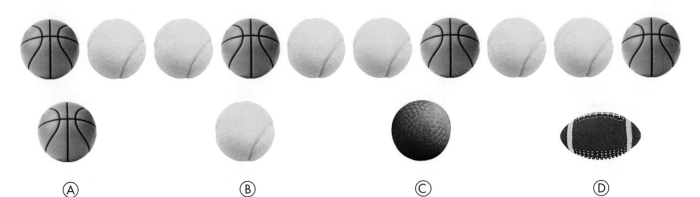
1 Which ball comes next in the pattern?

Ⓐ   Ⓑ   Ⓒ   Ⓓ

Which number is greater than 5?

     2   4   5   6

     Ⓐ   Ⓑ   Ⓒ   Ⓓ

Which shows the numbers in order from least to greatest?

3   3, 10, 5   9, 7, 10   5, 8, 12   6, 4, 11

     Ⓐ   Ⓑ   Ⓒ   Ⓓ

What is the missing number?

4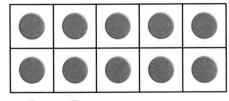

10 and 2 more is _____.

   8   9   11   12

   Ⓐ   Ⓑ   Ⓒ   Ⓓ

5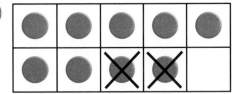

2 fewer than 9 is _____.

   11   8   7   6

   Ⓐ   Ⓑ   Ⓒ   Ⓓ

Growing Patterns

How do we make the next one?

Add one more square to the one before it.

   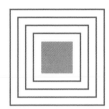

Circle what comes next in each pattern.

1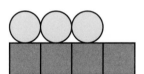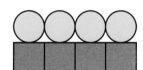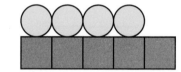

2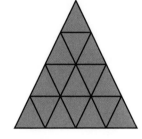

3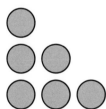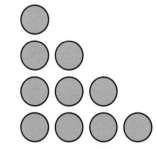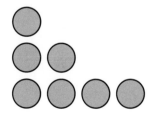

4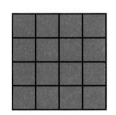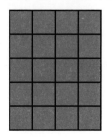

 Home Connection Your child decided what came next in each growing pattern. **Home Activity** Ask your child to tell you how each pattern grew.

Use the Keys of a Calculator

You can use a calculator to show numbers.
Press the keys. Write the numbers you see.

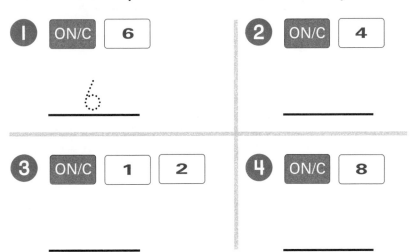

1 [ON/C] [6]

_____6_____

2 [ON/C] [4]

_____

3 [ON/C] [1] [2]

_____

4 [ON/C] [8]

_____

Use your calculator. Press [ON/C].

Show more numbers.
Write the numbers you press.

5 Show 10.

[1] [0]

6 Show 11.

[ ] [ ]

7 Show 12.

[ ] [ ]

8 Show 13.

[ ] [ ]

9 Show 14.

[ ] [ ]

10 Show 15.

[ ] [ ]

Think About It Number Sense

Which keys would you press to show
the number that is after 15?

Home Connection Your child practiced using a calculator to show
numbers. **Home Activity** Ask your child to explain how he or she could
show any number from 1 to 12 on a calculator.

Name_____

Understand the Question

Important words help you understand
what a question is asking.

Test-Taking Strategies

Understand the Question
Get Information for the Answer
Plan How to Find the Answer
Make Smart Choices
Use Writing in Math

1 Which number is greater than 5?

Ⓐ 0

Ⓑ 5

Ⓒ 2

Ⓓ 9

The most important words are **greater than.**
Fill in the answer bubble.

Your Turn

What are the most important words?
Fill in the answer bubble.

2 Which number is less than 10?

Ⓐ 8

Ⓑ 11

Ⓒ 10

Ⓓ 12

3 Which number is between 4 and 7?

Ⓐ 3

Ⓑ 6

Ⓒ 4

Ⓓ 7

I can do this!

Home Connection Your child prepared for standardized tests by
identifying the most important words in math problems. **Home Activity** Ask
your child which words he or she identified as being the most important
words in Exercises 2 and 3. *(Less than; between)*

thirty-nine **39**

Name_____

Discover Math in Your World

Speaking of Math...

Can you count from 1 to 10? Children around the world count in many different languages. This chart shows you how to count to 10 in English and in Spanish.

one	two	three	four	five	six	seven	eight	nine	ten
1	2	3	4	5	6	7	8	9	10
uno	dos	tres	cuatro	cinco	seis	siete	ocho	nueve	diez

Counting Around the Classroom

Use the chart. Solve each problem.

1 What is the English word for 1 more than 5? _____

2 What is the Spanish word for 1 less than 4? _____

3 What number is 1 more than **nueve**? _____

4 Write the numbers for these words in order
from least to greatest: **siete   diez   two**

_____

 **Take It to the NET
Video and Activities**
www.scottforesman.com

 Home Connection Your child learned the English and Spanish words for the numbers from 1 to 10. **Home Activity** Say any number, from 1 to 10, in English or in Spanish. Then ask your child to use the chart to find the number that is 1 more than, 1 less than, 2 more than, and 2 less than the number you said.

Chapter Test

Find the pattern. Circle the picture that comes next.

1

Draw a shape pattern in the top row.
Then make the same pattern using letters.

2

Predict: Will the scarf have more
red shapes or gold shapes?   more _____ shapes

3

Color the rest of the scarf.

How many red shapes does it have?   _____ red shapes

How many gold shapes does it have?   _____ gold shapes

Use counters and Workmat 1.
Draw the missing counters. Write the numbers.

4

7 is _____ and _____.

5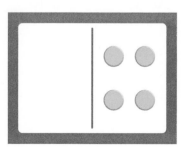

9 is _____ and _____.

Use counters and Workmat 2.
Draw the missing counters. Write the numbers.

6

10 is _____ and _____.

7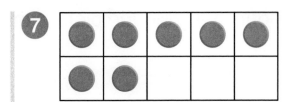

12 is _____ and _____.

Use counters and Workmat 2. Write the numbers.

8 6 and 1 more is _____.

9 6 and 2 more is _____.

10 1 fewer than 11 is _____.

11 2 fewer than 11 is _____.

Use cubes.
Write the numbers in order from least to greatest.

12

10	3	7

_____, _____, _____

13

9	12	6

_____, _____, _____

Use counters.
Write one way to put 9 berries into 3 bowls.

14 9 is _____ and _____ and _____.

Use cubes. Circle **less** or **greater**.

15 12 is _____ than 10.   **less**   **greater**

Dear Family,

Today my class started Chapter 2, **Understanding Addition and Subtraction.** I will learn that adding means joining things together and that subtracting means taking things away or comparing two groups. Here are some of the math words I will be learning and some things we can do to help me with my math.

Love,

_____

Math Activity to Do at Home

Gather a group of small toys or other objects. Together, use them to make up addition stories, such as *4 cars plus 6 cars equals 10 cars.* You can also make up subtraction stories, such as *9 cars minus 3 cars equals 6 cars.*

Books to Read Together

Reading math stories reinforces concepts. Look for these titles in your local library:

One More Bunny
By Rick Walton
(Lothrop, Lee & Shepard, 2000)

Twenty Is Too Many
By Kate Duke
(Dutton, 2000)

Take It to the NET
More Activities
www.scottforesman.com

My New Math Words

add

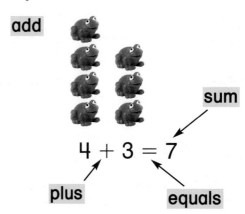

4 + 3 = 7

plus   sum   equals

subtract

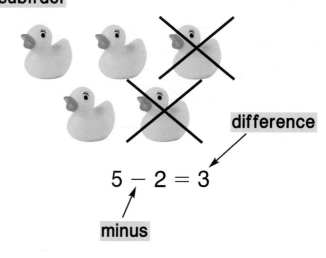

5 − 2 = 3

difference   minus

Cover the Beds

What You Need

paper clip
pencil
small game markers
for each player

How to Play

1. Spin and read the top spinner.
2. Spin and read the bottom spinner.
3. Cover the bed that has the answer on it.
4. Keep playing until you have covered all of the beds.

1 more than	2 less than
2 more than	1 less than

3	7
10	5

7   6   12   8   9   4   2   1   3   11   5

You can **add** to find the **sum**.

When we join parts,
we are adding.

__3__ and __2__ is __5__ in all.

5 is the sum of 3 and 2.

Check ✓

Use counters and Workmat 1 to find the sum.

Word Bank

add

sum

①

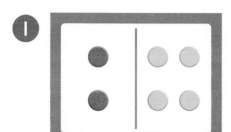

2 and 4 is _____ in all.

②

1 and 5 is _____ in all.

③

4 and 3 is _____ in all.

④

5 and 2 is _____ in all.

Think About It   Number Sense

Tell how to find the sum of 3 and 3.

Add to find the sum.
Use counters if you like.

 ⑤

___4___ and ___1___ is ___5___.

 ⑥

_____ and _____ is _____.

 ⑦

_____ and _____ is _____.

⑧

_____ and _____ is _____.

 ⑨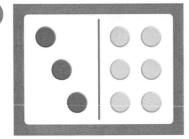

_____ and _____ is _____.

⑩

_____ and _____ is _____.

Problem Solving   Reasoning

⑪ Is the sum of 5 and 3 more or less than 7?

_____

 Home Connection Your child added to join two groups and find the sum.
Home Activity Use pieces of cereal as counters. Ask your child to show you two groups and tell how to join them to find the sum.

Name_____

 **Algebra**

> We write addition sentences to find how many there are in all. We use + and =.

2 and 4 is 6 in all.

2 **plus** 4 **equals** _6_.

_2_ + _4_ = _6_

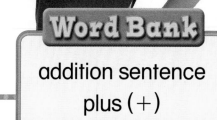

Word Bank

addition sentence

plus (+)

equals (=)

Check ✓

Tell how many in all.

Then write an addition sentence.

1

How many hats in all?

3 plus 1 equals _____.

____ + ____ = ____

2

How many masks in all?

1 plus 4 equals _____.

____ + ____ = ____

3

How many balls in all?

2 plus 6 equals _____.

____ + ____ = ____

4

How many bats in all?

1 plus 2 equals _____.

____ + ____ = ____

Think About It   Reasoning

What does + mean?

What does = mean?

Write an addition sentence for each workmat.

5

_1_ + _6_ = _7_

6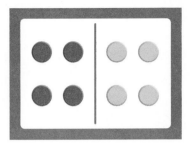

___ + ___ = ___

7

___ + ___ = ___

8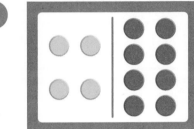

___ + ___ = ___

9

___ + ___ = ___

10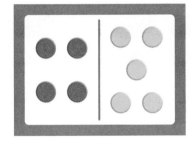

___ + ___ = ___

Problem Solving Algebra

11 Jan has 9 pets.

3 of her pets are cats.

The rest of her pets are dogs.

How many of Jan's pets are dogs?

_____ dogs

Name_____

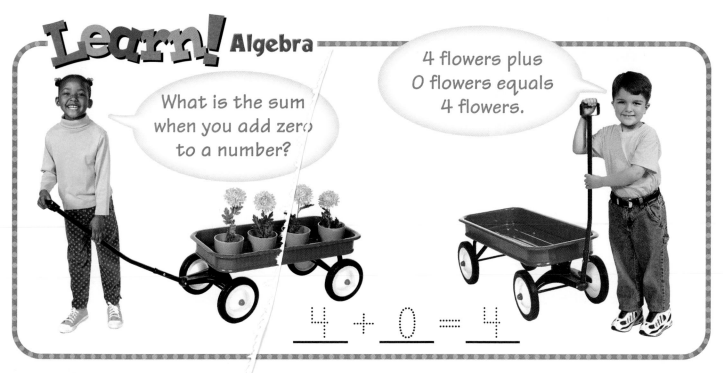

Learn! Algebra

What is the sum when you add zero to a number?

4 flowers plus 0 flowers equals 4 flowers.

$$4 + 0 = 4$$

Check ✓

Write an addition sentence.

①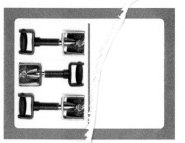

___ + ___ = ___

②

___ + ___ = ___

③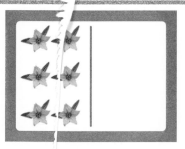

___ + ___ = ___

④

___ + ___ = ___

Think About It   Number Sense

What is the sum of $0 + 0$? Explain.

Write an addition sentence for each workmat.

5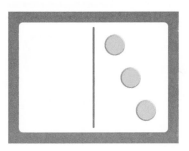

You can also add a number to zero.

$\underline{0} + \underline{3} = \underline{3}$

6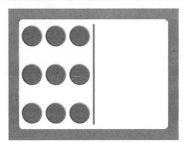

$\underline{} + \underline{} = \underline{}$

7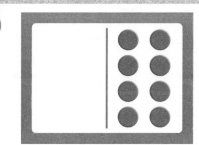

$\underline{} + \underline{} = \underline{}$

8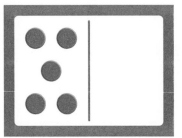

$\underline{} + \underline{} = \underline{}$

9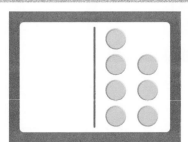

$\underline{} + \underline{} = \underline{}$

Problem Solving Mental Math

10 You have 3 dimes in one pocket.

You have none in the other pocket.

How many dimes do you have in all?   _____ dimes

Vertical Addition

Here are two ways to write an addition sentence.

$5 + 4 =$ ___9

$\begin{array}{r} 5 \\ + 4 \\ \hline 9 \end{array}$

Check ✓

Add to find the sum.

1

$4 + 6 =$ ___

$\begin{array}{r} 4 \\ + 6 \\ \hline \end{array}$

2

$5 + 6 =$ ___

$\begin{array}{r} 5 \\ + 6 \\ \hline \end{array}$

3

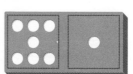

$7 + 1 =$ ___

$\begin{array}{r} 7 \\ + 1 \\ \hline \end{array}$

Think About It   Reasoning

What do the yellow lines in these addition sentences mean?

$8 + 3 = 11$

$\begin{array}{r} 8 \\ + 3 \\ \hline 11 \end{array}$

Add to find the sum.

4

$7 + 5 = \underline{12}$

$$\begin{array}{r} 7 \\ + 5 \\ \hline 12 \end{array}$$

5

$0 + 5 = \underline{}$

$$\begin{array}{r} 0 \\ + 5 \\ \hline \end{array}$$

6

$9 + 1 = \underline{}$

$$\begin{array}{r} 9 \\ + 1 \\ \hline \end{array}$$

7

$4 + 6 = \underline{}$

$$\begin{array}{r} 4 \\ + 6 \\ \hline \end{array}$$

8

$9 + 3 = \underline{}$

$$\begin{array}{r} 9 \\ + 3 \\ \hline \end{array}$$

9

$2 + 8 = \underline{}$

$$\begin{array}{r} 2 \\ + 8 \\ \hline \end{array}$$

Problem Solving **Algebra**

10 Complete the pattern.

$$\begin{array}{r} 2 \\ + 1 \\ \hline 3 \end{array} \qquad \begin{array}{r} 3 \\ + 1 \\ \hline 4 \end{array} \qquad \begin{array}{r} 4 \\ + 1 \\ \hline 5 \end{array} \qquad \begin{array}{r} 5 \\ + 1 \\ \hline \square \end{array} \qquad \begin{array}{r} \square \\ + \square \\ \hline \square \end{array}$$

Home Connection Your child worked with vertical addition sentences.
Home Activity Ask your child to show you two kinds of addition sentences. Read the sentences on this page aloud together.

Name_____

Identify the Main Idea

The main idea tells what a story problem is all about.

Knowing the main idea can help you solve story problems.

1 Read this story problem.

Luis has 2 puppets.
Alma has 2 puppets.
How many puppets do they have in all?

2 Circle what the story problem is all about.

3 Circle a good title for this story problem.

How Many Snacks?   **How Many Puppets?**   **My Friends**

4 Write the numbers in this story problem.

_____   _____

5 Solve this story problem.
Write a number sentence about the main idea.

_____ + _____ = _____ puppets

Think About It   Reasoning

Why did you add to solve this story problem?

6 Read another story problem.

Skipper had 3 dog treats.
Then he got 2 more treats.
How many treats does Skipper have now?

7 Circle what the story problem is all about.

8 Circle a good title for this story problem.

How Many Treats?   **Run Dog Run!**   **How Many Cats?**

9 Write the numbers in the story problem.

_____   _____

10 Solve this story problem.
Write a number sentence about the main idea.

_____ + _____ = _____ treats

Home Connection Your child identified the main idea in story problems and solved story problems by writing number sentences. **Home Activity** Make up story problems about adding two sets of objects. Ask your child to tell what the story problem is about, suggest a name for the story, and then write a number sentence to solve the problem.

Name_____

Learn! Algebra

Write a number sentence to solve the problem.

4 birds are singing.
7 more birds sing with them.
How many birds are singing in all?

Read and Understand

You need to find how many birds are singing in all.

Plan and Solve

You can write an addition sentence.

__4__ + __7__ = __11__ birds

Look Back and Check

Does your answer make sense?

Check ✓

Write an addition sentence to answer the question.

1 There are 8 squirrels in the tree.
 1 more squirrel jumps into the tree.
 How many squirrels are in the tree now?

____ + ____ = ____ squirrels

Think About It   Reasoning

What can you do to find how many in all?

Write an addition sentence to answer each question.

2 There are 2 bunnies eating lettuce.
7 more bunnies are eating carrots.
How many bunnies are in the garden?

__2__ + __7__ = __9__ bunnies

3 There are 9 bluejays on the fence.
2 more bluejays are in the birdbath.
How many bluejays are there altogether?

_____ + _____ = _____ bluejays

4 There are 8 chipmunks eating nuts.
2 more chipmunks are running.
How many chipmunks are there in all?

_____ + _____ = _____ chipmunks

5 There are 8 skunks walking to the left.
There are 3 skunks walking to the right.
How many skunks are walking?

_____ + _____ = _____ skunks

Home Connection Your child wrote number sentences to solve problems.
Home Activity When you are putting groceries away with your child, ask questions such as "How many did we have?" or "How many do we have now?" Have your child write number sentences to solve the problems.

Name _____

Add to find the sum.
Use counters if you like.

3 and 7 is _____.

②

5 and 5 is _____.

Write each addition sentence.

③

____ + ____ ⋯ ____

④

____ + ____ ⋯ ____

Add to find the sum.

⑤

$$\begin{array}{r} 6 \\ + 3 \\ \hline \end{array}$$

6 + 3 = ____

⑥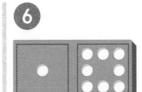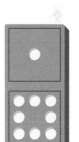

$$\begin{array}{r} 1 \\ + 8 \\ \hline \end{array}$$

1 + 8 = ____

Write an addition sentence to answer the question.

⑦ There are 8 dogs in the park.
2 more dogs join them.
How many dogs are there in all?

____ + ____ ⋯ ____ dogs

What is the missing number?

1

7 is 4 and _____.

3   4   5   7
Ⓐ   Ⓑ   Ⓒ   Ⓓ

2

10 is 8 and _____.

0   2   6   8
Ⓐ   Ⓑ   Ⓒ   Ⓓ

3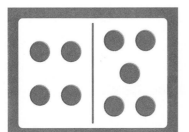

4 and 5 is _____.

1   8   9   10
Ⓐ   Ⓑ   Ⓒ   Ⓓ

4

$8 + 0 =$ ___

0   7   8   9
Ⓐ   Ⓑ   Ⓒ   Ⓓ

Solve the problem.

5 1 tiger is in the grass. 4 more tigers join it. How many tigers are there in all?

1 tiger   3 tigers   4 tigers   5 tigers
Ⓐ   Ⓑ   Ⓒ   Ⓓ

Learn!

5 children went to the beach.

3 of the children played in the water.

The rest played in the sand.

Our group separated into two parts.

How many children played in the sand?   2 children

Check ✓

Tell a separating story about the picture.
Use counters to answer the question.

1

How many boats stayed at the dock?   ☐ boats

Think About It   Reasoning

If one more boat sails away, will there be more boats
or fewer boats at the dock?

Use counters to answer each question.

There are 6 ladybugs.

4 ladybugs are eating a leaf.

How many ladybugs are not eating? | ladybugs

8 worms are on a plant.

2 worms crawl away.

How many worms did not crawl away? | worms

Problem Solving   Reasonableness

Use counters to choose the most reasonable answer.

4 There are 5 fireflies.

4 fireflies fly away.

How many fireflies did not fly away?

0 fireflies

9 fireflies

1 firefly

Home Connection Your child read and told separating stories.
Home Activity Hold up 5 fingers. Then curl down 2 fingers and ask how many fingers are left. Take turns doing this, each time changing the number of starting fingers.

You can **subtract** to find the **difference** .

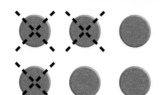

I take one group away to find how many are left.

There are 6 counters in all.

Take away 3 of them.

How many counters are left?

6 take away 3 is ___.

Word Bank

subtract

difference

Check ✔

Use counters.

Cross out the ones you take away.

Then write how many are left.

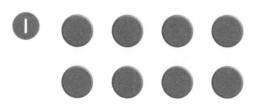

1 8 take away 3 is _____.

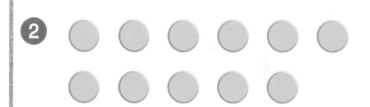

2 11 take away 7 is _____.

3 8 take away 1 is _____.

4 9 take away 7 is _____.

Think About It   **Number Sense**

How are Exercises 1 and 3 alike?

How are they different?

Subtract to find the difference.
Use counters if you like.

5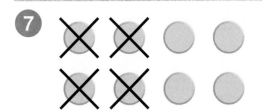

___5___ take away ___1___ is ___4___.

6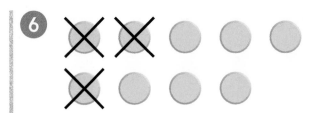

_____ take away _____ is _____.

7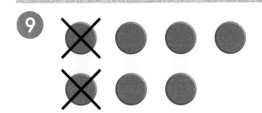

_____ take away _____ is _____.

8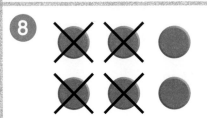

_____ take away _____ is _____.

9

_____ take away _____ is _____.

10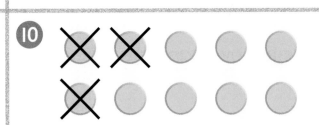

_____ take away _____ is _____.

Problem Solving   Number Sense

11 What is the most you can take away from 8 counters? Draw a picture to show that number.

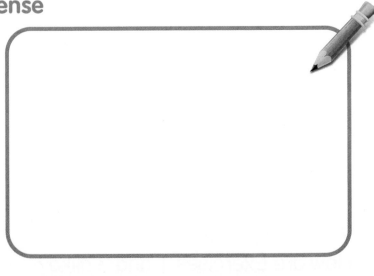

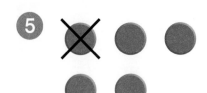

Home Connection Your child used counters to subtract and show how many are left. **Home Activity** Have your child show you how to use cereal pieces, coins, buttons, or other counters to act out "take away" stories. Take turns using counters to show subtraction stories you both make up.

Algebra

We can write *subtraction sentences* to find how many are left.

We use a minus (−) sign.

6 take away 1   is   5.
6 **minus**   1 equals 5.
6   −   1   =   5

Word Bank

subtraction sentence
minus (−)

Check ✓

Tell how many are left.
Then write a subtraction sentence.

1

How many backpacks are left?

5 minus 4   equals ____.

5 − 4 = 1
___ ___ ___ ___

2

How many coats are left?

9 minus 5   equals ____.

___ ___ ___ ___

Think About It   Number Sense

What subtraction sentences can you write with 2 left?

Write a subtraction sentence.

3

8 — 6 = 2

4

_____ .... _____ ::::::: _____

5

_____ .... _____ ::::::: _____

6

_____ .... _____ ::::::: _____

7

_____ .... _____ ::::::: _____

Problem Solving   Writing in Math

8 Draw a picture that shows subtraction.
Write a subtraction sentence to go with it.

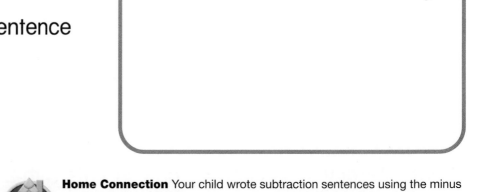

Home Connection Your child wrote subtraction sentences using the minus sign (−). **Home Activity** As you and your child clear the table, make up subtraction stories such as, "4 plates take away 3 plates is 1 plate left. So 4 minus 3 equals 1."

Name _____

Learn! Algebra

If you take away all, zero are left.

If you take away zero, all are left.

6 − 6 = 0

6 − 0 = 6

Check ✓

Write a subtraction sentence.

①

___ __ ___ __ ___

②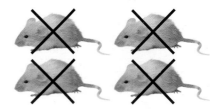

___ __ ___ __ ___

③

___ __ ___ __ ___

④

___ __ ___ __ ___

⑤

___ __ ___ __ ___

⑥

___ __ ___ __ ___

Think About It Reasoning

What do you always have left when you take away zero?

Write a subtraction sentence.

7

$$2 - 0 = 2$$

8

$$2 - 2 = 0$$

9

___ ___ ___

10

___ ___ ___

11

___ ___ ___

12

___ ___ ___

13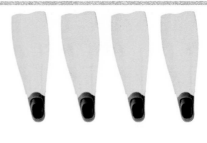

___ ___ ___

14

___ ___ ___

Problem Solving Mental Math

15 If $2 - 0 = 2$, then what is $20 - 0$? ___

If $2 - 2 = 0$, then what is $20 - 20$? ___

Home Connection Your child used zero in subtraction sentences.
Home Activity Give your child 6 pennies. Say "I'm going to take away zero pennies. Now how many pennies do you have left?" Repeat with different amounts of pennies, taking away all or none.

Name_____

 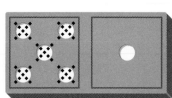

When you write a subtraction sentence this way, write the whole amount first.

When you write a subtraction sentence this way, write the whole amount on top.

$$6 - 5 = \underline{}$$

$$\begin{array}{r} 6 \\ -5 \\ \hline \end{array}$$

Check

Cross out the dots to show subtraction.

Subtract to find the difference.

1

$$9 - 1 = \underline{}$$

$$\begin{array}{r} 9 \\ -1 \\ \hline \end{array}$$

2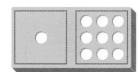

$$10 - 1 = \underline{}$$

$$\begin{array}{r} 10 \\ -1 \\ \hline \end{array}$$

3

$$7 - 0 = \underline{}$$

$$\begin{array}{r} 7 \\ -0 \\ \hline \end{array}$$

Think About It   Reasoning

How do you know which number to write first?

Subtract to find the difference.
Cross out the dots if you like.

$8 - 7 = \underline{}$

$\begin{array}{r} 8 \\ -\ 7 \\ \hline \end{array}$

$9 - 6 = \underline{}$

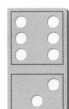

$\begin{array}{r} 9 \\ -\ 6 \\ \hline \end{array}$

$7 - 6 = \underline{}$

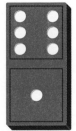

$\begin{array}{r} 7 \\ -\ 6 \\ \hline \end{array}$

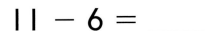

$11 - 6 = \underline{}$

$\begin{array}{r} 11 \\ -\ 6 \\ \hline \end{array}$

$10 - 4 = \underline{}$

$\begin{array}{r} 10 \\ -\ 4 \\ \hline \end{array}$

$12 - 6 = \underline{}$

$\begin{array}{r} 12 \\ -\ 6 \\ \hline \end{array}$

Problem Solving   Visual Thinking

Use the dominoes to fill in the missing numbers.

$12 - \boxed{} = 7$

$\boxed{} - 9 = 3$

Home Connection Your child worked with both horizontal and vertical subtraction sentences. **Home Activity** Ask your child to write subtraction sentences, such as $4 - 2 = 2$ and $6 - 1 = 5$, vertically.

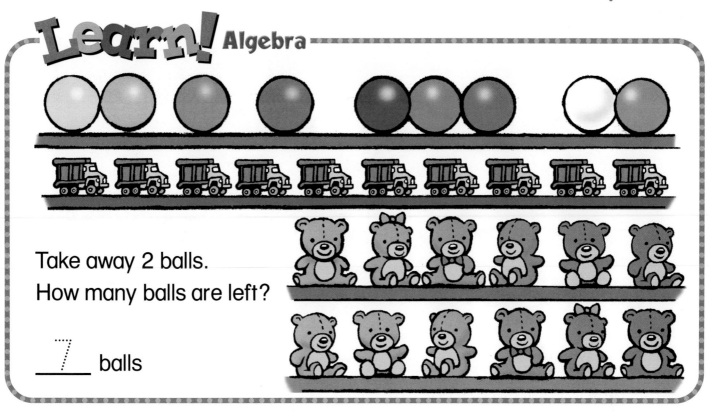

Take away 2 balls.
How many balls are left?

___7___ balls

Check ✓

Use the picture. Circle **add** or **subtract**.
Then write the answer.

1 How many teddy bears
are on both shelves?

add   subtract

_____ teddy bears

2 Jane takes 3 trucks from the shelf.
How many trucks are left?

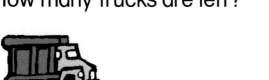

add   subtract

_____ trucks

Think About It   Reasoning

How can you decide whether to add or subtract?

Use the picture. Circle **add** or **subtract**.
Then write the answer.

3 There are 3 yellow chicks
and 5 white chicks.
How many chicks are there in all?

add   subtract

_____ chicks

4 7 cows live on the farm.
5 of the cows are eating.
How many cows are not eating?

add   subtract

_____ cows

5 There are 5 pigs on the farm.
4 pigs are in the mud.
How many pigs are not in the mud?

add   subtract

_____ pig

Home Connection Your child chose an operation to solve each problem.
Home Activity Point to a problem on the page. Ask your child to tell you
how he or she knew whether to add or subtract.

Name_____

Cross out the ones you take away.
Then write how many are left.

1

7 take away 6 is ____.

2

9 take away 4 is ____.

Write each subtraction sentence.

3

____ ___ ____ ___ ____

4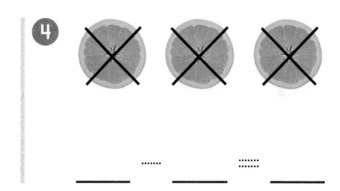

____ ___ ____ ___ ____

Subtract to find the difference.

5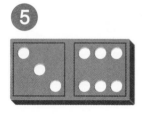
$$\begin{array}{r} 9 \\ -\ 3 \\ \hline \end{array}$$

$9 - 3 =$ ____

6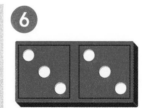
$$\begin{array}{r} 6 \\ -\ 3 \\ \hline \end{array}$$

$6 - 3 =$ ____

Circle **add** or **subtract**.
Then write the answer.

7 There are 6 goats eating grass.
5 more goats are sleeping.
How many goats are there altogether?

add   subtract

____ goats

1 What color block do you need to finish the wall?

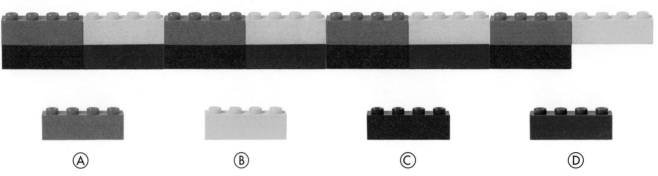

Ⓐ   Ⓑ   Ⓒ   Ⓓ

2 Which addition sentence tells how many birdhouses there are in all?

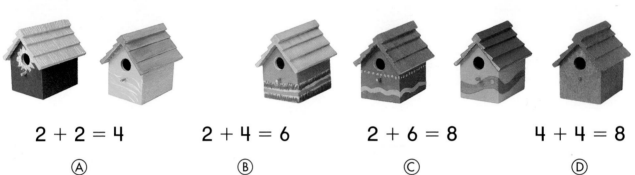

2 + 2 = 4   2 + 4 = 6   2 + 6 = 8   4 + 4 = 8

Ⓐ   Ⓑ   Ⓒ   Ⓓ

3 What is the sum?

$7 + 0 =$ ___

Ⓐ   0
Ⓑ   7
Ⓒ   8
Ⓓ   9

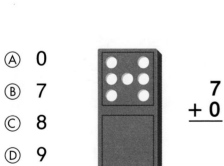

$$\begin{array}{r} 7 \\ + 0 \\ \hline \end{array}$$

4 What is the difference?

$8 - 3 =$ ___

Ⓐ   3
Ⓑ   5
Ⓒ   8
Ⓓ   11

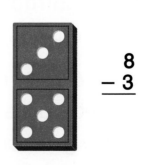

$$\begin{array}{r} 8 \\ - 3 \\ \hline \end{array}$$

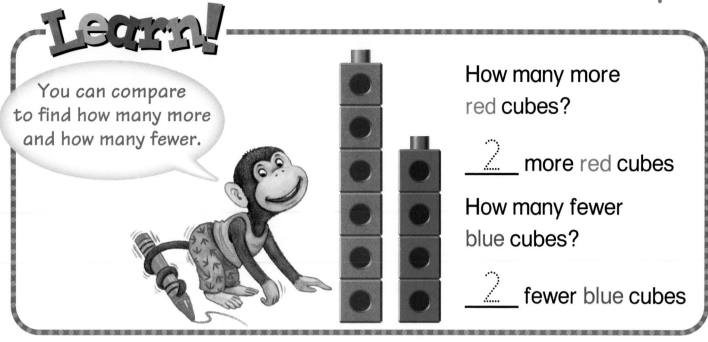

Learn!

You can compare to find how many more and how many fewer.

How many more red cubes?

_2_ more red cubes

How many fewer blue cubes?

_2_ fewer blue cubes

Check ✓

Use cubes. Color to show the cubes.
Then write how many more and how many fewer.

3 red cubes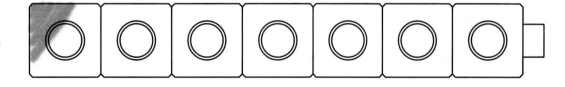

6 blue cubes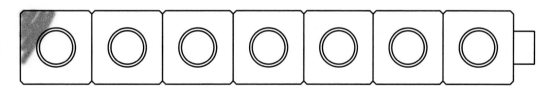

1 How many more blue cubes? _____ more blue cubes

2 How many fewer red cubes? _____ fewer red cubes

Think About It   Reasoning

Tell how to compare 5 red cubes and 2 blue cubes.

Write how many red cubes and how many blue cubes.
Then write how many more or how many fewer cubes.

3

____3____ red cubes

____2____ blue cubes

____1____ fewer blue cube

4

_____ red cubes

_____ blue cubes

_____ fewer blue cubes

5

_____ red cubes

_____ blue cubes

_____ more blue cubes

6

_____ red cube

_____ blue cubes

_____ more blue cubes

Problem Solving   Visual Thinking

Draw a picture to solve.

7 Rena has 7 shells.
June has 5 shells.
How many more shells
does Rena have than June?

_____ more shells

Home Connection Your child used cubes to compare and find out how many more and how many fewer. **Home Activity** Ask your child to tell you how many windows and doors there are in your home. Then talk about how many more windows there are than doors.

 **Algebra**

How many more red cubes than blue cubes?

You can write a subtraction sentence to compare.

_8_ ⊖ _3_ ⊜ _5_

There are __5__ more red cubes than blue cubes.

Check ✓

Write a subtraction sentence.
Then write how many fewer.

1 How many fewer yellow cubes than green cubes?

___ ◯ ___ ◯ ___

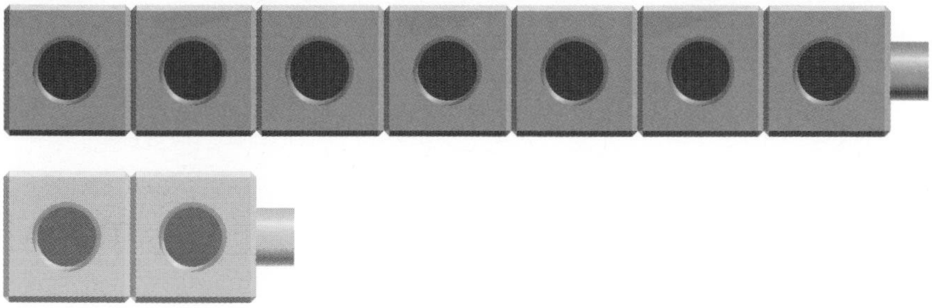

There are _____ fewer yellow cubes than green cubes.

Think About It   Number Sense

There are 4 more red cubes than blue cubes.
How many fewer blue cubes are there?

Write each subtraction sentence.

Then write how many more or how many fewer.

2 How many fewer pots than lids?

<u>8</u> ⊖ <u>6</u> ⊜ <u>2</u>   <u>2</u> fewer pots

3 How many more cups than plates?

____ ◯ ____ ◯ ____   ____ more cups

4 How many more forks than spoons?

____ ◯ ____ ◯ ____   ____ more forks

Problem Solving   Estimation

Answer each question.

5 Does your classroom have more crayons or more children?

_____

6 Does your classroom have fewer children or fewer teachers?

_____

Home Connection Your child used subtraction to compare.
Home Activity Ask your child to write a subtraction sentence to compare a number of plates to a different number of cups.

Name _____

Dorling Kindersley

Do You Know...
that stinkbugs have glands that make bad smells when the stinkbugs are in danger?

1 3 stinkbugs sit on a log.
2 more stinkbugs join them.
How many stinkbugs are there now?

3 and 2 more is ____.

2 2 butterflies are resting on a plant.
0 butterflies are flying.
How many butterflies are there in all?

____ + ____ = ____

3 4 caterpillars hatch from a butterfly's eggs.
5 more caterpillars hatch.
How many caterpillars hatched?

____ + ____ = ____

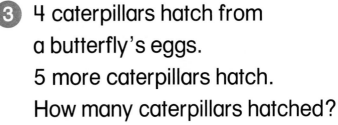

4 There are 11 stinkbugs and 9 thorn bugs.
How many fewer thorn bugs are there?

_____ fewer thorn bugs

5 9 thorn bugs are on a stick.
A bird eats 0 thorn bugs.
How many thorn bugs are left on the stick?

_____ − _____ = _____ thorn bugs

6 There are 3 stinkbugs and
9 thorn bugs in the tree.
How many more thorn bugs are there?

There are _____ more thorn bugs
than stinkbugs.

Fun Fact!

This bug is called a
thorn bug because
it looks like a thorn
on a twig.

7 **Writing in Math**

Write an addition sentence or
a subtraction sentence.

Write a story about your number sentence.
Then draw a picture.

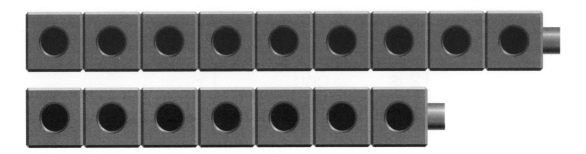

1 How many fewer blue cubes? _____ fewer blue cubes

2 How many more red cubes? _____ more red cubes

Write a subtraction sentence.
Then write how many fewer butterflies.

3

____ ◯ ____ ◯ ____   _____ fewer butterflies

Write a subtraction sentence.
Then write how many more birds.

4

____ ◯ ____ ◯ ____   _____ more birds

1 What is one way you can put 12 eggs into 2 cartons?

12 is _____ and _____.

6 and 3	5 and 7	5 and 4	7 and 7
Ⓐ	Ⓑ	Ⓒ	Ⓓ

2 Which shows the numbers in order from **least** to **greatest?**

11, 8, 5	8, 5, 11	5, 8, 11	8, 11, 5
Ⓐ	Ⓑ	Ⓒ	Ⓓ

3 Which addition sentence answers the question?

5 kangaroos are resting.
5 kangaroos are hopping.
How many kangaroos are
there altogether?

5 + 5 = 10	5 + 2 = 7	4 + 5 = 9	5 + 1 = 6
Ⓐ	Ⓑ	Ⓒ	Ⓓ

4 How many fewer blue cubes are there than red cubes?

1 fewer	2 fewer	3 fewer	4 fewer
Ⓐ	Ⓑ	Ⓒ	Ⓓ

Name_____

Find the Missing Number

> If you know an addition fact,
> you also know a subtraction fact.

$$4 + \bigcirc = 5$$

$$5 - \bigcirc = 4$$

Add the green cube.
4 and 1 more is 5.

Take away the green cube.
5 take away 1 is 4.

Make each train with cubes.
Then complete the number sentences.

1

$$4 + \triangle = 7$$

$$7 - \triangle = 4$$

2

$$3 + \hexagon = 5$$

$$5 - \hexagon = 3$$

3

$$5 + \square = 9$$

$$9 - \square = 5$$

4

$$2 + \bigcirc = 8$$

$$8 - \bigcirc = 2$$

 Home Connection Your child found missing numbers in number sentences.
Home Activity Ask your child to tell how the number sentences in Exercise 1
are the same and how they are different.

Name_____

Choose an Operation Using a Calculator

Use your calculator. Make a true number sentence.

Press ON/C . Press the keys that you see below.

Press + or − for the blank key.

Draw + or − to show the key you pressed.

1. 4 +̈ 6 = 10

2. 9 ☐ 5 = 4

3. 1 1 ☐ 1 = 10

4. 6 ☐ 6 = 12

5. 3 ☐ 4 = 7

6. 1 1 ☐ 1 = 12

7. 1 0 ☐ 1 = 9

8. 1 2 ☐ 1 2 = 0

Think About It   Reasoning

How did you decide whether to press

+ or − ?

Home Connection Your child used a calculator to decide whether to add or subtract in order to make true number sentences. **Home Activity** Point to a problem on the page. Ask your child to explain how he or she used a calculator to decide whether to add or subtract.

Name _____

Get Information for the Answer

Pictures may help you solve math problems.

Test-Taking Strategies

Understand the Question

Get Information for the Answer

Plan How to Find the Answer

Make Smart Choices

Use Writing in Math

1 Which number sentence tells how many fewer red cubes there are?

$7 - 2 = 5$ $\quad$ $7 - 5 = 2$ $\quad$ $5 - 2 = 3$ $\quad$ $7 - 3 = 4$

Ⓐ $\qquad$ Ⓑ $\qquad$ Ⓒ $\qquad$ Ⓓ

Look at the cubes. How many more yellow cubes are there? Use this information to answer the question. Then fill in the answer bubble.

Your Turn

Look at the picture to get information.
Then fill in the answer bubble.

2 Which number sentence tells how many more blue cubes there are?

$6 - 4 = 2$ $\quad$ $8 - 4 = 4$ $\quad$ $2 - 2 = 0$ $\quad$ $6 - 2 = 4$

Ⓐ $\qquad$ Ⓑ $\qquad$ Ⓒ $\qquad$ Ⓓ

Home Connection Your child prepared for standardized tests by using pictures to solve math problems. **Home Activity** Ask your child to describe how he or she used the picture to answer the question in Exercise 2.

Name _____

Who's on First?

Which sports do you like to play? Do you know some of the rules for those sports? Every sport has rules. One rule tells how many players can be on each team.

Teams by the Numbers

Use counters to show the players. Then solve.

1 Each soccer team has 1 goalie. How many goalies are on the field during a game?

_____ goalies

2 Doubles tennis has 2 players on each side of the court. How many players are on the court during a match?

_____ players

3 Both basketball teams have 5 players on the court at a time. How many players are on the floor at a time?

_____ players

4 There are 12 players ready for a game. How many of these players are on each team?

_____ players

Take It to the NET
Video and Activities
www.scottforesman.com

Home Connection Your child solved problems about the number of players on sports teams. **Home Activity** Ask your child to solve similar kinds of problems. For example, ask your child how many players are on the field during a football game at any given time. *(11 players from each team; 22 players in all)*

© Pearson Education, Inc.

Write each addition sentence.

___ + ___ = ___

___ + ___ = ___

Write each subtraction sentence.

 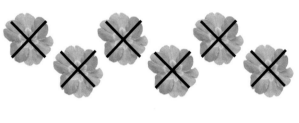

___ - ___ = ___

___ - ___ = ___

Add to find the sum.

$$\begin{array}{r} 5 \\ + 7 \\ \hline \end{array}$$

5 + 7 = ___

$$\begin{array}{r} 4 \\ + 6 \\ \hline \end{array}$$

4 + 6 = ___

Subtract to find the difference.

$$\begin{array}{r} 9 \\ - 7 \\ \hline \end{array}$$

9 - 7 = ___

$$\begin{array}{r} 8 \\ - 5 \\ \hline \end{array}$$

8 - 5 = ___

Write an addition sentence to answer the question.

9 Meg had 7 toy cars.
Pat gave her 4 more toy cars.
How many toy cars does Meg have now?

_____ $+$ _____ $=$ _____ toy cars

Circle **add** or **subtract**.
Then write the answer.

10 Ty has 8 toy boats.
He put 7 of the boats in the bathtub.
How many boats are not
in the bathtub?

add   subtract

_____ toy boat

---

11 How many fewer red cubes?

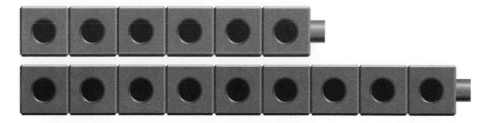

_____ fewer red cubes

---

12 Write a subtraction sentence.
Then write how many more planes.

_____ ◯ _____ ◯ _____

_____ more planes

What is the missing number?

1

7 is 5 and _____.

2	3	4	5
Ⓐ	Ⓑ	Ⓒ	Ⓓ

2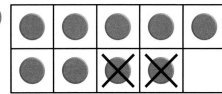

2 fewer than 9 is _____.

5	7	9	11
Ⓐ	Ⓑ	Ⓒ	Ⓓ

3 Which part of the pattern repeats?

Ⓐ

Ⓒ

Ⓑ

Ⓓ

4 Which addition sentence tells how many bears in all?

8 + 0 = 8	2 + 6 = 8	1 + 8 = 9	8 + 2 = 10
Ⓐ	Ⓑ	Ⓒ	Ⓓ

5 Which number sentence tells how many parrots are left if Selena buys 3?

8 + 3 = 11	10 − 3 = 7	11 − 3 = 8	2 + 1 = 3
Ⓐ	Ⓑ	Ⓒ	Ⓓ

Draw the missing counters.
Then write the numbers.

12 is _____ and _____.

10 is _____ and _____.

Write each addition sentence.

___ + ___ = ___

___ + ___ = ___

Cross out the ones you take away.
Then write how many are left.

10 take away 3 is _____.

9 − 9 = ___

Write a subtraction sentence.
Then write how many fewer bunnies.

____ − ____ = ____

____ fewer bunnies

88B

Where Can 12 Friends Play?

Written by **Tina Martin** • Illustrated by **John Patience**

This Math Storybook belongs to

_____

3A

Can **2** birds play in this tree?
Yes, they can, as you can see.
2 birds can play in this tree.

3B

Can **2** squirrels also play in this tree?
Yes, they can, as you can see.
2 birds and **2** squirrels
can play in this tree.

3C

Can **3** bears also play in this tree?
Yes, they can, as you can see.
2 birds and **2** squirrels and
3 bears can play in this tree.

Can **5** elephants also play in this tree?
There is no room, as you can see!
They need a place where
12 friends can be.

3E

Can **12** friends play around this tree?
Yes, they can, as you can see.
12 friends can play around this tree.

3F

Home-School Connection

Dear Family,

Today my class started Chapter 3, **Strategies for Addition Facts to 12.** I will learn different ways to add numbers with sums to 12. Here are some of the new math words I will be learning and some things we can do to help me with my math.

Love,

_____

Math Activity to Do at Home

Have your child cut out pictures of people from magazines. Then have him or her glue different sets (groups) of people to sheets of paper and write addition stories about the people in the pictures.

Books to Read Together

Reading math stories reinforces concepts. Look for these titles in your local library:

Freight Train
By Donald Crews
(Morrow, 1992)

Animals on Board
By Stuart J. Murphy
(HarperCollins, 1998)

My New Math Words

count on Use this strategy to add 1, 2, or 3 to a number.

$$5 + 2 = 7$$

Start at 5.
Count on 6, 7.

number line A number line can help you count on.

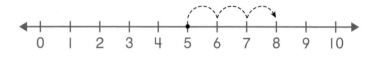

$$5 + 3 = 8$$

doubles A doubles fact has 2 equal addends.

$$4 + 4 = 8$$

Name _____

Leafy Addition

How to Play

1. Toss the cubes. Count the dots.
2. Put markers over those two numbers **or** over the sum of those two numbers.
3. Once a number is covered, you may not use it again.
4. Continue playing until you have covered all of the numbers.

Name_____

You can **count on** to add.

Start at 5.
Count on 3: 6, 7, 8.
$5 + 3 = 8$

There are 5 counters in the bowl.
Add 3 counters.

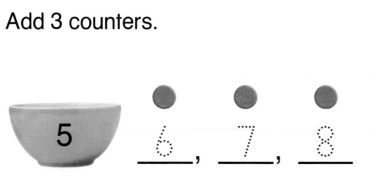

5   __6__, __7__, __8__

Word Bank

count on

Check ✓

Use counters. Count on to find each sum.

1

4   ____, ____

$4 + 2 =$ ___

2

5   ____

$5 + 1 =$ ___

3

8   ____, ____, ____

$8 + 3 =$ ___

4

7   ____, ____

$7 + 2 =$ ___

Think About It   Reasoning

Is it easier to count on $6 + 5$ or $6 + 3$? Explain.

Count on to find each sum.
Use counters if you like.

> 9 counters are in the bowl. Count on 2 more: 10, 11.

5

9 + 2 = 11

6

8 + 1 = ___

7

6 + 2 = ___

8

7 + 3 = ___

9

6 + 1 = ___

10

8 + 2 = ___

11

9 + 1 = ___

Problem Solving   Number Sense

Count on to solve.

12 Sam has 5 snacks.
Then he gets 2 more.
How many snacks does
Sam have in all?

_____ snacks

13 Spot has 9 bones.
Jill gives him 3 more.
How many bones does
Spot have now?

_____ bones

Home Connection Your child counted on to add 1, 2, or 3 to a number.
Home Activity Use pennies or other household items to help your child
count on 1, 2, or 3 from different numbers.

92 ninety-two

Name_____

 **Algebra**

You can change the order of the **addends** and get the same sum.

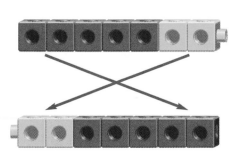

$$\underline{5} + \underline{2} = \underline{7}$$
$$\underline{2} + \underline{5} = \underline{7}$$
addend   addend   sum

Word Bank

addend

Check ✓

Color to show the addends in a different order.
Then write the addition sentences.

1

___ + ___ = ___   ___ + ___ = ___

2

___ + ___ = ___   ___ + ___ = ___

3

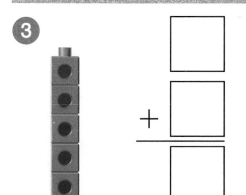

☐
+ ☐
___
☐

☐
+ ☐
___
☐

Think About It   Reasoning

How can you use cubes to show that
2 + 7 is the same as 7 + 2?

Chapter 3 ★ Lesson 2   ninety-three   **93**

Add. Then write an addition sentence with
the addends in a different order.

4
$$6 + 1 = \boxed{7}$$ 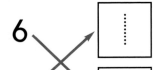 $$+ \boxed{6} = \boxed{7}$$

5
$$3 + 5 = \boxed{}$$ $$+ \boxed{} = \boxed{}$$

6
$$2 + 8 = \boxed{}$$ $$+ \boxed{} = \boxed{}$$

7
$$5 + 0 = \boxed{}$$ $$+ \boxed{} = \boxed{}$$

8
$$3 + 9 = \boxed{}$$ $$+ \boxed{} = \boxed{}$$

9
$$9 + 1 = \boxed{}$$ $$+ \boxed{} = \boxed{}$$

10
$$6 + 2 = \underline{}$$
$$\underline{} + \underline{} = \underline{}$$

11
$$3 + 7 = \underline{}$$
$$\underline{} + \underline{} = \underline{}$$

Problem Solving   Visual Thinking

12   Write two different addition sentences
that tell about the picture.

$$\underline{} + \underline{} = \underline{}$$

$$\underline{} + \underline{} = \underline{}$$

7 Crayons

Home Connection Your child learned that facts such as 2 + 7 and
7 + 2 always have the same sum. **Home Activity** Ask your child to tell
you other addition facts using the same numbers as 5 + 3 = 8 *(3 + 5 = 8)* and
6 + 1 = 7 *(1 + 6 = 7)*.

It is easy to count on when you start with the greater number!

6 is the greater number. Say 6. Then count on.

$(6) + 2 = 8$

$2 + (6) = 8$

Check

Circle the greater number.
Then count on to add.

$9 + 3 = $ ___

$3 + 9 = $ ___

2

$5 + 2 = $ ___

$2 + 5 = $ ___

3

$8 + 1 = $ ___

$1 + 8 = $ ___

Think About It   Reasoning

Why should you count on from the greater number?

Circle the greater number.
Then count on to add.

4 (6) + 3 = _9_   7 + 3 = ___   4 + 1 = ___

5 8 + 1 = ___   3 + 6 = ___   1 + 6 = ___

6 2 + 8 = ___   5 + 3 = ___   2 + 9 = ___

7 1 + 4 = ___   4 + 2 = ___   9 + 3 = ___

8

4	7	9	1	6	2
+ 3	+ 1	+ 3	+ 5	+ 2	+ 7

9

2	7	1	2	8	3
+ 3	+ 2	+ 9	+ 4	+ 2	+ 8

Problem Solving Algebra

Finish the picture and complete the addition sentence.

10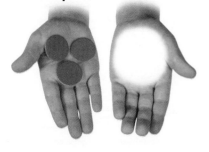

3 + ___ = 4

11

4 + ___ = 6

 Home Connection Your child selected the greater number and then counted on from that number to add 1, 2, or 3. **Home Activity** Say a number between 4 and 9 and ask your child to add 1, 2, or 3 to that number.

You can use a **number line**
to count on.

Start at 6.
Count on 3:
7, 8, 9.

$$6 + 3 = \underline{9}$$

Check ✓

Word Bank

number line

Add 1, 2, or 3.
Use the number line to help you.

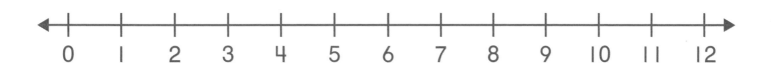

1 $1 + 4 = \underline{}$ $2 + 3 = \underline{}$ $6 + 1 = \underline{}$

2 $3 + 7 = \underline{}$ $1 + 3 = \underline{}$ $8 + 2 = \underline{}$

3 $2 + 2 = \underline{}$ $9 + 1 = \underline{}$ $2 + 5 = \underline{}$

4 $2 + 7 = \underline{}$ $1 + 6 = \underline{}$ $3 + 8 = \underline{}$

Think About It   Reasoning

How do you use a number line to find a sum?

Add 1, 2, or 3.
Use the number line to help you.

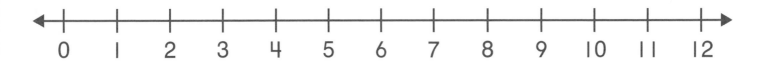

0 1 2 3 4 5 6 7 8 9 10 11 12

5

5	4	2	4	8	5
+ 1	+ 2	+ 1	+ 3	+ 1	+ 2
6					

6

8	5	7	9	1	3
+ 3	+ 3	+ 2	+ 1	+ 2	+ 1

7

1	9	2	4	6	3
+ 7	+ 3	+ 3	+ 1	+ 2	+ 2

Problem Solving Visual Thinking

8 Draw jumps to show the addition on the number line.
Then write the sum.

0 1 2 3 4 5 6 7 8 9 10

$$3 + 5 = \underline{\quad}$$

Name_____

Read carefully.

Carl sees 8 fish.

~~He sees 2 cats.~~

Then he sees 3 more fish.

How many fish does Carl see in all?

___8___ + ___3___ = ___11___ fish

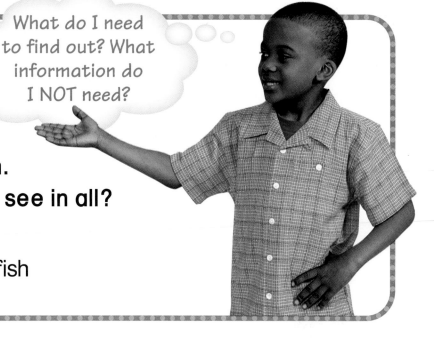

What do I need to find out? What information do I NOT need?

Check ✅

Cross out the extra information.

Then write a number sentence to solve the problem.

① There are 2 dogs at home.

8 more dogs are at the park.

3 cats are at home.

How many dogs are there in all?   ____ + ____ = ____ dogs

② 2 lizards rest on a rock.

4 boys watch the lizards.

5 other lizards play in the sand.

How many lizards are there?   ____ + ____ = ____ lizards

Think About It   Reasoning

How do you know which sentence to cross out?

Cross out the extra information.

Then write a number sentence to solve the problem.

3 ~~Ali visits the pet store 2 times.~~

There are 4 orange cats.

There are 3 black cats.

How many cats are there in all?

___4___ + ___3___ = ___7___ cats

4 The dog has 6 red toys.

He also has 1 blue toy.

The boy has 5 toy cars.

How many toys does the dog have?

_____ + _____ = _____ toys

5 3 birds are singing.

4 girls are singing.

7 more birds are asleep.

How many birds are there in all?

_____ + _____ = _____ birds

6 9 crabs are eating.

2 more crabs are digging.

Sal wants to buy 2 pets.

How many crabs are there?

_____ + _____ = _____ crabs

Home Connection Your child identified and excluded unnecessary information when solving a problem. **Home Activity** Create a word problem that contains extra information. Ask your child to identify the information that is not needed to solve the problem.

Name_____

Count on to find the sum.

  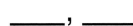

____, ____

6   +   2   = ____

Write two addition sentences that tell about the picture.

___ + ___ = ___   ___ + ___ = ___

Add. Use the number line if you like.

0   1   2   3   4   5   6   7   8   9   10   11   12

③ $4 + 2 =$ ___ $7 + 1 =$ ___ $5 + 3 =$ ___

Add.

④

$$\begin{array}{cc} 5 \\ +\,2 \end{array} \quad \begin{array}{cc} 7 \\ +\,0 \end{array} \quad \begin{array}{cc} 2 \\ +\,9 \end{array} \quad \begin{array}{cc} 8 \\ +\,2 \end{array} \quad \begin{array}{cc} 6 \\ +\,1 \end{array} \quad \begin{array}{cc} 8 \\ +\,3 \end{array}$$

Cross out the extra information.
Then write a number sentence to solve the problem.

⑤   There are 7 boats in the bay.
4 girls are fishing in the bay.
2 more boats sail into the bay.
How many boats are there now?   ____ + ____ = ____ boats

Name_____

What is the missing number?

1
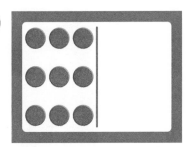

9 is 9 and _____.

0	2	4	6
Ⓐ	Ⓑ	Ⓒ	Ⓓ

2
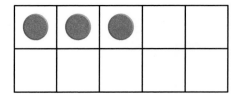

11 is 3 and _____.

3	4	5	8
Ⓐ	Ⓑ	Ⓒ	Ⓓ

3 Which number is less than 4?

3	5	7	9
Ⓐ	Ⓑ	Ⓒ	Ⓓ

Solve the problem.

4 5 turtles are on a rock.
1 turtle swims away.
How many turtles are
on the rock now?

1 turtle	2 turtles	3 turtles	4 turtles
Ⓐ	Ⓑ	Ⓒ	Ⓓ

5 How many more mice are there than cats?

1 more mouse	6 more mice	7 more mice	8 more mice
Ⓐ	Ⓑ	Ⓒ	Ⓓ

Name _____

 **Learn!**

You can use a **double** to help you add.

_5_ + _5_ = _10_   _4_ + _4_ = _8_

Word Bank

double

Check ✓

Write the addition sentence for each double.

1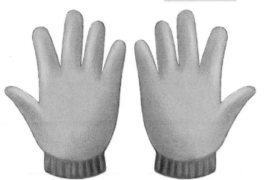

___ + ___ = ___

2

___ + ___ = ___

3

___ + ___ = ___

4

___ + ___ = ___

Think About It   Number Sense

Can you use doubles to make 9? Explain.

Chapter 3 ★ Lesson 6   one hundred three   **103**

Circle the doubles. Then add.

5.
(circled)
```
  1
+ 1
———
  2
```

```
  1
+ 8
———
```

```
  5
+ 2
———
```

```
  9
+ 2
———
```

```
  4
+ 4
———
```

```
  3
+ 6
———
```

6.
```
  6
+ 0
———
```

```
  3
+ 3
———
```

```
  7
+ 1
———
```

```
  0
+ 0
———
```

```
  9
+ 1
———
```

```
  6
+ 6
———
```

7.
```
  9
+ 3
———
```

```
  2
+ 7
———
```

```
  5
+ 5
———
```

```
  2
+ 2
———
```

```
  3
+ 5
———
```

```
  6
+ 1
———
```

8. 6 + 2 = ___   4 + 4 = ___   0 + 8 = ___

9. 6 + 6 = ___   4 + 3 = ___   8 + 3 = ___

Problem Solving   Visual Thinking

Write a number sentence that tells how many
apples there are in all.

10.

11.

___ + ___ = ___   ___ + ___ = ___

Name_____

 **Learn!** ········· Add the doubles.
Then add 1 more.

You can use doubles
to add other facts.

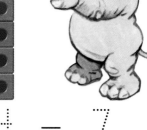

3 + 3 = 6

3 + 4 = 7

Check ✓

Write the addition sentences.
Use cubes if you like.

1

___ + ___ = ___

___ + ___ = ___

2

___ + ___ = ___

___ + ___ = ___

3

___ + ___ = ___

___ + ___ = ___

Think About It   Number Sense

How does knowing 5 + 5 = 10 help you find 5 + 6?

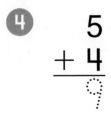

Find each sum.
Use cubes if you like.

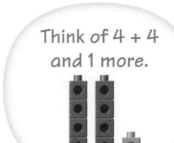

Think of 4 + 4
and 1 more.

④
$$\begin{array}{r} 5 \\ + 4 \\ \hline 9 \end{array}$$

⑤
$$\begin{array}{r} 3 \\ + 3 \\ \hline \end{array}$$
$$\begin{array}{r} 4 \\ + 3 \\ \hline \end{array}$$
$$\begin{array}{r} 5 \\ + 5 \\ \hline \end{array}$$
$$\begin{array}{r} 2 \\ + 2 \\ \hline \end{array}$$
$$\begin{array}{r} 1 \\ + 1 \\ \hline \end{array}$$
$$\begin{array}{r} 3 \\ + 2 \\ \hline \end{array}$$

⑥
$$\begin{array}{r} 2 \\ + 3 \\ \hline \end{array}$$
$$\begin{array}{r} 2 \\ + 1 \\ \hline \end{array}$$
$$\begin{array}{r} 6 \\ + 6 \\ \hline \end{array}$$
$$\begin{array}{r} 3 \\ + 4 \\ \hline \end{array}$$
$$\begin{array}{r} 4 \\ + 4 \\ \hline \end{array}$$
$$\begin{array}{r} 6 \\ + 5 \\ \hline \end{array}$$

⑦
$$\begin{array}{r} 1 \\ + 0 \\ \hline \end{array}$$
$$\begin{array}{r} 1 \\ + 2 \\ \hline \end{array}$$
$$\begin{array}{r} 0 \\ + 0 \\ \hline \end{array}$$
$$\begin{array}{r} 5 \\ + 6 \\ \hline \end{array}$$
$$\begin{array}{r} 4 \\ + 5 \\ \hline \end{array}$$
$$\begin{array}{r} 0 \\ + 1 \\ \hline \end{array}$$

Problem Solving **Algebra**

Write addends so that each fact is a double
or a doubles plus 1.

⑧

$$\begin{array}{r} \square \\ + \square \\ \hline 8 \end{array}$$
$$\begin{array}{r} \square \\ + \square \\ \hline 9 \end{array}$$
$$\begin{array}{r} \square \\ + \square \\ \hline 10 \end{array}$$
$$\begin{array}{r} \square \\ + \square \\ \hline 11 \end{array}$$
$$\begin{array}{r} \square \\ + \square \\ \hline 12 \end{array}$$

 Home Connection Your child used doubles to solve problems that are one more than a double, such as 3 + 4. **Home Activity** Give your child some doubles-plus-1 problems, such as 4 + 5, and have him or her tell you the doubles facts that helped solve the problems.

Name_____

You can use a ten-frame to learn sums of 10.

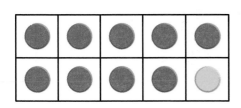

___9___ + ___1___ = 10

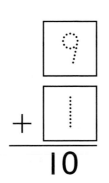

Check ✓

Write the addition sentences for each sum.
Use ten-frames and counters to help you.

1

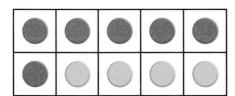

___ + ___ = 10

2

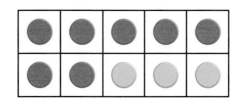

___ + ___ = 10

3

___ + ___ = 10

4

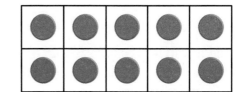

___ + ___ = 10

Think About It   Number Sense

Is 3 + 8 greater than 10, equal to 10, or less
than 10? Explain.

Fill in the missing numbers to find each sum of 10.
Use ten-frames and counters if you like.

5

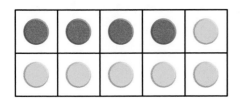

4

$+$ 6

10

6

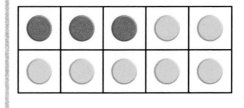

3

$+$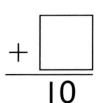

10

7

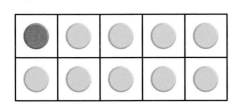

1

$+$

10

8

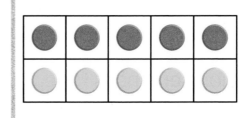

5

$+$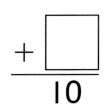

10

9

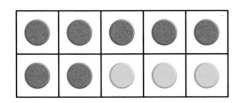

7

$+$

10

10

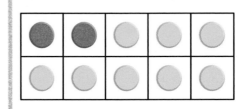

2

$+$

10

Problem Solving   Mental Math

Circle the card that shows your answer.

11 Jon is 3 years old.
How many years is it until
he is 10 years old?

Home Connection Your child used ten-frames to find sums of 10.
Home Activity Ask your child to make a list of all of the sums of 10.

Visualize

You can picture what is happening in a story problem.

1 Read this story problem. Picture it in your mind.

> **There are 5 oranges on the tree.**
> **There are 5 oranges under the tree.**
> **How many oranges are there in all?**

2 Finish the picture of the story problem by drawing the oranges.

How many oranges are on the tree? _____

How many oranges are under the tree? _____

3 Write an addition sentence for the story problem. Count the oranges in the picture to find the sum.

_____ + _____ = _____ oranges

Think About It   Reasoning

How can you use the picture to check that your answer is correct?

4 Read this story problem. Picture it in your mind.

There are 6 worms in the ground.
There are 4 worms on the plant.
How many worms are there in all?

5 Finish the picture of the story problem by drawing the worms.

6 Write an addition sentence for the story problem.
Use the picture to help you.

_____ + _____ = _____ worms

---

7 Read this story problem. Picture it in your mind.

There are 3 bees on the flowers.
There are 8 bees in the air.
How many bees are there in all?

8 Finish the picture of the story problem by drawing the bees.

9 Write an addition sentence for the story problem.
Use the picture to help you.

_____ + _____ = _____ bees

Home Connection Your child read story problems, pictured the problems in his or her mind, drew pictures of the problems, and then used the pictures to write addition sentences. **Home Activity** Tell your child story problems with sums no greater than 12. For each problem, ask your child to picture it in his or her mind, draw a picture, and then write an addition sentence.

Name_____

There are 8 red apples.

There are 4 green apples.

How many apples are there in all?

Read and Understand

You need to find how many
apples there are in all.

Plan and Solve

You can draw a picture.

Then you can write a number sentence.

Count the pictures to find the sum.

___8___ + ___4___ = ___12___ apples

Look Back and Check

How can you be sure your answer is correct?

$$8 + 4 = 12$$

Check ✓

Draw a picture.

Then write a number sentence.

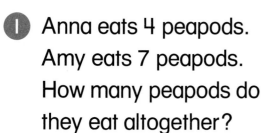

1 Anna eats 4 peapods.
Amy eats 7 peapods.
How many peapods do
they eat altogether?

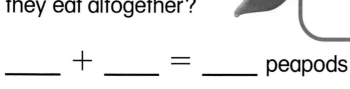

____ + ____ = ____ peapods

Think About It Reasoning

How did the picture help you write the number sentence?

Draw a picture.
Then write a number sentence.

2 There were 7 slices
of watermelon.
Mom cut 5 more slices.
How many slices are there now?

__7__ + __5__ = __12__ slices

3 Chris ate 4 green grapes.
Then he ate 8 red grapes.
How many grapes did he
eat in all?

____ + ____ = ____ grapes

4 Juan bought 7 pints of blueberries
and 4 pints of raspberries.
How many pints of berries
did Juan buy?

____ + ____ = ____ pints

5 There were 5 carrots in the soup.
Dad added 7 more carrots.
How many carrots are there now?

____ + ____ = ____ carrots

Home Connection Your child drew simple pictures to solve problems.
Home Activity Give your child an addition problem and ask him or her to
draw a picture to help solve it.

Name _____

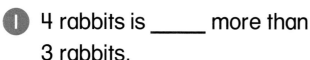 Dorling Kindersley

Do You Know...
that rabbits like to eat lettuce and clover?

1 4 rabbits is _____ more than 3 rabbits.

2 2 rabbits are brown.
1 rabbit is white.
How many rabbits are there in all?

_____ rabbits

3 There are 10 rabbits.
5 of them are brown.
The rest are white.
How many rabbits are white?

_____ + 5 = 10 rabbits

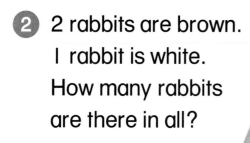

Fun Fact!
Tiny baby rabbits are called kittens.

4 5 big rabbits are eating.
2 ants are eating.
3 little rabbits are eating.
How many rabbits are eating?

_____ + _____ = _____ rabbits

5 4 rabbits hop in the grass.
5 more rabbits join them.
How many rabbits are there in all?

There are _____ rabbits in all.

Very long rabbit ears pick up at sounds of danger!

6 3 rabbits are resting.
3 more rabbits sit with them.
How many rabbits are there in all?

There are _____ rabbits in all.

7 10 rabbits are in the garden.
The rabbits are in two groups.
One group has 7 rabbits.
How many rabbits are in the other group?

There are _____ rabbits in the other group.

8 Writing in Math

Draw a picture to show 10 rabbits in two groups.
Write an addition sentence for your picture.

© Pearson Education, Inc.

Home Connection Your child learned to solve problems by applying his or her math skills. **Home Activity** Talk to your child about how he or she solved the problems on these two pages.

Name_____

Use doubles to add.

1 2 + 2 = ___

2 + 3 = ___

2 3 + 3 = ___

3 + 4 = ___

Write each addition sentence.

3

___ + ___ = ___

4

___ + ___ = ___

Add.

5
$$\begin{array}{r} 5 \\ + 5 \\ \hline \end{array} \qquad \begin{array}{r} 1 \\ + 2 \\ \hline \end{array} \qquad \begin{array}{r} 4 \\ + 5 \\ \hline \end{array} \qquad \begin{array}{r} 8 \\ + 2 \\ \hline \end{array} \qquad \begin{array}{r} 5 \\ + 0 \\ \hline \end{array} \qquad \begin{array}{r} 4 \\ + 6 \\ \hline \end{array}$$

Draw a picture.
Then write a number sentence.

6 Rick has 9 hats.
He buys 3 more hats.
How many hats does
Rick have now?

____ + ____ = ____ hats

What is the missing number?

1

5 and I more is _____.

5	6	7	8
Ⓐ	Ⓑ	Ⓒ	Ⓓ

2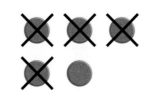

5 take away 4 is _____.

0	I	2	3
Ⓐ	Ⓑ	Ⓒ	Ⓓ

---

3 Which subtraction sentence tells how many butterflies are left?

$2 - 0 = 2$	$4 - 4 = 0$	$4 - 3 = 1$	$4 - 2 = 2$
Ⓐ	Ⓑ	Ⓒ	Ⓓ

---

4 Count on. What is the sum?

$8 + 3 = \underline{}$

9	10	I I	12
Ⓐ	Ⓑ	Ⓒ	Ⓓ

---

5 Which addition fact shows the same addends in a different order?

$$9 + 2 = 11$$

$2 + 9 = 11$	$3 + 8 = 11$	$6 + 3 = 9$	$4 + 2 = 6$
Ⓐ	Ⓑ	Ⓒ	Ⓓ

Name _____

Following Directions

Follow the directions.
Then tell where the children land.

1 Alex starts on 3.
Double it.

3 + 3 = 6

Go back 5.

Alex is at _____.

2 Benito starts on 10.
Go back 9.
Add 3.

Benito is at _____.

3 Carla starts on 3.
Go back 2.
Add 5.

Carla is at _____.

4 Daniel starts on Carla's number.
Double it.
Count on 2.

Daniel is at _____.

5 Writing in Math

Start on 8. Write three directions so that
you land between Benito and Carla.

Home Connection Your child followed directions to solve problems.
Home Activity Give your child a series of directions to follow. Check to see
that he or she listens carefully.

Add 1, 2, or 3 Using a Calculator

You can use a calculator to add 1, 2, or 3.

Press ON/C . Press the keys that you see below.

Then write the number you see in the display.

1  7 + 1 = 8

2  4 + 2 = ____

3  5 + 2 = ____

4  8 + 3 = ____

Press ON/C . Press the keys that you see below.

Write what the display shows each time you press = .

5

 7 + 3 = = =

Display: ____ ____ ____

6

 9 + 2 = = =

Display: ____ ____ ____

7

 1 0 + 2 = = = = = = = =

Display: ____ ____ ____ ____ ____ ____ ____

Think About It   Number Sense

In Exercise 5, what number did you add

each time you pressed = ? Explain.

 Home Connection Your child used a calculator to add 1, 2, or 3 to a greater addend. **Home Activity** Ask your child to explain how to use a calculator to find the sum of 5 + 3.

Name _____

Plan How to Find the Answer

Sometimes you need to decide when to add and when to subtract.

Test-Taking Strategies

Understand the Question

Get Information for the Answer

Plan How to Find the Answer

Make Smart Choices

Use Writing in Math

1. Shannon has 7 dolls. She buys 3 more dolls. Which number sentence tells how many dolls she has now?

   Ⓐ $7 + 3 = 10$

   Ⓑ $7 + 2 = 9$

   Ⓒ $7 - 3 = 4$

   Ⓓ $10 - 3 = 7$

Plan to **add** if you are joining two groups together.

Plan to **subtract** if you are separating two groups.

Also plan to subtract if you are comparing two groups.

What does this question ask you to do?

Your Turn

Do you need to add or subtract?

Fill in the correct answer bubble.

2. Tony has 6 markers. Maria has 8 markers. Which number sentence tells how many more markers Maria has?

   Ⓐ $2 + 8 = 10$

   Ⓑ $8 + 6 = 14$

   Ⓒ $8 - 1 = 7$

   Ⓓ $8 - 6 = 2$

Home Connection Your child prepared for standardized tests by determining whether to add or subtract to solve a given math problem.
Home Activity Ask your child how he or she determined whether to add or subtract in Exercise 2.

Name _____

Got Math?

Have you ever been to a dairy farm?
Cows are raised on dairy farms.
From cows we get the milk we drink.

"Moo"ving the Milk

Write number sentences to learn more about how
milk moves from the dairy farm to the grocery store.

1 Most dairy cows produce 7 gallons of milk a day.
One cow produced only 5 gallons.
How many more gallons does she need
to produce to catch up to the other cows?

____ − ____ = ____ more gallons

2 Each dairy cow is milked every 12 hours.
One cow was milked 8 hours ago.
How many more hours will go by
before that cow is milked again?

____ − ____ = ____ more hours

3 Milk goes from the dairy farm to a factory.
From there, the milk is taken to the grocery store.
How many different places is that?

____ + ____ + ____ = ____ different places

Take It to the NET
Video and Activities
www.scottforesman.com

Home Connection Your child solved problems about milk production by writing number sentences. **Home Activity** Ask your child to solve math problems about drinking milk at home. For example, ask your child to find the total number of cups of milk he or she drank in the past two days.

© Pearson Education, Inc.

Name_____

Count on to find the sum.

1

5

_____, _____

5   +   2   = _____

Add. Use the number line if you like.

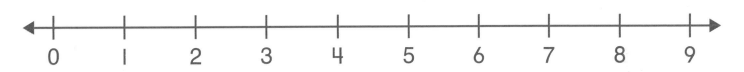

0   1   2   3   4   5   6   7   8   9

2 7 + 2 = _____   6 + 1 = _____   2 + 3 = _____

Add.

3
$\begin{array}{r} 6 \\ +2 \\ \hline \end{array}$ $\begin{array}{r} 8 \\ +0 \\ \hline \end{array}$ $\begin{array}{r} 8 \\ +3 \\ \hline \end{array}$ $\begin{array}{r} 7 \\ +1 \\ \hline \end{array}$ $\begin{array}{r} 4 \\ +2 \\ \hline \end{array}$ $\begin{array}{r} 9 \\ +3 \\ \hline \end{array}$

Draw a picture.
Then write a number sentence.

4   Olga has 6 dolls.
    She gets 3 more dolls.
    How many dolls does
    Olga have now?

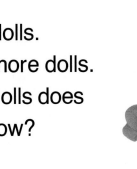

_____ + _____ = _____ dolls

Use doubles to add.

 5 + 5 = ___

5 + 6 = ___

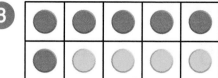 **4 + 4 = ___**

4 + 5 = ___

Write each addition sentence.

 7

___ + ___ = ___

8

___ + ___ = ___

Write two different addition sentences that tell about the picture.

9

___ + ___ = ___   ___ + ___ = ___

Cross out the extra information.
Then write a number sentence to solve the problem.

10 8 rabbits are in the yard.
    1 more rabbit hops into the yard.
    3 cats are in the yard.
    How many rabbits are in the yard now?

____ + ____ = ____ rabbits

Read Together

Count Back, Jack

Written by Paul Evans   Illustrated by   Karen Stormer Brooks

This Math Storybook belongs to

_____

Counting back is really great.
Now we know the answer is 8.
Counting back is fun to do.
You will like to do it too!

Home-School Connection

Dear Family,

Today my class started chapter 4, **Strategies for Subtraction Facts to 12.** I will learn ways to subtract from the numbers 1 through 12. Here are some of the new math words I will be learning and some things we can do to help me with my math.

Love,

_____

Math Activity to Do at Home

Make a group of pennies and a group of nickels, each with fewer than 12 coins. Ask your child to write subtraction sentences to compare the coins. For example, if you give your child 8 pennies and 3 nickels, your child should write $8 - 3 = 5$ to show that there are 5 more pennies.

Books to Read Together

Reading math stories reinforces concepts. Look for these books in your local library:

Turtle Splash
by Cathryn Falwell
(Greenwillow, 2001)

Subtraction Action
by Loreen Leedy
(Holiday House, 2000)

Take It to the NET
More Activities
www.scottforesman.com

My New Math Words

count back Use this strategy to subtract 1 or 2 from a number.

$$6 - 2 = 4$$

Start at 6.
Count back 5, 4.

related facts Addition and subtraction facts are related if they use the same numbers.

$$4 + 3 = 7$$
$$\text{so } 7 - 4 = 3$$

fact family A fact family is a group of related addition and subtraction facts.

$$4 + 5 = 9$$
$$5 + 4 = 9$$
$$9 - 5 = 4$$
$$9 - 4 = 5$$

Name _____

Counting Back

How to Play

1. Take turns spinning the spinner.
   Name the number you land on.
   Then count back 1.
2. Place a marker on the answer
   on the number line.
3. Play until every number is covered.
4. Play again and count back 2.
   If the spinner lands on 1,
   skip a turn.

What You Need

paper clip
pencil
2 kinds of game markers

124   one hundred twenty-four

Name

You can use a number line to **count back**.
Count back to subtract.

Start on 8.
Count back 2: 7, 6.

$$8 - 2 = \underline{6}$$

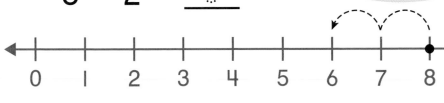

0 I 2 3 4 5 6 7 8 9 10 II 12

Word Bank

count back

Check ✓

Use the number line.
Count back to find each difference.

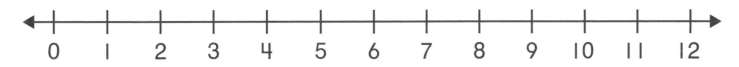

0 I 2 3 4 5 6 7 8 9 10 II 12

1 $7 - 2 = \underline{}$ $10 - 1 = \underline{}$ $4 - 1 = \underline{}$

2 $6 - 1 = \underline{}$ $5 - 2 = \underline{}$ $11 - 2 = \underline{}$

3 $9 - 2 = \underline{}$ $7 - 1 = \underline{}$ $3 - 2 = \underline{}$

4 $8 - 1 = \underline{}$ $10 - 2 = \underline{}$ $2 - 1 = \underline{}$

5 $4 - 2 = \underline{}$ $9 - 1 = \underline{}$ $6 - 2 = \underline{}$

Think About It Reasoning

How is adding on a number line different from
subtracting on a number line?

Chapter 4 ★ Lesson 1

Count back to subtract.

Use the number line if you like.

```
◄──┼──┼──┼──┼──┼──┼──┼──┼──┼──┼──┼──┼──┼──►
   0  1  2  3  4  5  6  7  8  9  10 11 12
```

6

7	11	6	10	3	9
− 1	− 2	− 1	− 2	− 1	− 1

6

7

8	1	4	2	9	2
− 2	− 1	− 2	− 2	− 2	− 1

8

7	5	4	6	10	8
− 2	− 1	− 1	− 2	− 1	− 1

Problem Solving   Algebra

Use the number line to subtract.

Write the missing numbers. Then look for a pattern.

```
◄──┼──┼──┼──┼──┼──┼──┼──┼──┼──┼──┼──┼──┼──►
   0  1  2  3  4  5  6  7  8  9  10 11 12
```

9

9	8	7	☐	5	☐
− ☐	− 2	− ☐	− 2	− 2	− 2
7	☐	5	4	☐	2

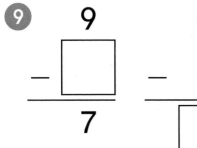

Home Connection Your child used a number line to count back 1 and 2.
Home Activity Point to a number greater than 2 on the number line at the top of this page. Ask your child to count back 1 or 2 from that number.

Name_____

You can count back to subtract 1 or 2.

4 − 1 = 3

Start at 4.
Count back 1: 3.

Check ✔

Count back to subtract 1 or 2.
Use counters if you like.

①

6 − 2 = ___

②

5 − 1 = ___

③

8 − 2 = ___

④

3 − 2 = ___

⑤

10 − 2 = ___

⑥

7 − 1 = ___

Think About It   Reasoning

Is it easier to count back for 7 − 2 or 7 − 4? Explain.

Count back to subtract.
Use counters if you like.

7

$$9$$
$$-\ 1$$
$$8$$

8

6	5	2	8	4	1
$-\ 2$	$-\ 1$	$-\ 2$	$-\ 1$	$-\ 2$	$-\ 1$

9

6	11	10	3	7	7
$-\ 1$	$-\ 2$	$-\ 1$	$-\ 1$	$-\ 2$	$-\ 1$

10

2	5	8	9	4	10
$-\ 1$	$-\ 2$	$-\ 2$	$-\ 2$	$-\ 1$	$-\ 2$

Problem Solving   Number Sense

Use the clues to answer each question.

11 Joy counted back 2.
Her answer was 7.
On what number did
Joy start?

____

12 Mick counted back 1.
His answer was 9.
On what number did
Mick start?

____

 Home Connection Your child counted back to subtract 1 or 2.
Home Activity Ask your child to explain how to count back to show 8 − 2.

Name_____

Learn!

You can use doubles to help you subtract.

Since I know 4 + 4 = 8,
I also know 8 − 4 = 4.

Think 4 + 4 = __8__

so 8 − 4 = __4__

Check ✓

Add the doubles.
Then use the doubles to help you subtract.

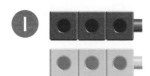

①

Think 3 + 3 = ___

so 6 − 3 = ___

②

Think 5 + 5 = ___

so 10 − 5 = ___

③

Think 6 + 6 = ___

so 12 − 6 = ___

④

Think 2 + 2 = ___

so 4 − 2 = ___

Think About It   Number Sense

Can doubles help you subtract 12 − 5? Explain.

Add the doubles.

Then use the doubles to help you subtract.

5

$$\begin{array}{r} 5 \\ + 5 \\ \hline 10 \end{array} \qquad \begin{array}{r} 10 \\ - 5 \\ \hline 5 \end{array}$$

6

$$\begin{array}{r} 1 \\ + 1 \\ \hline \end{array} \qquad \begin{array}{r} 2 \\ - 1 \\ \hline \end{array}$$

7

$$\begin{array}{r} 4 \\ + 4 \\ \hline \end{array} \qquad \begin{array}{r} 8 \\ - 4 \\ \hline \end{array}$$

8

$$\begin{array}{r} 6 \\ + 6 \\ \hline \end{array} \qquad \begin{array}{r} 12 \\ - 6 \\ \hline \end{array}$$

9

$$\begin{array}{r} 3 \\ + 3 \\ \hline \end{array} \qquad \begin{array}{r} 6 \\ - 3 \\ \hline \end{array}$$

Problem Solving   Visual Thinking

Write an addition sentence and a
subtraction sentence for the picture.

10

___ + ___ = ___

___ − ___ = ___

Home Connection Your child used doubles to subtract. **Home Activity**
Ask your child to use buttons or other small objects to show a doubles fact.
Then have him or her name the subtraction problem that can be solved
using the doubles fact.

Name_____

Identify the Main Idea

Knowing the main idea in a story problem
can help you solve it.

1 Read this story problem.

**There were 8 apples in a bowl.
Mike ate 2 apples.
How many apples are left?**

2 Circle what this story is all about.

   a bowl   apples   a girl

3 Circle the main idea in the story problem.
  a. Mike likes apples.
  b. How many apples are left?
  c. Apples are in a bowl.

4 How many apples were in the bowl? _____

How many apples did Mike eat? _____

5 Solve this story problem.
Write a subtraction sentence about the main idea.

____ − ____ = ____ apples

Think About It   Reasoning

Why did you subtract to solve this
story problem?

6 Read this story problem.

A farmer had 6 pumpkins.
He sold 5 pumpkins.
How many pumpkins are left?

7 Circle the main idea in the story problem.
   a. Pumpkins are orange.
   b. How many pumpkins are left?
   c. A farmer grows pumpkins.

8 How many pumpkins did the farmer have? _____

How many pumpkins did the farmer sell? _____

9 Solve the story problem.
Write a subtraction sentence about the main idea.

_____ − _____ = _____ pumpkin

---

10 Read this story problem.

A farmer had 7 flowers.
She sold 6 flowers.
How many flowers does she have now?

11 How many flowers did the farmer have? _____

How many flowers did the farmer sell? _____

12 Solve the story problem.
Write a subtraction sentence about the main idea.

_____ − _____ = _____ flower

Home Connection Your child identified the main idea in story problems and solved the problems by writing subtraction sentences. **Home Activity** Make up story problems that involve subtracting a number from 12 or any number less than 12. Ask your child what the main ideas of the problems are and have your child write subtraction sentences to solve the problems.

 **Algebra**

There are 8 children on the bus.
2 children get off the bus.
How many children are left?

Read and Understand

You need to find how many children
are left on the bus.

Plan and Solve

Write a subtraction sentence.
Count back to find the difference.

 children

Look Back and Check

Does your answer make sense?

Check ✓

Write a subtraction sentence to answer the question.

1 There are 5 children playing with jacks.
2 children are playing with clay.
How many more children are
playing with jacks than with clay?

____ .... ____ ::::::: ____ more children

Think About It   Reasoning

How can you prove that your answer is correct?

Write a subtraction sentence to answer each question.

2 Rita had 10 crayons.
She gave 5 crayons to Luz.
How many crayons
does Rita have left?

__10__ – __5__ = __5__ crayons

---

3 Ben has 8 pencils
and 4 erasers.
How many more pencils than
erasers does he have?

_____ – _____ = _____ more pencils

---

4 There are 7 boys and
2 girls painting pictures.
How many more boys
than girls are painting pictures?

_____ – _____ = _____ more boys

---

5 12 children are playing with the blocks.
6 children move to the art table.
How many children are left playing
with blocks?

_____ – _____ = _____ children

Home Connection Your child wrote subtraction sentences to solve problems. **Home Activity** When you are eating with your child, ask questions such as, "How many crackers did you have? How many did you eat? How many do you have left?" Have your child write subtraction sentences for each problem.

Name_____

Count back to subtract.
Use counters if you like.

1

$$3 - 2 = \underline{\quad}$$

2

$$8 - 1 = \underline{\quad}$$

Add the doubles.
Then use the doubles to help you subtract.

3

$$\begin{array}{r} 2 \\ + 2 \\ \hline \end{array} \qquad \begin{array}{r} 4 \\ - 2 \\ \hline \end{array}$$

4

$$\begin{array}{r} 6 \\ + 6 \\ \hline \end{array} \qquad \begin{array}{r} 12 \\ - 6 \\ \hline \end{array}$$

Count back to subtract.
Use the number line if you like.

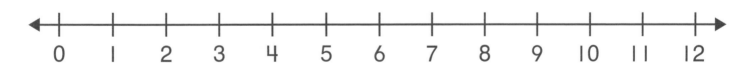

0 1 2 3 4 5 6 7 8 9 10 11 12

5 $7 - 2 = \underline{\quad}$ $\qquad$ $10 - 1 = \underline{\quad}$ $\qquad$ $2 - 2 = \underline{\quad}$

Write a subtraction sentence to answer the question.

6 6 horses are in the barn.
2 horses walk away.
How many horses are left
in the barn?

$\underline{\quad\quad} \underset{\cdots}{\underline{\quad\quad}} \underline{\quad\quad} \underset{\cdots}{\underline{\quad\quad}} \underline{\quad\quad}$ horses

Name_____

What is the missing number?

1

2 fewer than 7 is _____.

2	5	7	9
Ⓐ	Ⓑ	Ⓒ	Ⓓ

2

$4 - 4 =$ ___

0	1	4	6
Ⓐ	Ⓑ	Ⓒ	Ⓓ

---

3 Which addition sentence matches the picture?

$4 + 1 = 5$	$2 + 2 = 4$	$2 + 4 = 6$	$4 + 4 = 8$
Ⓐ	Ⓑ	Ⓒ	Ⓓ

---

4 Which addition sentence matches the picture?

$3 + 3 = 6$	$4 + 4 = 8$	$3 + 4 = 7$	$3 + 5 = 8$
Ⓐ	Ⓑ	Ⓒ	Ⓓ

---

5 Which addition sentence answers the question?

Diego has 4 shells.
He finds 8 more shells.
How many shells does Diego have now?

$7 + 3 = 10$	$4 + 8 = 12$	$8 + 3 = 11$	$8 + 0 = 8$
Ⓐ	Ⓑ	Ⓒ	Ⓓ

Name_____

 **Algebra**

Addition and subtraction facts are related if they use the same numbers.

These are related facts.

$$5 \quad + \quad 4 \quad = \quad \underline{9}$$

$$\underline{9} \quad - \quad \underline{4} \quad = \quad 5$$

Word Bank

related facts

Check ✓

Add.

Then write a related subtraction fact.

1 $1 \quad + \quad 6 \quad = \quad \underline{}$

$\underline{} \quad - \quad \underline{} \quad = \quad \underline{}$

2  $5 \quad + \quad 6 \quad = \quad \underline{}$

$\underline{} \quad - \quad \underline{} \quad = \quad \underline{}$

3  $3 \quad + \quad 6 \quad = \quad \underline{}$

$\underline{} \quad - \quad \underline{} \quad = \quad \underline{}$

Think About It   Reasoning

What two subtraction facts are related to $6 + 4 = 10$?

Write related addition and subtraction
facts for each picture.

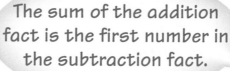

The sum of the addition
fact is the first number in
the subtraction fact.

$$6 + 5 = 11$$
$$11 - 5 = 6$$

5

___ + ___ = ___

___ − ___ = ___

6

___ + ___ = ___

___ − ___ = ___

7

___ + ___ = ___

___ − ___ = ___

8

___ + ___ = ___

___ − ___ = ___

Problem Solving   Writing in Math

Draw a picture to show these related facts.

9 $4 + 5 = 9$ $9 - 5 = 4$

Home Connection Your child wrote related addition and subtraction facts.
Home Activity Set out two groups of small objects. Ask your child to write
an addition fact and a subtraction fact for the groups. Then switch roles and
repeat.

© Pearson Education, Inc.

Name_____

Learn! Algebra

These four related facts make up a **fact family**.

The numbers in this fact family are 3, 7, and 10.

$7 + \underline{3} = \underline{10}$ $10 - \underline{3} = \underline{7}$

$3 + \underline{7} = \underline{10}$ $10 - \underline{7} = \underline{3}$

Word Bank

fact family

Check ✓

Complete each fact family.
Use cubes if you like.

1

$4 + \underline{} = \underline{}$ $12 - \underline{} = \underline{}$

$8 + \underline{} = \underline{}$ $12 - \underline{} = \underline{}$

2

$4 + \underline{} = \underline{}$ $6 - \underline{} = \underline{}$

$2 + \underline{} = \underline{}$ $6 - \underline{} = \underline{}$

Think About It   Reasoning

This fact family has only two facts. Tell why.

$3 + 3 = 6$

$6 - 3 = 3$

Write each fact family.
Use cubes if you like.

Most fact families have 4 facts.

3

$\underline{2} + \underline{3} = \underline{5}$ $\underline{5} - \underline{3} = \underline{2}$

$\underline{3} + \underline{2} = \underline{5}$ $\underline{5} - \underline{2} = \underline{3}$

4

$\underline{} + \underline{} = \underline{}$ $\underline{} - \underline{} = \underline{}$

$\underline{} + \underline{} = \underline{}$ $\underline{} - \underline{} = \underline{}$

5

$\underline{} + \underline{} = \underline{}$ $\underline{} - \underline{} = \underline{}$

$\underline{} + \underline{} = \underline{}$ $\underline{} - \underline{} = \underline{}$

6

$\underline{} + \underline{} = \underline{}$ $\underline{} - \underline{} = \underline{}$

$\underline{} + \underline{} = \underline{}$ $\underline{} - \underline{} = \underline{}$

Problem Solving   Algebra

7 Write the missing signs to complete the fact family.

$7 \bigcirc 3 = 4$ $4 \bigcirc 3 = 7$

$3 \bigcirc 4 = 7$ $7 \bigcirc 4 = 3$

Home Connection Your child wrote the number sentences in addition and subtraction fact families. **Home Activity** Give your child an addition sentence. Ask him or her to tell you the rest of the facts in that fact family.

 **Algebra**

You can use addition to help you subtract.

If $1 + 7 = 8$,
then $8 - 7 = 1$.

Think $\quad 1 + 7 =$ __8__

so $\quad 8 - 7 =$ __1__

Check ✓

Add.

Then use the addition fact to help you subtract.

1

Think $\quad 5 + 7 =$ ___

so $\quad 12 - 5 =$ ___

2

Think $\quad 9 + 2 =$ ___

so $\quad 11 - 9 =$ ___

3

Think $\quad 8 + 3 =$ ___

so $\quad 11 - 8 =$ ___

4

Think $\quad 9 + 3 =$ ___

so $\quad 12 - 9 =$ ___

Think About It Number Sense

Which two addition facts could help you subtract $7 - 4$?

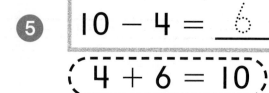

Circle the addition fact that will help you subtract.
Then subtract.

5 | 10 − 4 = __6__
(4 + 6 = 10)
3 + 8 = 11

6 | 11 − 7 = ___
9 + 3 = 12
4 + 7 = 11

7 | 12 − 9 = ___
9 + 3 = 12
7 + 1 = 8

8 | 12 − 5 = ___
5 + 7 = 12
5 + 6 = 11

9 | 5 − 4 = ___
5 + 3 = 8
4 + 1 = 5

10 | 6 − 5 = ___
5 + 1 = 6
6 + 1 = 7

11 | 10 − 9 = ___
9 + 1 = 10
2 + 8 = 10

12 | 9 − 8 = ___
8 + 1 = 9
1 + 7 = 8

Problem Solving Mental Math

13 Dan had 11 stamps.
He gave away 6 stamps.
How many stamps does Dan have left?

_____ stamps

Home Connection Your child used addition facts to help solve subtraction problems. **Home Activity** Write a subtraction problem on a piece of paper. Ask your child to write an addition fact to use that will help find the difference.

© Pearson Education, Inc.

Should I add or subtract?

Maria planted 7 seeds.

Then she planted 3 more seeds.

How many seeds did Maria plant in all?

(add)   subtract

__7__ (+) __3__ = __10__ seeds

Check ✓

Circle **add** or **subtract**.

Then write a number sentence.

1 Rob grew 8 red peppers
and 6 green peppers.
How many more red peppers
did Rob grow than green peppers?

add   subtract

____ ◯ ____ = ____ more red peppers

2 Tom dug up 11 potatoes.
He gave away 5 potatoes.
How many potatoes does
Tom have left?

add   subtract

____ ◯ ____ = ____ potatoes

Think About It Reasoning

In the problem about potatoes, how did you
decide to subtract?

Circle **add** or **subtract**.

Then write a number sentence.

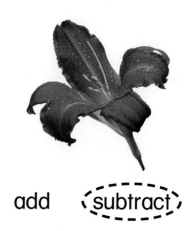

3 12 flowers were growing in the garden.
Jay picked 9 of them.
How many flowers are left
in the garden?

add (subtract)

_12_ ⊝ _9_ = _3_ flowers

4 There were 9 holes in the garden.
Sari dug 1 more hole.
How many holes are there
in the garden now?

add   subtract

____ ◯ ____ = ____ holes

5 There are 7 plants.
Alma watered 6 plants.
How many plants are there
left to water?

add   subtract

____ ◯ ____ = ____ plant

6 There are 2 small pumpkins
and 7 big pumpkins.
How many pumpkins
are there in all?

add   subtract

____ ◯ ____ = ____ pumpkins

Home Connection Your child decided whether to add or subtract and wrote a number sentence to solve each problem. **Home Activity** Point to a problem on the page. Ask your child to explain why he or she chose to add or subtract.

Name _____

Dorling Kindersley

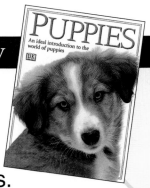
PUPPIES
An ideal introduction to the world of puppies

Do You Know...
that a dog's hair is called its coat? Some dogs have soft coats. Some dogs have stiff, wiry coats.

1. Here are some puppies. How many more puppies do you need to have 10 in all?

$$4 + \underline{\hspace{1cm}} = 10$$

2. There are 6 puppies playing. 3 more puppies join them. How many puppies are there now?

There are _____ puppies now.

Fun Fact!
A dog learns about new things by smell. A dog's sense of smell is better than most people's sense of smell.

3. 9 puppies are playing together. 7 puppies are running after a ball. How many puppies are not running after a ball?

$$\underline{\hspace{1cm}} - \underline{\hspace{1cm}} = \underline{\hspace{1cm}}$$

4. The fuzzy puppy has 5 toys.
The spotted puppy has 7 toys.
How many more toys does
the spotted puppy have?

____ − ____ = ____

The spotted puppy has _____ more toys.

5. The puppies were playing with 12 toys.
They lost 6 of the toys.
How many toys are left?

____ − ____ = ____

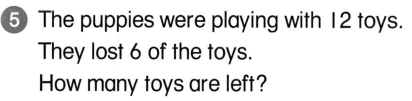

An adult Labrador
retriever can act
as a guide dog for
people with visual
impairments.

6. Which doubles fact helped
you solve Exercise 5?

____ + ____ = ____

7. **Writing in Math**

Write a subtraction story about puppies.
Use pictures, numbers, or words.

Home Connection Your child learned to solve problems by applying
his or her math skills. **Home Activity** Talk to your child about how he
or she solved the problems on these two pages.

Name_____

Write related addition and subtraction
facts for the picture.

1

___ + ___ = ___

___ − ___ = ___

Write the fact family.

2

___ + ___ = ___   ___ − ___ = ___

___ + ___ = ___   ___ − ___ = ___

Circle **add** or **subtract**.
Then write a number sentence.

3 Saul has 10 baseballs and 4 bats.
How many more baseballs
does he have than bats?

add   subtract

___ ◯ ___ = ___ more baseballs

Circle the addition fact that will help you subtract.
Then subtract.

4
┌─────────────────┐
│ 10 − 8 = ___   │
└─────────────────┘

9 + 2 = 11

8 + 2 = 10

5
┌─────────────────┐
│ 12 − 3 = ___   │
└─────────────────┘

9 + 3 = 12

1 + 9 = 10

Name_____

Add or subtract. Use the number line if you like.

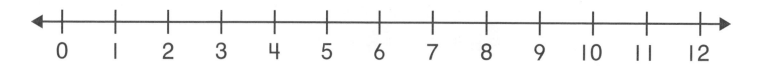

```
0   1   2   3   4   5   6   7   8   9   10   11   12
```

1 6 + 3 = ___

| 7 | 8 | 9 | 10 |
| Ⓐ | Ⓑ | Ⓒ | Ⓓ |

2 11 − 2 = ___

| 7 | 8 | 9 | 10 |
| Ⓐ | Ⓑ | Ⓒ | Ⓓ |

3 7 − 1 = ___

| 6 | 7 | 8 | 9 |
| Ⓐ | Ⓑ | Ⓒ | Ⓓ |

4 9 + 2 = ___

| 9 | 10 | 11 | 12 |
| Ⓐ | Ⓑ | Ⓒ | Ⓓ |

5 Which subtraction sentence answers the question?

Jake had 9 snow globes.
He gave 4 of them to Kay.
How many snow globes does Jake have left?

4 − 4 = 0   5 − 4 = 1   9 − 2 = 7   9 − 4 = 5
   Ⓐ   Ⓑ   Ⓒ   Ⓓ

6 Which number sentence answers the question?

Lena had 8 peaches.
She ate 1 peach.
How many peaches does Lena have now?

8 + 1 = 9   8 − 1 = 7   9 − 2 = 7   1 + 2 = 3
   Ⓐ   Ⓑ   Ⓒ   Ⓓ

Many Names for a Number

There are many ways to name 6. Can you think of another way?

$$12 - 6$$

$$2 + 4$$

$$9 - 3$$

Circle all of the names for each number.

$(2 + 9)$	$5 + 6$	$8 + 3$
$1 + 1$	$7 + 4$	$10 - 1$

$4 + 5$	$10 - 3$	$7 - 0$
$12 - 6$	$1 + 6$	$3 + 4$

$12 - 3$	$4 + 4$	$7 + 2$
$11 - 2$	$5 - 4$	$1 + 8$

$6 + 6$	$9 + 3$	$1 + 2$
$10 - 2$	$7 + 5$	$8 + 4$

5 **Writing in Math**

Make a list of different ways to name 10.

How many ways can you find?

Home Connection Your child found many ways to name different numbers.
Home Activity Have your child tell three different ways to name 8.

Name_____

Subtract Using a Calculator

You can use a calculator to subtract.

Press ON/C . Press the keys that you see below.

Write the number you see in the display after you press = .

1 8 − 2 = 6

2 5 − 1 = _____

3 4 − 3 = _____

4 9 − 5 = _____

Press ON/C each time you begin.

Write what the display shows each time you press = .

5 6 − 1 = = =   Display: _____ _____ _____

6 1 0 − 2 = = =   Display: _____ _____ _____

7 2 0 − 4 = = =   Display: _____ _____ _____

8 3 0 − 5 = = =   Display: _____ _____ _____

Think About It   Number Sense

In Exercise 6, how many more times would you need to

press = before the display would show 0?

Home Connection Your child used a calculator to learn how to subtract the same amount over and over again. **Home Activity** Ask your child to explain how many times he or she would need to subtract 10 to get from 50 back to 0. *(5 times)* 40? *(4 times)* 30? *(3 times)* 20? *(2 times)* 10? *(1 time)*

Chapter 4

Make Smart Choices

When you take a math test,
you need to make good choices
and mark your answers correctly.

Test-Taking Strategies

Understand the Question

Get Information for the Answer

Plan How to Find the Answer

Make Smart Choices

Use Writing in Math

1 Use the number line.
Count back to subtract.
Fill in the answer bubble.

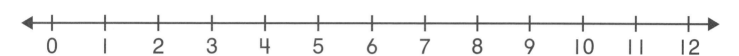

$$10 - 1 = \_\_\_$$

Ⓐ 7   Ⓑ 8   Ⓒ 9   Ⓓ 10

After you counted backward, did you
fill in the correct answer bubble?

Your Turn

Solve the problem and fill in the answer bubble.

2 Use the number line. Count back to subtract.

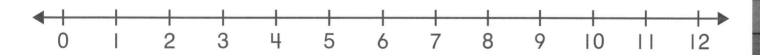

$$6 - 2 = \_\_\_$$

Ⓐ 4   Ⓑ 5   Ⓒ 6   Ⓓ 7

Home Connection Your child prepared for standardized tests by learning how to
mark answer choices. **Home Activity** Ask your child how he or she knows that
the answer bubble for Exercise 2 was filled in correctly. *(Possible answer: I colored
in the bubble completely and didn't make any marks outside of the bubble.)*

Name _____

Discover Math in Your World

Countdown!

Have you ever watched a Space Shuttle launch on TV? Pretend that you are going on a flight.

Subtracting ... 3, 2, 1

Solve each problem. Use the number line to help you.

1 Your mission is supposed to last 10 days. But on Day 6, one of the computers has a problem. Mission Control tells you to land on Day 7. How many more days was your mission supposed to last?

$$\underline{10} - \underline{7} = \underline{\quad} \text{ more days}$$

2 There are going to be 12 flights this year. Your team is on the 10th flight. How many more flights will there be this year?

$$\underline{12} - \underline{10} = \underline{\quad} \text{ more flights}$$

3 There are 7 people on your mission. 1 is the commander, 1 is the pilot, and 2 are mission specialists. The rest are payload specialists. How many people are payload specialists?

$$\underline{1} + \underline{1} + \underline{2} + \underline{\quad} = \underline{7} \text{ people in all}$$

_____ people are payload specialists.

15
14
13
12
11
10
9
8
7
6
5
4
3
2
1
0

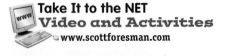
Take It to the NET
Video and Activities
www.scottforesman.com

Home Connection Your child solved problems about an imaginary Space Shuttle mission by using a number line and by writing number sentences. **Home Activity** Ask your child to explain how using a number line helps him or her solve subtraction problems.

Name _____

Count back to subtract.
Use the number line if you like.

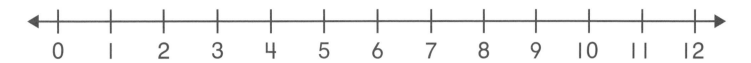

1 10 − 2 = ___   8 − 1 = ___   11 − 2 = ___

Write related addition and subtraction facts
for the picture.

2

      ___ + ___ = ___

___ − ___ = ___

Count back to subtract.
Use counters if you like.

3

5 − 2 = ___

4

10 − 1 = ___

Add the doubles.
Then use the doubles to help you subtract.

5

```
  5    10
+ 5  −  5
```

6

```
  3     6
+ 3  −  3
```

Circle the addition fact that will help you subtract.
Then subtract.

7 | $12 - 7 =$ ___ |

$5 + 1 = 6$

$5 + 7 = 12$

8 | $11 - 8 =$ ___ |

$5 + 3 = 8$

$3 + 8 = 11$

Write the fact family.

9

___ $+$ ___ $=$ ___   ___ $-$ ___ $=$ ___

___ $+$ ___ $=$ ___   ___ $-$ ___ $=$ ___

Write a subtraction sentence to answer the question.

10 There are 5 puppies.
There are 3 kittens.
How many fewer kittens
are there than puppies?

____ $-$ ____ $=$ ____ fewer kittens

Circle **add** or **subtract**.
Then write a number sentence.

11 Matt has 9 baseball cards.
He gets 3 more cards.
How many cards does
he have in all?

add   subtract

____ $\bigcirc$ ____ $=$ ____ cards

Name_____

1 Which letters show the same pattern as the toys?

Ⓐ A B B A B B A B B A

Ⓑ A B A B A B A B A B

Ⓒ A B C A B C A B C A

Ⓓ A B C D A B C D A B

2 Which addition fact completes this fact family?

$$8 + 2 = 10 \qquad 10 - 8 = 2 \qquad 10 - 2 = 8$$

| $2 + 6 = 8$ | $2 + 8 = 10$ | $5 + 3 = 8$ | $5 + 5 = 10$ |
| Ⓐ | Ⓑ | Ⓒ | Ⓓ |

3 Which addition fact will help you subtract?

$$7 - 1 = \underline{}$$

| $1 + 6 = 7$ | $7 + 1 = 8$ | $1 + 9 = 10$ | $7 + 2 = 9$ |
| Ⓐ | Ⓑ | Ⓒ | Ⓓ |

What is the missing number?

 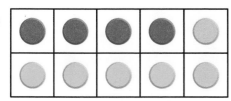

$$4 + \underline{} = 10$$

| 2 | 4 | 5 | 6 |
| Ⓐ | Ⓑ | Ⓒ | Ⓓ |

5

$$5 + \underline{} = 10$$

| 2 | 3 | 4 | 5 |
| Ⓐ | Ⓑ | Ⓒ | Ⓓ |

How many fewer red cubes than blue cubes?

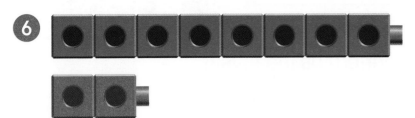

6

_____ fewer red cubes

Write two different addition sentences that tell
about this picture.

7

___ + ___ = ___   ___ + ___ = ___

Subtract.
Use the number line if you like.

0   1   2   3   4   5   6   7   8   9   10   11   12

8 9 − 2 = ___   6 − 2 = ___   8 − 1 = ___

Cross out the extra information.
Then write a number sentence.

9 There are 2 toy chests in Robert's room.
One toy chest has 6 toys.
The other toy chest has 3 toys.
How many toys are there in all?

___ + ___ = ___ toys

154B

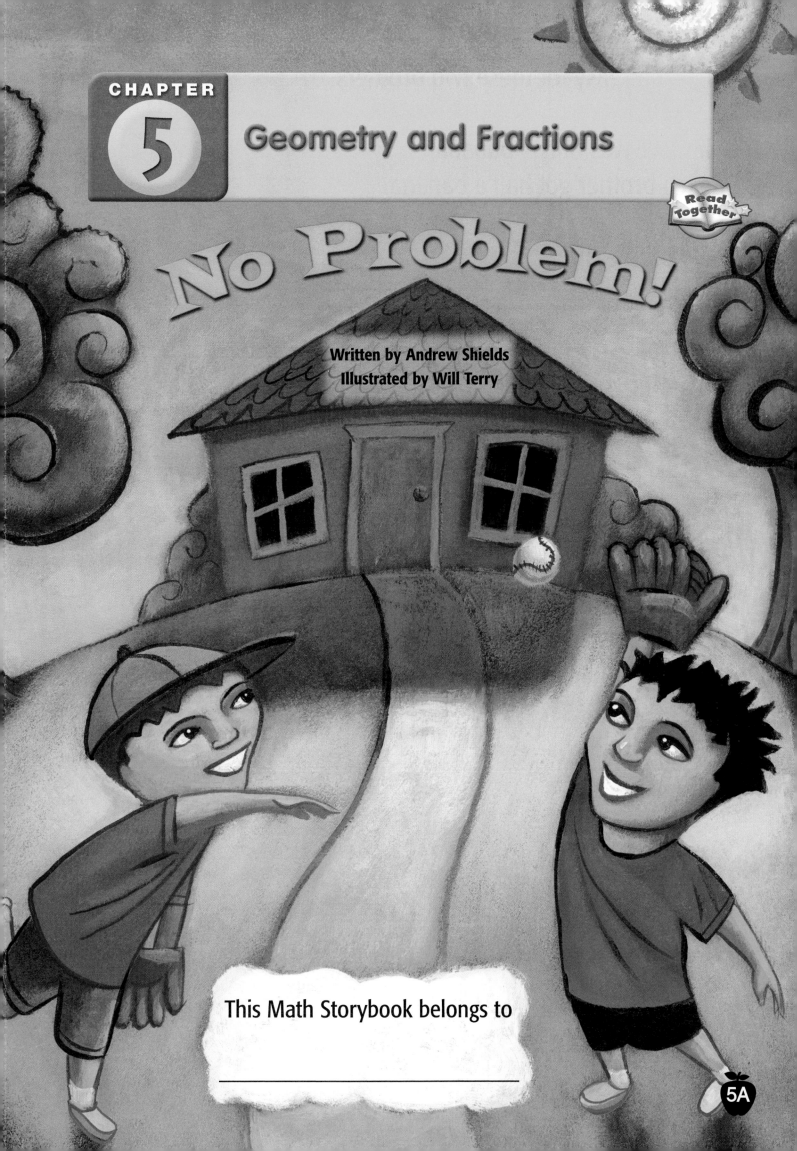

No Problem!

Written by Andrew Shields
Illustrated by Will Terry

This Math Storybook belongs to

_____

Life was easy for these two brothers.

If there was only 1 banana,
each brother got half a banana.

No problem!

5B

If there were a dozen strawberries, each brother got half a dozen.

No problem!

Even when their new baby sister was born, no problem.

She was too little to eat fruit.

But then one day, while the two brothers
were sharing a dozen grapes,
their little sister said,

"Hey! Where's mine?"

Uh-oh! Big problem!

5E

But they solved it. Here's how.

If there were a dozen grapes, they did this:

If there was only ▌ banana, they did this:

No problem!

Home-School Connection

Dear Family,

Today my class started Chapter 5, **Geometry and Fractions.** I will learn about solid figures like a cube and a cone, and also about plane shapes like a triangle and a square. I will learn about fractions and talk about halves, thirds, and fourths. Here are some of the math words I will be learning and some things we can do to help me with my math.

Love,

_____

Math Activity to Do at Home

Help your child create a plane-shapes collage. Cut out several triangles, rectangles, circles, and squares. Have your child color the shapes and use them to make a picture. Glue the shapes to a sheet of paper.

Books to Read Together

Reading math stories reinforces concepts. Look for these titles in your local library:

Rabbit and Hare Divide an Apple
By Harriet Ziefert
(Viking Penguin, 1997)

Shape Space
By Cathryn Falwell
(Houghton, 1992)

 Take It to the NET
More Activities
www.scottforesman.com

My New Math Words

solid figures A solid figure is a 3-D shape.

 cube   sphere   cone

 rectangular prism   cylinder

plane shape A plane shape is a flat shape.

 triangle   rectangle   circle   square

symmetry Two parts that match show symmetry.

line of symmetry

vertex A vertex is a corner of a solid figure or a plane shape.

face A face is the flat side of a cube or a prism.

Name _____

Fraction Concentration

How to Play

1. Place the squares on the gameboard.
2. Take turns. Remove 2 squares.
3. If you find a match, keep both squares.
4. If you do not find a match, put the squares back.
5. Keep playing until you have made all of the matches.
6. Don't forget to concentrate!

Learn!

We see these kinds of shapes everywhere!

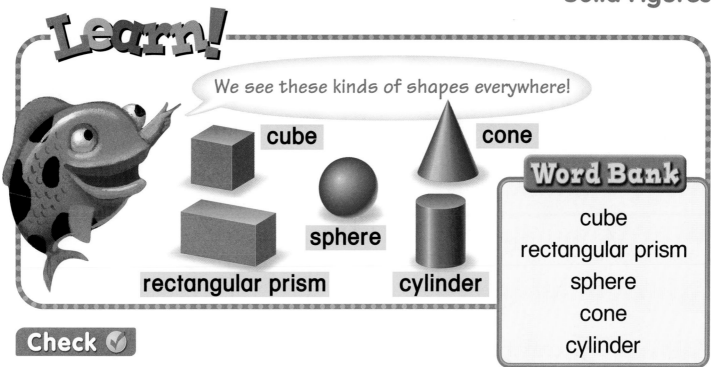

cube

cone

sphere

rectangular prism

cylinder

Word Bank

cube
rectangular prism
sphere
cone
cylinder

Check ✓

Look at the solid figure.

Then circle the objects that have the same shape.

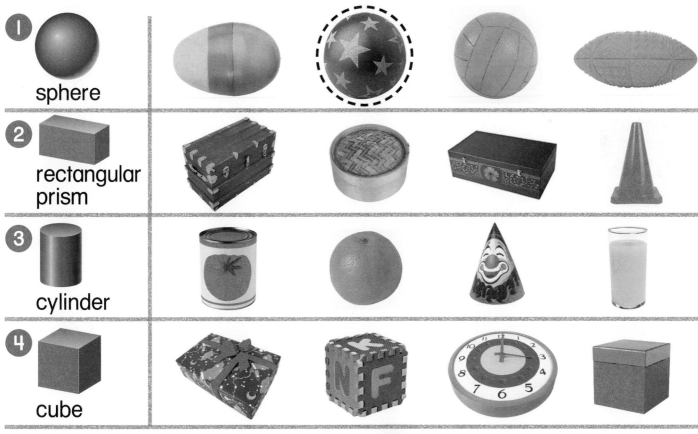

1 sphere

2 rectangular prism

3 cylinder

4 cube

Think About It Reasoning

Which of these rectangular prisms
look like cubes? How do you know?

5 Color each solid figure below.
Now put an **X** on each cube.

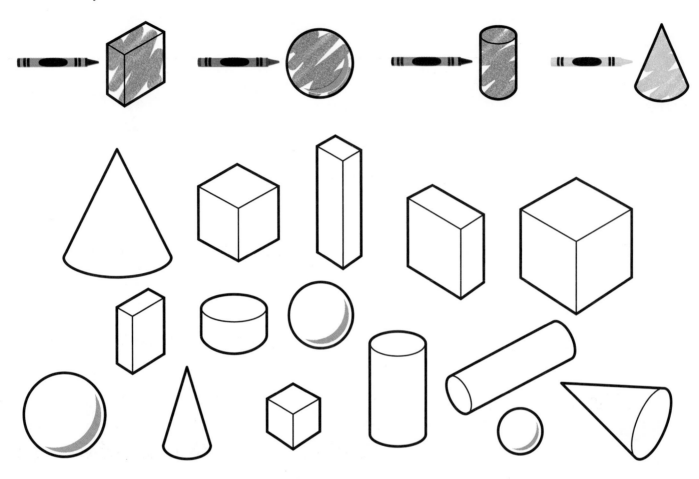

Problem Solving Visual Thinking

6 Finish drawing the cube.

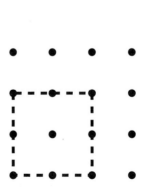

Home Connection Your child identified solid figures. **Home Activity** Be on the lookout for everyday objects that have the same shapes as these solid figures.

Name_____

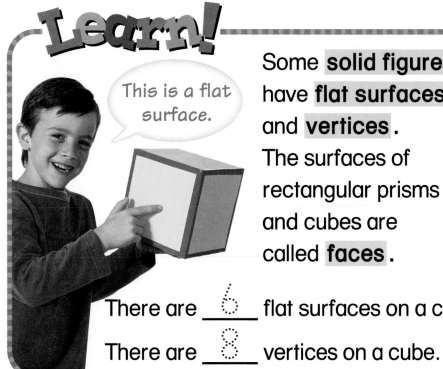

Learn!

This is a flat surface.

Some **solid figures** have **flat surfaces** and **vertices** .
The surfaces of rectangular prisms and cubes are called **faces** .

This is a vertex.

There are ____6____ flat surfaces on a cube.

There are ____8____ vertices on a cube.

Word Bank

solid figure

flat surface

vertex (vertices)

face

corner

Check ✓

Use solid figures to complete the table.

Solid Figure	Number of flat surfaces:	Number of vertices (**corners**):
❶		
❷		
❸		
❹		

Think About It Number Sense

Which solid figures have the same number of flat surfaces as vertices?

Chapter 5 ★ Lesson 2

one hundred fifty-nine **159**

Circle the solid figure that answers each question.

5 Which solid figure has 1 flat surface and 0 vertices?

6 Which solid figures have 6 flat surfaces and 8 vertices?

7 Which solid figure has 2 flat surfaces and 0 vertices?

8 Which solid figure has 0 flat surfaces and 0 vertices?

Problem Solving   Reasoning

Use the clues to answer each question.

9 I have 2 flat surfaces.
I have no vertices.
Which solid figure am I?

_____

10 I have no flat surfaces.
I have no vertices.
Which solid figure am I?

_____

 Home Connection Your child counted the corners and flat surfaces on solid figures. **Home Activity** Count corners and flat surfaces on solid figures you find at home.

Name_____

When you trace around the flat surface of a solid figure, you get a shape that you may already know.

The flat surface of a cylinder is a circle.

Check ✓

Use solid figures.
Circle the solid figures you could trace to make each shape.

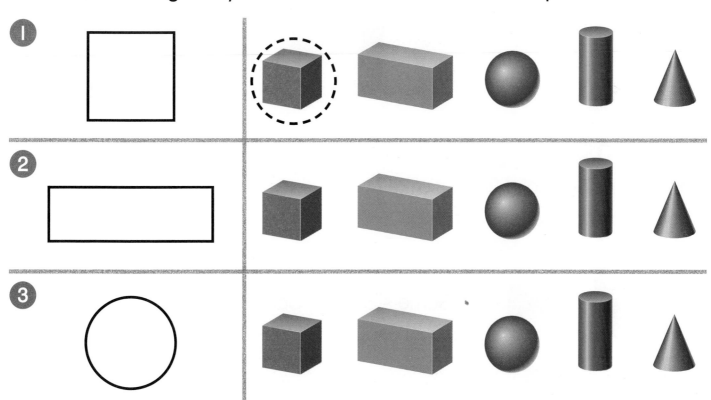

Think About It   Reasoning

Which shapes can be traced from more than one solid figure? Explain.

Look at the shape.

Then circle the objects you could trace to make the shape.

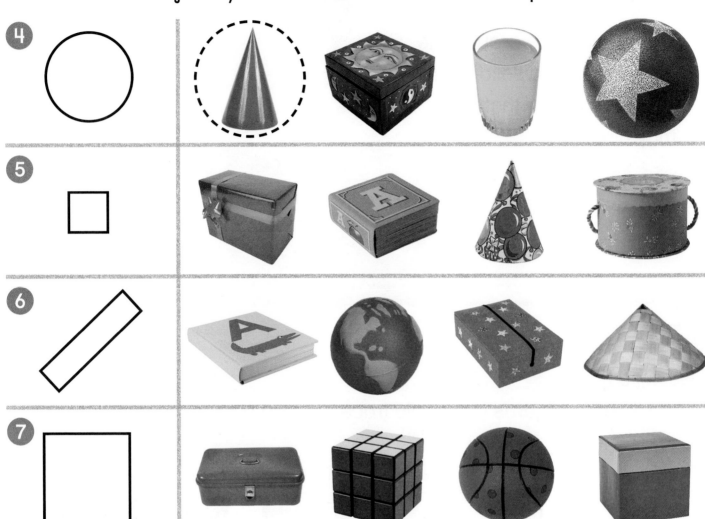

Problem Solving   Reasoning

How are the two solid figures alike?

Circle each correct answer.

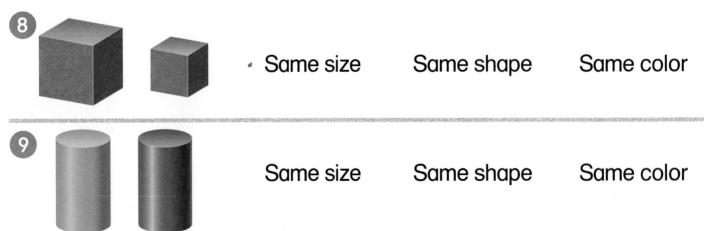

8   Same size   Same shape   Same color

9   Same size   Same shape   Same color

Home Connection Your child matched solid figures to the shapes of their flat surfaces. **Home Activity** Have your child trace around common household objects to make squares, rectangles, and circles.

Name_____

1 Circle all of the cylinders.

2 Circle all of the cubes.

3 Circle the solid figure that has 1 flat surface and 0 vertices.

4 Circle the solid figures that you could trace to make a circle.

5 Circle the shape you would make if you traced a cube.

Name_____

1 Which number sentence answers the question?

Tim has 5 oranges.
Sally has 4 oranges.
Mom has 3 apples.
How many oranges are there in all?

$5 + 4 = 9$ $5 + 3 = 8$ $4 + 3 = 7$ $4 + 4 = 8$

(A)   (B)   (C)   (D)

---

2 Which doubles fact will help you subtract?

$8 - 4 =$ _____

(A) $2 + 2 = 4$

(B) $3 + 3 = 6$

(C) $4 + 4 = 8$

(D) $5 + 5 = 10$

---

3 Which fact is a related subtraction fact?

$3 + 4 = 7$

(A) $9 - 2 = 7$

(B) $10 - 6 = 4$

(C) $8 - 3 = 5$

(D) $7 - 4 = 3$

---

4 Which fact completes this fact family?

$5 + 3 = 8$
$3 + 5 = 8$
$8 - 5 = 3$

(A) $8 + 3 = 11$

(B) $8 - 3 = 5$

(C) $5 + 5 = 10$

(D) $8 - 8 = 0$

Learn!

Flat shapes are called **plane shapes** .

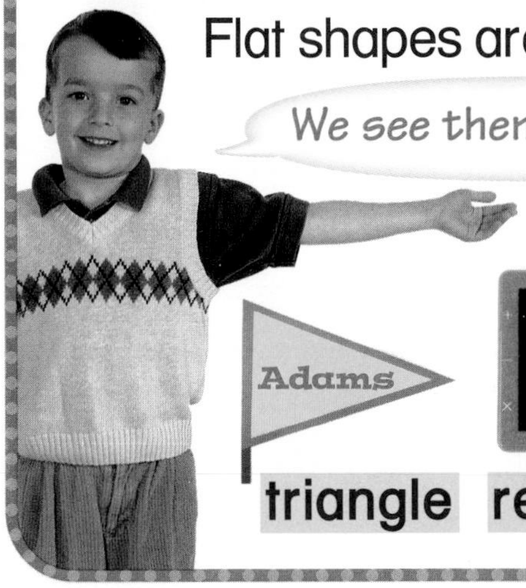

We see them everywhere!

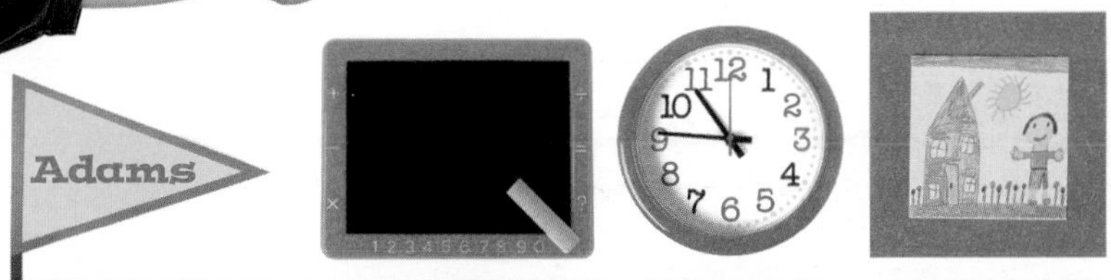

Adams

triangle   rectangle   circle   square

Check ✓

1 Color all of the circles.

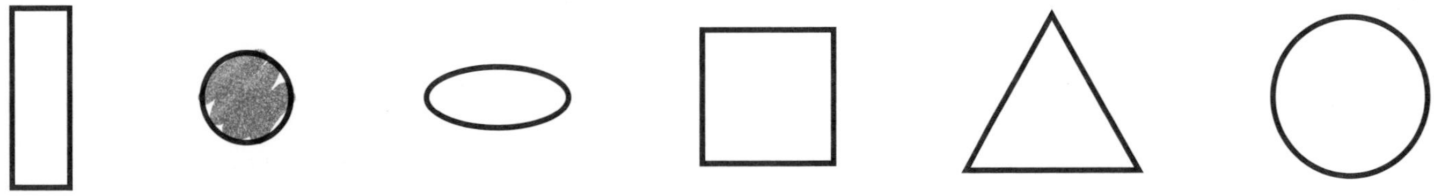

2 Color all of the squares.

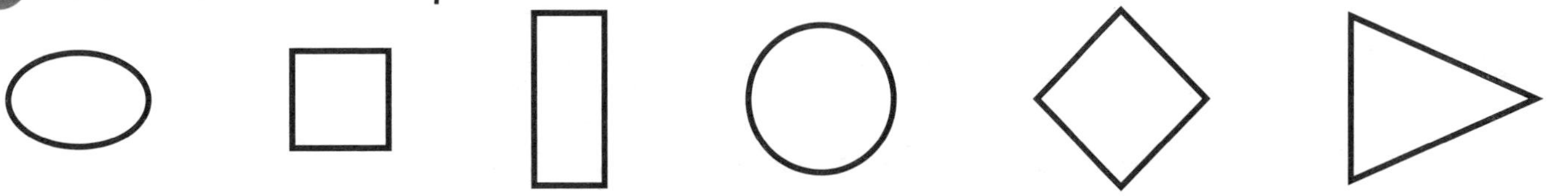

3 Color all of the triangles.

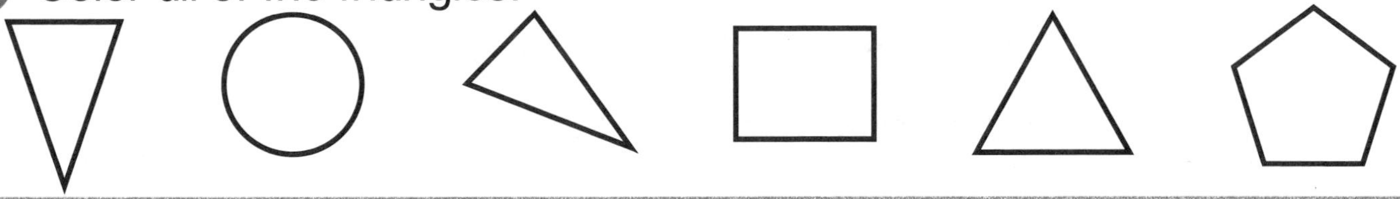

4 Color all of the rectangles.

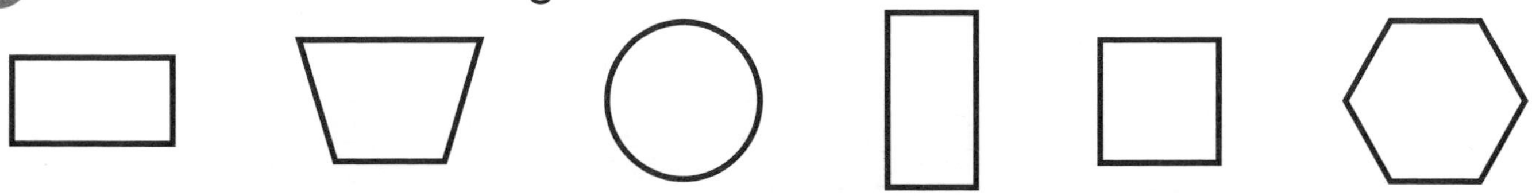

Think About It   Reasoning

Is this shape a rectangle? Explain.

5 Draw a square.

6 Draw a circle.

7 Draw a rectangle.

8 Draw a triangle.

Problem Solving **Algebra**

Draw the shape that comes next in the pattern.

9

Home Connection Your child learned to recognize and draw plane shapes. **Home Activity** Take your child on a shapes hunt to look for plane shapes in your home or neighborhood.

Learn!

You can ask questions to help you sort shapes.
Do these shapes have straight **sides** and **vertices**?

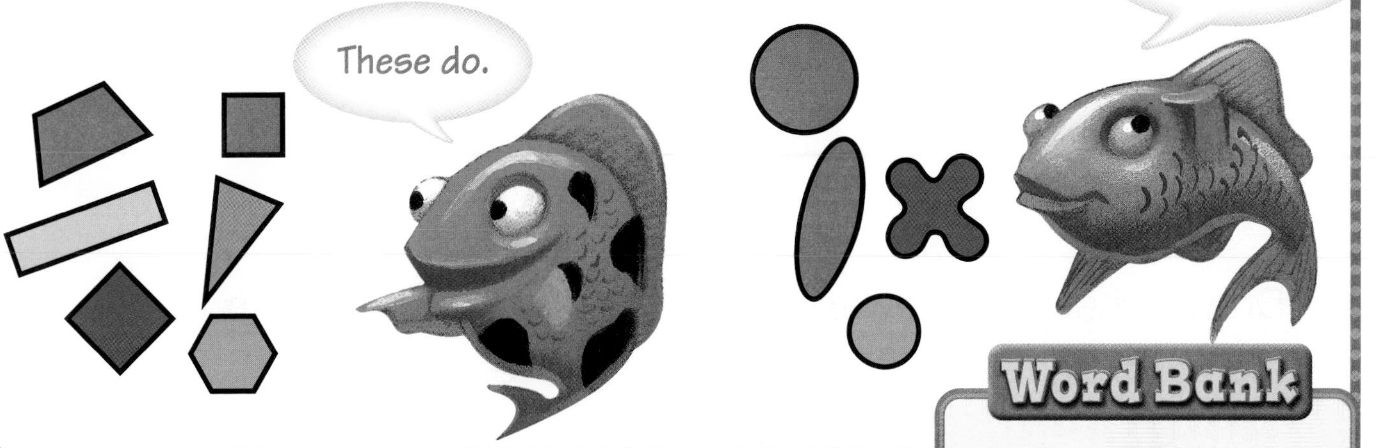

These do.

These do not. They have curves.

Word Bank

side
vertex (vertices)

Check ✓

Write **Yes** or **No** to complete the table.

Plane Shape	Does it have 4 straight sides?	Does it have 4 vertices?
❶ ⬛	Yes	Yes
❷ ⬤		
❸ ▲		
❹ ▬		

Think About It   Reasoning

What are some other ways you can sort plane shapes?

5 Draw a shape with 3 vertices.

6 Draw a shape with more than 4 straight sides.

7 Draw a shape with fewer than 5 straight sides.

8 Draw a shape with 5 vertices.

Problem Solving   Reasonableness

Here is the way that Sarah sorted some plane shapes.

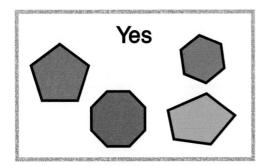

Yes

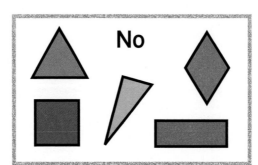

No

9 Circle the question that Sarah might have asked.

Does it have more than 4 vertices?

Does it have fewer than 4 straight sides?

 Home Connection Your child identified plane shapes and sorted them by the number of vertices and straight sides. **Home Activity** Cut out some shapes for your child to sort into groups. Then talk about the sorting rule.

Learn!

These shapes match—they are the **same size** and the **same shape**.

These shapes do not match.

Word Bank

same size

same shape

Check ✓

Do the two shapes match?

Circle **Yes** or **No**.

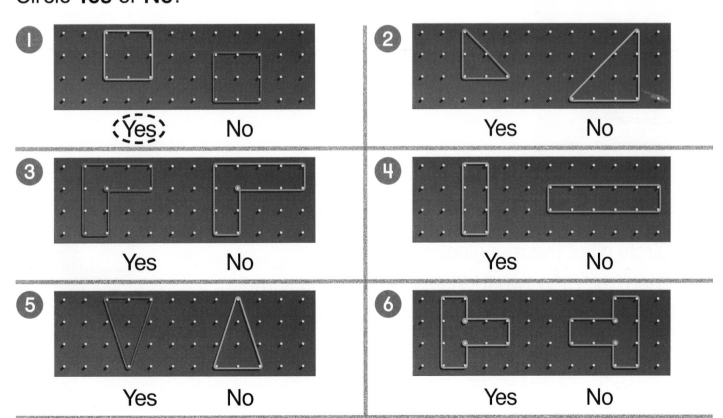

1. (Yes)   No

2. Yes   No

3. Yes   No

4. Yes   No

5. Yes   No

6. Yes   No

Think About It   Reasoning

How can you tell if two shapes match?

Look at the first shape.
Then draw two shapes that match it.

7

8

9

10

Problem Solving   Visual Thinking

11   Circle all of the triangles.
Then color the two triangles that are the same
size and the same shape.

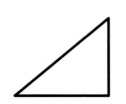  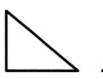 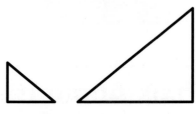

© Pearson Education, Inc.

 Home Connection Your child recognized when plane shapes are the same
size and the same shape. **Home Activity** Ask your child to draw two
shapes that are the same size and the same shape.

Name _____

Wow! Look at that heart! The two parts match. They show symmetry.

The fold is a line of symmetry.

Word Bank

symmetry
line of symmetry

Check ✓

Color the shapes if the parts will match when you fold on the line.

1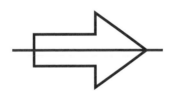

2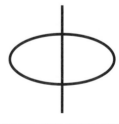

3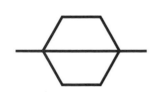

Think About It Reasoning

Is the dotted line a line of symmetry? Explain.

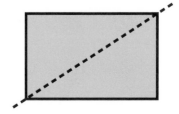

Draw a **line of symmetry** to make two matching parts.

④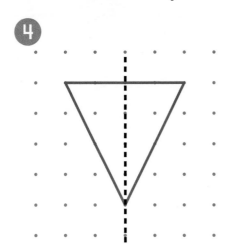

⑤

⑥

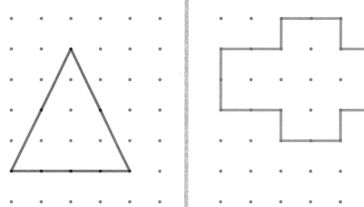

⑦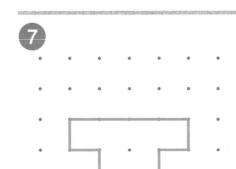

⑧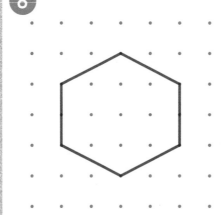

⑨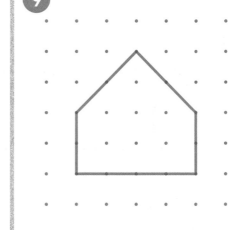

Problem Solving   Visual Thinking

⑩ Draw a different line of symmetry on each square.

Home Connection Your child learned that a shape has symmetry if it can be folded to make two matching parts. **Home Activity** Have your child cut out some shapes and then fold them to find out whether or not they have symmetry.

Name_____

Here are some ways to move a shape.

Word Bank

slide
flip
turn

Check ✓

Slide, flip, or turn each pattern block.

Then draw to show how it was moved.

Use this shape.	Slide it.	Flip it.	Turn it.
❶			
❷			

Think About It Reasoning

Was this shape flipped or turned?

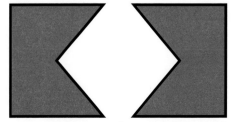

Is it a **slide,** a **flip,** or a **turn?**
Circle the answer.

3

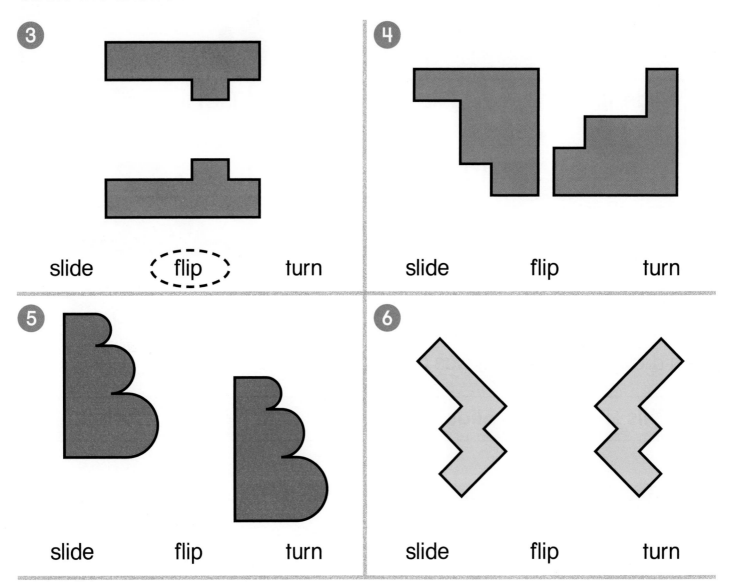

slide ⟨ flip ⟩ turn

4

slide flip turn

5

slide flip turn

6

slide flip turn

Problem Solving Visual Thinking

7 Circle the shapes that will look the same
after they are flipped.

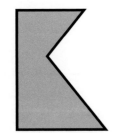   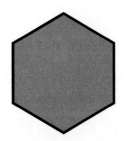

Home Connection Your child learned the difference between a slide, a flip, and a turn. **Home Activity** Slide, flip, or turn objects. Then ask your child to tell how you moved the objects.

Reading for Math Success

Understand Graphic Sources: Lists

Look at these flowers.

How many of each flower did the children pick?

The answers are in the list below.

Read the list with your teacher.

Flowers Picked			
	🌹	🌼	🌸
Anna	1	2	3
Pedro	2	3	1
Yukio	3	1	2

1 How many 🌹 did Anna pick? _____

2 How many 🌼 did Pedro pick? _____

3 How many 🌸 did Yukio pick? _____

Think About It   Reasoning

Why might you put information in a list?

Use this list to answer the questions.

Leaves Collected	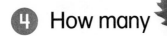	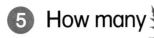	
Thomas	4	3	2
Carmen	3	2	4
Jade	2	4	3

4 How many 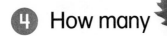 did Carmen collect? ____

5 How many 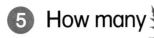 did Thomas collect? ____

6 How many  did Jade collect? ____

Use this list to answer the questions.

Shells Collected			
Luis	1	3	5
Alvin	3	5	1
Pam	5	1	3

7 How many did Pam collect? ____

8 How many did Luis collect? ____

9 How many did Alvin collect? ____

Home Connection Your child used information found in lists to answer questions. **Home Activity** Ask your child to explain some of the information in each list.

Make an Organized List

Name_____

1 How many ways can you make this shape using pattern blocks?

Read and Understand

You need to find all the ways to use pattern blocks to make the shape.

Plan and Solve

Make a list to keep track of the different ways you find.

Write how many of each shape you use.

Ways to Make ⬛			
	⬛	◆	▲
Way 1	1	0	0
Way 2			
Way 3			

Look Back and Check

Did you find all the ways?
How do you know?

Think About It   Reasoning

How does making an organized list help you?

2 How many ways can you make this shape using pattern blocks? Complete the list.

Ways to Make ⬡				
	⬡	⬟	◆	▲
Way 1	1	0	0	0
Way 2				
Way 3				
Way 4				
Way 5				
Way 6				
Way 7				
Way 8				

Writing in Math

3 How many ways can you use the pattern blocks to make ▲? Explain.

_____

_____

Home Connection Your child made a list of all the solutions to a problem.
Home Activity Ask your child to explain how he or she made the list in Exercise 2, above.

Name _____

1 Circle the shape that has 3 straight sides and 3 vertices.

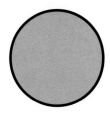  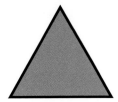  

2 Circle the shapes that match the first shape.

   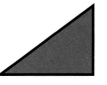

3 Draw a line of symmetry on each shape to show two matching parts.

 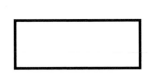 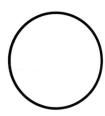 

4 Circle the shape that shows a flip of the first shape.

 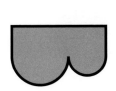   

5 Circle the **two** shapes that could be used to make the first shape.

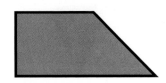 

Name_____

What is the missing number?

1

$8 + \underline{\hphantom{00}} = 10$

2	3	4	5
Ⓐ	Ⓑ	Ⓒ	Ⓓ

2

$9 - 1 = \underline{\hphantom{00}}$

6	7	8	9
Ⓐ	Ⓑ	Ⓒ	Ⓓ

---

3 Which object has the same shape as a cone?

Ⓐ   Ⓑ   Ⓒ   Ⓓ

---

4 Which solid figure has 2 flat surfaces and 0 vertices?

Ⓐ   Ⓑ   Ⓒ   Ⓓ

---

5 Which solid figure could you trace to make this shape? [ ]

Ⓐ   Ⓑ   Ⓒ   Ⓓ

Name_____

Sometimes things are divided into equal parts.

Sometimes they are not.

Word Bank

equal parts

Check ✓

Circle all the shapes that show equal parts.

1.

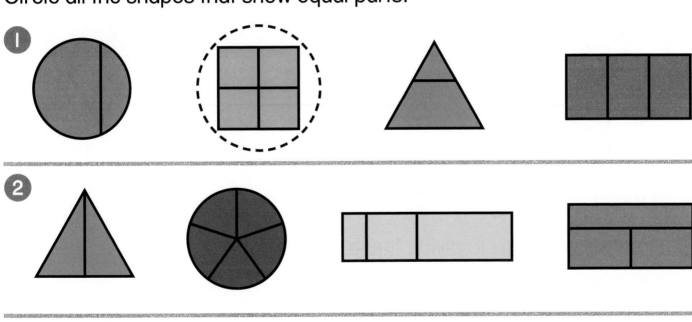

2.

3.

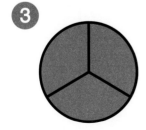 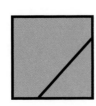 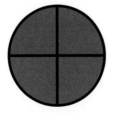 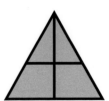

Think About It Reasoning

Is this rectangle divided into equal parts?

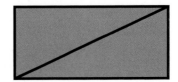

Color the shapes that show equal parts.

Then write the number of equal parts for all of the shapes.

④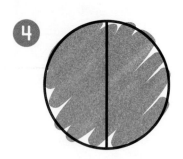

2

⑤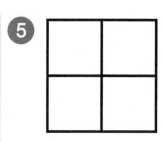

_____

⑥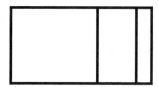

_____

⑦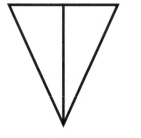

_____

⑧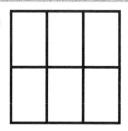

_____

⑨

_____

⑩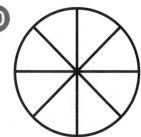

_____

⑪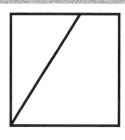

_____

⑫

_____

Problem Solving   Visual Thinking

⑬ Draw straight lines to divide these shapes
into equal parts.

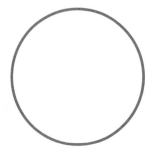

4 equal parts   4 equal parts   2 equal parts

Home Connection Your child decided which shapes were divided into equal parts. **Home Activity** Have your child draw a simple geometric shape and then divide it into equal parts.

Name_____

 **Learn!**

You can use a **fraction** to name equal parts of a **whole**.

These are not halves.

When something has **2** equal parts, each part is **one half** of the whole.

These are halves.

We write **one half** or $\frac{1}{2}$.

Word Bank

fraction

whole

halves

one half ($\frac{1}{2}$)

Check ✓

Circle each shape that shows one half shaded.

1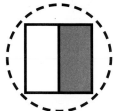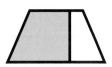

2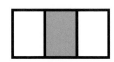

3

Think About It   Number Sense

These shapes do **not** have $\frac{1}{2}$ shaded.
Tell how you know.

Chapter 5 ★ Lesson 11

one hundred eighty-three   **183**

Draw a straight line on each shape
to show halves.

4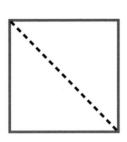

5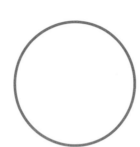

6

7

8

9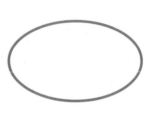

10

11

12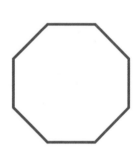

Problem Solving   Mental Math

Answer the question.

13 Jack, James, and David shared 1 apple for their snack.

Jack ate $\frac{1}{2}$ of the apple.

James ate $\frac{1}{2}$ of the apple.

Was there any apple left for David?

_____

Home Connection Your child divided shapes in half. **Home Activity** With your child, draw a series of four identical rectangles and then divide them in half four different ways.

184   one hundred eighty-four

Name _____

Look at this one! It is divided into **fourths**, and **one fourth** is shaded.

Look! This rectangle is divided into **thirds**, and **one third** is shaded.

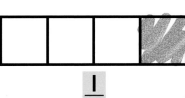

$\frac{1}{4}$

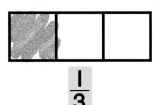

$\frac{1}{3}$

Word Bank

thirds

one third ($\frac{1}{3}$)

fourths

one fourth ($\frac{1}{4}$)

Check ✓

Circle each shape that shows one third shaded.

1

2

Circle each shape that shows one fourth shaded.

3

4

Think About It Number Sense

How many thirds equal one whole?

How many fourths equal one whole?

Color 1 part of each shape.
Then circle the fraction.

5

$\left(\dfrac{1}{3}\right)$ $\dfrac{1}{4}$

6

$\dfrac{1}{3}$ $\dfrac{1}{4}$

7

$\dfrac{1}{3}$ $\dfrac{1}{4}$

8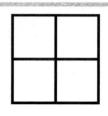

$\dfrac{1}{3}$ $\dfrac{1}{4}$

9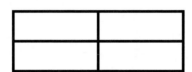

$\dfrac{1}{3}$ $\dfrac{1}{4}$

10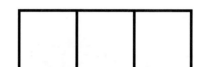

$\dfrac{1}{3}$ $\dfrac{1}{4}$

Problem Solving   Number Sense

Answer the question.

11 Patty has $\dfrac{1}{3}$ of a glass of juice.

Raul has $\dfrac{1}{4}$ of a glass of juice.

The glasses are the same size.

Who has more juice? _____

$\dfrac{1}{3}$ $\dfrac{1}{4}$

Patty's glass   Raul's glass

 Home Connection Your child identified and shaded one third or one fourth of different shapes. **Home Activity** With your child, draw two circles, two squares, and two triangles. Then divide each pair of shapes into thirds and fourths.

 **Learn!**

1 green apple

2 apples in all

$\frac{1}{2}$ of the apples is green.

1 out of 2 is green.

1 green tomato

3 tomatoes in all

$\frac{1}{3}$ of the tomatoes is green.

1 out of 3 is green.

1 green pepper

4 peppers in all

$\frac{1}{4}$ of the peppers is green.

1 out of 4 is green.

Check ✓

Circle the fraction that tells what part of the set is green.

 1

$\frac{1}{2}$ $\frac{1}{3}$ $\left(\frac{1}{4}\right)$

2

$\frac{1}{2}$ $\frac{1}{3}$ $\frac{1}{4}$

 3

$\frac{1}{2}$ $\frac{1}{3}$ $\frac{1}{4}$

4

$\frac{1}{2}$ $\frac{1}{3}$ $\frac{1}{4}$

Think About It Reasoning

How is finding a fraction of a **set**
like finding a fraction of a **shape?**

Chapter 5 ★ Lesson 13

Color 1 object in each set. Then circle the fraction.

5

$\frac{1}{2}$  $\frac{1}{4}$

6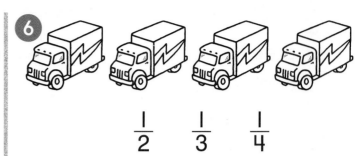

$\frac{1}{2}$ $\frac{1}{3}$ $\frac{1}{4}$

7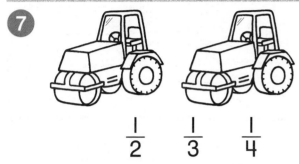

$\frac{1}{2}$ $\frac{1}{3}$ $\frac{1}{4}$

8

$\frac{1}{2}$ $\frac{1}{3}$ $\frac{1}{4}$

9

$\frac{1}{2}$ $\frac{1}{3}$ $\frac{1}{4}$

10

$\frac{1}{2}$ $\frac{1}{3}$ $\frac{1}{4}$

Problem Solving Writing in Math

Draw pictures to solve.

11 Jenny has a basket of apples. $\frac{1}{4}$ of them are red. Draw Jenny's apples.

12 David has a basket of apples. $\frac{1}{3}$ of them are green. Draw David's apples.

Home Connection Your child learned that a group of things can be divided into equal parts. **Home Activity** Have your child gather 12 of an object, such as 12 spoons, and show *one half, one third,* and *one fourth* of the objects.

Name_____

Fractions can name more than one equal part.

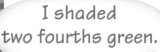

I shaded two fourths green.

So did I.

Check ✓

Circle the fraction that tells how much is colored.

1

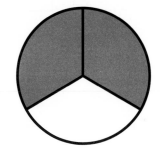

$\frac{1}{3}$ ⬚$\frac{2}{3}$⬚ $\frac{3}{4}$

2

$\frac{1}{4}$ $\frac{2}{4}$ $\frac{3}{4}$

3

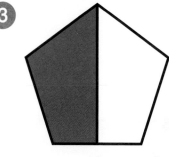

$\frac{1}{2}$ $\frac{2}{3}$ $\frac{3}{4}$

4

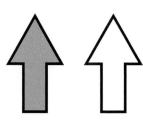

$\frac{3}{4}$ $\frac{2}{3}$ $\frac{1}{2}$

5

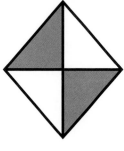

$\frac{2}{4}$ $\frac{1}{4}$ $\frac{3}{4}$

6

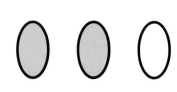

$\frac{3}{4}$ $\frac{2}{3}$ $\frac{1}{3}$

Think About It   Number Sense

How could you show $\frac{3}{6}$ on this shape?

Chapter 5 ★ Lesson 14

one hundred eighty-nine   **189**

Write the fraction that tells how much is colored.

7 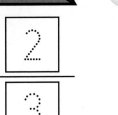  Both show $\frac{2}{3}$!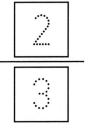

$\frac{2}{3}$ $\frac{2}{3}$

8  $\frac{}{}$

9  $\frac{}{}$

10 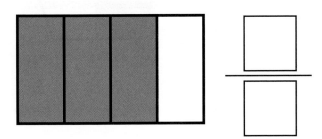 $\frac{}{}$

11 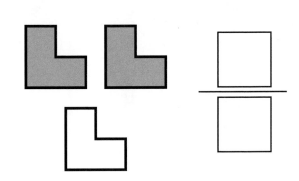 $\frac{}{}$

Problem Solving Number Sense

12 Color to show $\frac{3}{8}$ of both.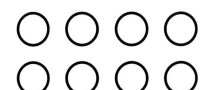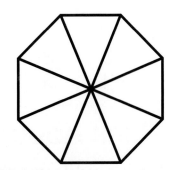

Home Connection Your child named fractions for shapes and for groups of objects. **Home Activity** Have your child tell how he or she solved the problems on this page.

 **Algebra**

We can use a chart to help solve problems.

How can you give an **equal share** of erasers to each of 3 children?

The chart shows that there are 12 erasers.

Use 12 counters.

Give them out equally.

School Supplies	
Erasers	12
Pencils	8
Crayons	9
Brushes	12

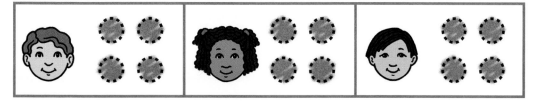

Each child gets _____4_____ erasers.

Word Bank

equal share

Check ✓

Use the chart and counters to solve.
Draw the equal shares.

1. 4 children want to share the pencils equally.

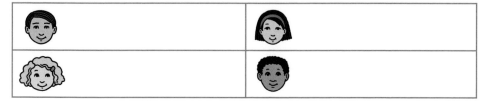

Each child gets _____ pencils.

Think About It Number Sense

Could 2 children share the crayons equally?
Explain?

Use the chart and counters to solve.
Draw the equal shares.

School Supplies	
Erasers	12
Pencils	8
Crayons	9
Brushes	12

2 3 children want to share the crayons equally.

Each child gets _____ crayons.

3 2 children want to share the pencils equally.

Each child gets _____ pencils.

4 4 children want to share the erasers equally.

Each child gets _____ erasers.

5 6 children want to share the brushes equally.

Each child gets _____ brushes.

 Home Connection Your child used information from a chart to solve problems. **Home Activity** Give your child a problem that can be solved only by referring to a chart, such as the nutrition label on a package of food.

Dorling Kindersley

1. Circle each sphere.

2. Draw a box around each cube.

Do You Know...
that all cubes are rectangular prisms but not all rectangular prisms are cubes?

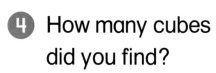
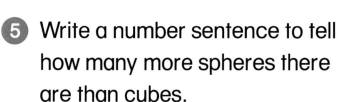

3. How many spheres did you find?

_____ spheres

4. How many cubes did you find?

_____ cubes

5. Write a number sentence to tell how many more spheres there are than cubes.

____ ◯ ____ = ____

_____ more spheres

Fun Fact!
Earth, our planet, is a sphere. Sometimes Earth is called the "big blue marble."

6 Fill in the missing shapes in the quilt pattern.

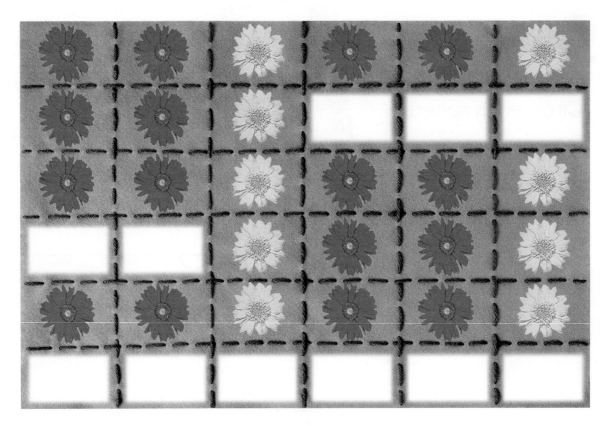

7 Draw a line on each shape to show half.

8 **Writing in Math**

Count the cones and cylinders in your classroom.
Draw a picture of each one that you find.
Did you find more cylinders or more cones?
How many more?

Name_____

1 Circle the shapes that show one half shaded.

 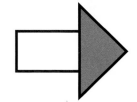  

2 Circle the shape that shows one third shaded.

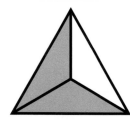 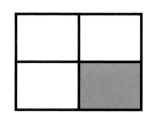 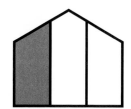 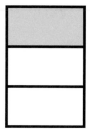

3 Color one fourth of the butterflies.

4 Circle the fraction that tells what part of the set is red.

$\frac{1}{2}$ $\frac{2}{4}$ $\frac{3}{4}$ $\frac{1}{3}$

Use the chart and counters to solve.

5 If 4 children share the blocks equally, how many blocks will each child get?

School Toys	
Blocks	12

Each child gets _____ blocks.

Name_____

Add.

1
```
   2
 + 9
```

9	10	11	12
Ⓐ	Ⓑ	Ⓒ	Ⓓ

2
```
   3
 + 6
```

3	6	9	12
Ⓐ	Ⓑ	Ⓒ	Ⓓ

3 Which addition fact will help you subtract?

$$11 - 7 = \underline{\quad}$$

$7 + 4 = 11$	$3 + 7 = 10$	$9 + 3 = 12$	$3 + 4 = 7$
Ⓐ	Ⓑ	Ⓒ	Ⓓ

4 Which shape is a square?

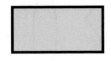

Ⓐ	Ⓑ	Ⓒ	Ⓓ

5 Which pair of shapes shows a flip?

Ⓐ
Ⓑ
Ⓒ
Ⓓ

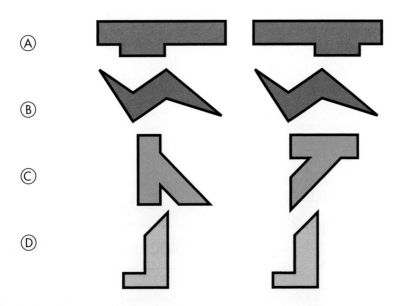

Name_____

Open and Closed Shapes

The bug cannot get out of a closed shape!

  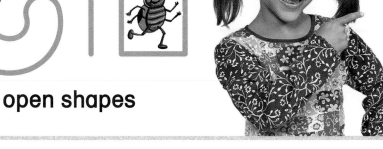  

open shapes   **closed shapes**

Circle **open** or **closed**.

If the shape is open, draw a line to close it.

1

   (open)   closed

2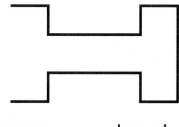

  open   closed

3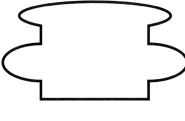

  open   closed

4

  open   closed

5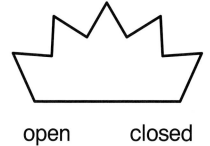

  open   closed

6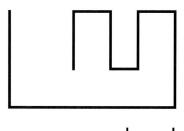

  open   closed

 Home Connection Your child learned about open and closed shapes.
Home Activity Have your child draw and label examples of open shapes
and closed shapes.

Slide, Flip, and Turn Shapes Using a Computer

You can use a computer to slide, flip, and turn a shape.

1 Go to the Geometry Shapes eTool.

2 Pick a shape. Place it in the workspace. Draw it on your paper.

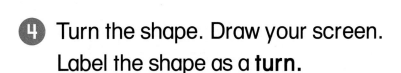

3 Flip the shape. Draw your screen. Label the shape as a **flip.**

4 Turn the shape. Draw your screen. Label the shape as a **turn.**

5 Slide the shape. Draw your screen. Label the shape as a **slide.**

6 Turn your paper over and repeat Steps 2–5, using a different shape.

Think About It   Reasoning

How are a turn and a slide the same?
How are they different?

Home Connection Your child used a computer to move shapes by flipping, sliding, and turning them. **Home Activity** Ask your child to draw a shape and then to draw the shape after it has been flipped, turned, and slid.

Name _____

 Read Together

Understand the Question

Some math problems have special words such as NOT.

1 Which shape does not have $\frac{1}{3}$ shaded?

Ⓐ  Ⓑ Ⓒ   Ⓓ

Circle the word NOT in this question. Choose the shape that is **not** divided into 3 equal parts. Fill in the answer bubble.

Your Turn

Underline the word NOT in this math problem. Solve the problem. Fill in the answer bubble.

2 Which shape does not show a line of symmetry?

Ⓐ   Ⓑ   Ⓒ   Ⓓ

I need to think about this!

Home Connection Your child prepared for standardized tests by identifying and applying the meaning of the word NOT to math problems.
Home Activity Ask your child what the word NOT means in Exercise 2.

Name _____

Math Music

Today you will play in the Hand-Clap Band.
Your teacher will divide the class
into three groups.

First, the whole class will practice
counting 1 - 2 - 3 - 4, 1 - 2 - 3 - 4.
Try to count the numbers, or beats,
at the same pace. Now …

Musical Parts

1 Group 1 will clap only on beat 1.
Group 1 will be clapping 1 out of
every 4 beats. Write this as a fraction.

_____

2 Group 2 will clap only on beats 1 and **3.**
Group 2 will be clapping 2 out of every 4 beats.
Write this as a fraction.

_____

3 Group 3 will clap on **every** beat.
Group 3 will be clapping 4 out of every 4 beats.
Write this as a fraction.

_____

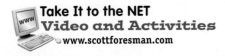
Take It to the NET
Video and Activities
www.scottforesman.com

Home Connection Your child solved problems about music by writing fractions. **Home Activity** Ask your child what fraction he or she would write to show clapping 3 out of every 4 beats. $\left(\frac{3}{4}\right)$

1 Circle the rectangular prism.

2 Circle the sphere.

3 How many flat surfaces does this solid figure have?

_____ flat surfaces

4 Draw the shape that is the flat surface of a cube.

5 Circle the rectangle.

 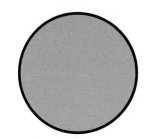 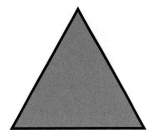 

6 How many straight sides does this triangle have?

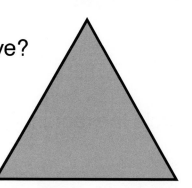

_____ straight sides

7 Look at the first shape.
Circle the shape that matches it.

8 Draw a line of symmetry on each shape.

 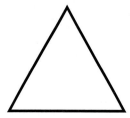 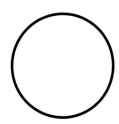

9 Divide this rectangle into thirds.

10 Divide this square into fourths.

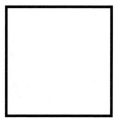

11 Divide this group in half.

Read Together

Late for School Again?

Written by Martha Bowles Illustrated by Jason Wolff

This Math Storybook belongs to

_____

Bunny jumped up out of bed.
It was 6:30.

"Oh, no! I know I'm going to be
late for school again!" she said.

Bunny brushed her teeth.
She washed her face and ears.
She made her bed.

She looked at her clock.
It was 7:00.

"Why is it so quiet?" wondered Bunny.
"I don't hear Mother calling me."

"Where are my socks?
Where are my shoes?
I can't find anything!"

Oh, no! It was already 7:30.

Bunny hopped down the stairs.
She was almost out of breath.

"It's time for breakfast," said Bunny.
"I have to hurry! It's already 8:00!"

6E

Then Bunny remembered. It was Saturday!

"There is no school today!" said Bunny. "Silly, silly me! Oh, well."

Bunny ate her breakfast and read some books until her mom and dad woke up.

Dear Family,

Today my class started Chapter 6, **Time.** I will learn about time to the hour and to the half hour. I will also learn about the days of the week and the months of the year by using a calendar. Here are some of the math words I will be learning and some things we can do to help me with my math.

Love,

_____

Math Activity to Do at Home

Help your child keep a picture diary of one activity he or she did each day for a week. Ask your child to write the name of the day and the time the activity was done beside each picture. Discuss with your child about how long each activity took.

Books to Read Together

Reading math stories reinforces concepts. Look for these titles in your local library:

10 Minutes till Bedtime
By Peggy Rathmann
(G.P. Putnam's Sons, 1998)

Bunny Day: Telling Time from Breakfast to Bedtime
By Rick Walton
(HarperCollins, 2002)

My New Math Words

hour There are 60 minutes in an hour.

 3 o'clock

 minute hand / hour hand

half hour A half hour is 30 minutes.

 3:30

calendar

JUNE						
Sunday	Monday	Tuesday	Wednesday	Thursday	Friday	Saturday
	1	2	3	4	5	6
7	8	9	10	11	12	13

month
days

year A year has 12 months.

Take It to the NET
More Activities
www.scottforesman.com

Spin for Time

What You Need

paper clip ✐
pencil ✏
12 game markers ●

How to Play

1. Pretend that the paper clip is the **hour hand** on a clock.

2. Take turns spinning the spinner. Say the time.

3. Place a marker on the clock that shows that time.

4. If you land on the clock that Bunny is holding, you get an extra turn!

5. Keep playing until you and your partner cover all of the clocks.

Name_____

Some activities take less than 1 **minute**.
Other activities take more than 1 minute.

How long does this activity take?

less than 1 minute

more than 1 minute

Word Bank

minute

Check ✔

How long does each activity take?
Circle the correct answer.

1

less than 1 minute

more than 1 minute

2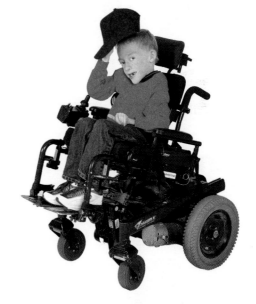

less than 1 minute

more than 1 minute

Think About It Reasoning

Would you take more or less than 1 minute to
drink a glass of milk? Explain.

Chapter 6 ★ Lesson 1 two hundred five **205**

How long does each activity take?
Circle the correct answer.

less than 1 minute

(more than 1 minute)

less than 1 minute

more than 1 minute

less than 1 minute

more than 1 minute

less than 1 minute

more than 1 minute

Problem Solving   Estimation

7 Draw a picture to show something that you can do
in about the same time as it takes to write your name.

Home Connection Your child decided if activities take more or less than
1 minute. **Home Activity** Before you and your child do an activity, ask your
child to predict whether it will take more or less than 1 minute. Then time
yourselves to see if he or she was correct.

The **hour hand** points to the **hour**.

When the **minute hand** points to 12, we say **o'clock**.

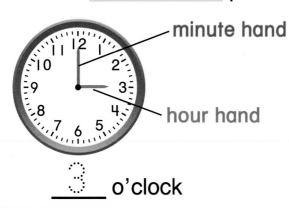

minute hand

hour hand

There are 60 minutes in 1 hour.

3 o'clock

Word Bank

hour
hour hand
minute hand
o'clock

Check ✓

Write the time shown on each clock.

_____ o'clock

_____ o'clock

_____ o'clock

_____ o'clock

_____ o'clock

_____ o'clock

Think About It   Reasoning

Does the hour hand or the minute hand move around the clock faster? Explain.

Draw an hour hand and a minute hand to show each time.

7

12 o'clock

The shorter hand points to the hour.

8

4 o'clock

9

6 o'clock

10

3 o'clock

11

7 o'clock

12

5 o'clock

13

10 o'clock

Problem Solving Mental Math

Write the next two hours.

14 3 o'clock   _____ o'clock   _____ o'clock

15 10 o'clock   _____ o'clock   _____ o'clock

 Home Connection Your child told time to the hour and then drew hands on clocks to show the times. **Home Activity** When the time is on the hour, ask your child to read a clock and tell you the time.

Name_____

Learn!

You can show the time in different ways.

It's 6 o'clock! That's when I eat dinner.

Check ✓

Draw hands on each clock face.

Then write the time on the other clock.

1. 8 o'clock

2. 11 o'clock

3. 5 o'clock

4. 3 o'clock

Think About It   Reasoning

How far does the hour hand move in
one hour? How far does the minute
hand move in one hour?

Draw lines to match the clocks that show
the same time.

5

6

Problem Solving   Algebra

Look for the pattern. Then write each missing time.

7 9:00, 10:00, _____:_____, 12:00, 1:00, _____:_____

8 11:00, 12:00, _____:_____, 2:00, 3:00, _____:_____

Home Connection Your child told and wrote time to the hour on analog
and digital clocks. **Home Activity** When the time is on the hour, ask your
child to look at a clock or watch and then tell and write the time.

Name_____

The hour hand is between __4__ and __5__.

The minute hand is on __6__.

30 minutes = one **half hour**

Check ✓

Complete each sentence.
Then write the time.

1

The hour hand is between _____ and _____.

The minute hand is on _____.

2

The hour hand is between _____ and _____.

The minute hand is on _____.

Think About It   Reasoning

Why is the hour hand between 3 and 4 when
it is 3:30?

Write the time shown on each clock.

When the minute hand points to 6, it is 30 minutes past the hour.

3 12:30

4 :

5 :

6 :

7 :

8 :

9 :

Problem Solving   Visual Thinking

10 Show 6 o'clock on the first clock.

On the second clock, show the time it will be in 30 minutes.

Home Connection Your child told and wrote time to the half hour on analog and digital clocks. **Home Activity** Notice whenever your clock at home shows time on the half hour. Ask your child to tell and write the time.

© Pearson Education, Inc.

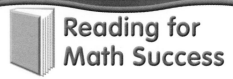
Visualize

Read this math problem. Picture what is happening.

The bus picks up the children at 8:00.
It takes I hour to get to school.
What time do the children arrive at school?

1 Show the starting time on your clock.
Draw hands to show the time on the first clock.
Write the time below it.

2 Move the hands on your clock to
show that I hour has passed.
Draw hands to show the time on the second clock.
Write the time below it.

_____ o'clock ⟶ I hour ⟶ _____ o'clock

3 What time did the children get to school? _____

Think About It Reasoning

How do the hands on a clock show that I hour
has gone by?

Read the problem. Picture what is happening.

Lunch starts at 12:00.
It lasts for 1 hour.
What time does lunch end?

4 Use a clock if you like.

Write the starting time and the ending time.

Then draw the hands to show each time.

_____ o'clock ⟶ 1 hour ⟶ _____ o'clock

Read the problem. Picture what is happening.

The play starts at 2:00.
It lasts for 1 hour.
What time does the play end?

5 Use a clock if you like.

Write the starting time and the ending time.

Then draw the hands to show each time.

_____ o'clock ⟶ 1 hour ⟶ _____ o'clock

 Home Connection Your child solved problems about starting times and ending times of activities that last 1 hour. **Home Activity** Ask your child to explain the passing of time for family activities. For example, dinner starts at 6:00. It lasts 1 hour. What time does dinner end? *(7:00)*

214 two hundred fourteen

Name_____

Storytime starts at 7 o'clock. It lasts for 1 hour.

What time does storytime end?

Read and Understand

You need to find what time it will be 1 hour after 7 o'clock.

Plan and Solve

You can use a clock to act it out.

____7____ o'clock ⟶ 1 hour ⟶ ____8____ o'clock

Look Back and Check

Does your answer make sense?

Check ✓

Use a clock. Write the starting time and the ending time.

Then draw the hands on the clock to show the ending time.

1

_____ o'clock ⟶ 1 hour ⟶ _____ o'clock

Think About It   Number Sense

If a movie started at 2:00 and ended at 4:00,

how long did it last?

Use a clock. Write the starting time and the ending time.
Then draw the hands on the clock to show the ending time.

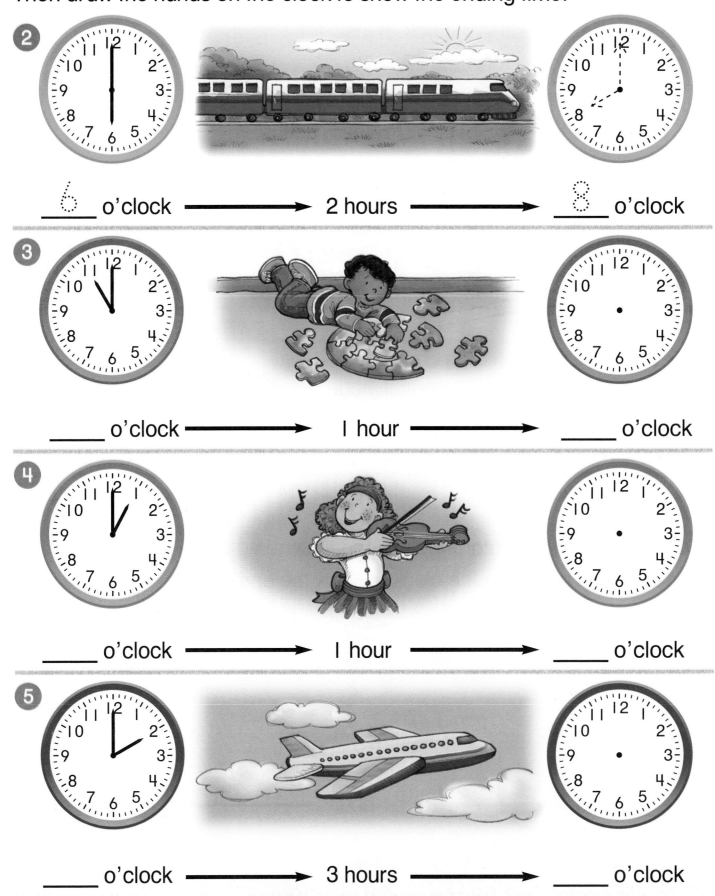

2

___6___ o'clock ⟶ 2 hours ⟶ ___8___ o'clock

3

_____ o'clock ⟶ I hour ⟶ _____ o'clock

4

_____ o'clock ⟶ I hour ⟶ _____ o'clock

5

_____ o'clock ⟶ 3 hours ⟶ _____ o'clock

Home Connection Your child used a clock to solve problems about the
passage of time. **Home Activity** Ask your child to explain how he or she
did the exercises on this page.

Name_____

Draw the hands on each clock face.
Then write the time on the other clock.

1 8 o'clock

2 1 o'clock

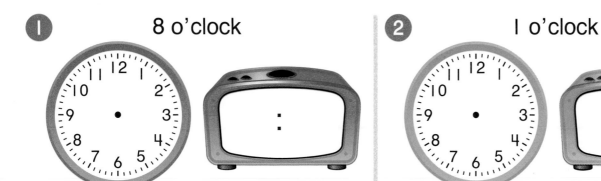

Write the same time.

3

4

How long does this activity take?
Circle the correct answer.

5

less than 1 minute

more than 1 minute

Write the starting time and the ending time.
Then draw the hands on the clock to show the ending time.

6

_____ o'clock ⟶ 2 hours ⟶ _____ o'clock

Name _____

1 Which subtraction sentence tells how many birds are left?

$4 - 3 = 1$	$3 - 1 = 2$	$5 - 2 = 3$	$4 - 2 = 2$
Ⓐ	Ⓑ	Ⓒ	Ⓓ

2 Which number sentence answers the question?

2 birds built a nest.
Then 5 baby birds hatched.
How many birds are there in all?

$5 - 2 = 3$	$2 + 3 = 5$	$2 + 5 = 7$	$7 - 4 = 3$
Ⓐ	Ⓑ	Ⓒ	Ⓓ

3 Use the chart and counters to solve.

If 2 children share the oranges equally, how many oranges will each child get?

Fruits		
	apples	7
	oranges	6
	bananas	5

2 oranges	3 oranges	5 oranges	6 oranges
Ⓐ	Ⓑ	Ⓒ	Ⓓ

4 Which shape shows equal parts?

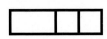

Ⓐ	Ⓑ	Ⓒ	Ⓓ

Name_____

What time of day do these things happen?

morning

afternoon

night

Word Bank

morning

afternoon

night

Check ✓

When did each of these things happen?
Draw lines to match.

- morning

- afternoon

- night

- morning

- afternoon

- night

③

- morning

- afternoon

- night

Think About It   Reasoning

In the exercises above, which happened first,
next, and last?

When did each of these things happen?
Draw lines to match.

4

· morning   · afternoon   · night

5

· morning   · afternoon   · night

Problem Solving *Writing in Math*

6 Draw a picture to show something you like to do. Write **morning, afternoon,** or **night** to match your picture.

Home Connection Your child decided if a pictured event happened in the morning, in the afternoon, or at night. **Home Activity** Help your child make three lists of activities that your family does under the headings *Morning, Afternoon,* and *Night.* Display the lists and add to them for several days.

Name_____

You can estimate about how long an activity takes.

about 1 minute

about 1 hour

about 1 day

Check ✓

About how long does each activity take?
Draw lines to match.

1

about 1 minute   about 1 hour   about 1 day

2

about 2 minutes   about 2 hours   about 2 days

Think About It   Reasoning

Put the activities in Exercise 2 in order starting
with the one that took the least time.

About how long does each activity take?
Draw lines to match.

3

about 1 minute   about 1 day   about 1 hour

4

about 3 minutes   about 3 hours   about 3 days

Problem Solving   Estimation

Answer each question.

5 Paúlo wants to do a 50-piece puzzle. Will he work for about 1 minute or about 1 hour?

_____

6 Sara wants to be a good soccer player. Should she practice each day for about 2 minutes or about 2 hours?

_____

Home Connection Your child estimated how long different activities might take. **Home Activity** Ask your child about how long it will take to eat dinner. Then check the time to see how close his or her guess was.

Name _____

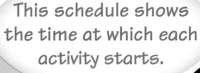

This schedule shows the time at which each activity starts.

| Community Center After-School Schedule ||
Time	Activity
3:00	Reading
3:30	Art
4:00	Sports
4:30	Clean Up

Check ✓

Circle the activity that starts at the time shown on each clock.

1.

Reading   (Art)   Clean Up

2.

Sports   Clean Up   Art

3.

Art   Sports   Reading

Think About It Reasoning

What happens 1 hour before Clean Up starts?

Chapter 6 ★ Lesson 8   two hundred twenty-three **223**

Use the schedule to answer the questions.

Mrs. Lopez's Class Schedule	
Time	**Activity**
8:00	Calendar Time
8:30	Reading
9:00	Centers
9:30	Math
10:00	Recess

4 What activity do children do just before recess?

_____

5 What does the class do just after reading?

_____

6 What time does math begin?

_____

Reasonableness

Use the schedule to solve the problem.

7 The class is about to start centers.
Jan wants to know how long it is until recess.
Peg says it is 2 hours.
Is she correct?

_____

Home Connection Your child used a schedule to answer questions.
Home Activity Work with your child to make a schedule of activities that you might do on a Saturday afternoon.

Name_____

This **calendar** shows the **days** and **weeks** in the **month** of November.

November

Sunday	Monday	Tuesday	Wednesday	Thursday	Friday	Saturday
	1	2	3	4	5	6
7	8	9	10	11	12	13
14	15	16	17	18	19	20
21	22	23	24	25	26	27
28	29	30				

Word Bank

calendar
day
week
month

Check ✓

Use the calendar above to answer the questions.

1 How many days are in 1 week? _____

2 How many days are in November? _____

3 On what day does this November begin? _____

4 If today is Thursday, what day will tomorrow be? _____

5 If today is Tuesday, what day was yesterday? _____

Think About It   Reasoning

On what day of the week will the next month begin? Explain.

6 Circle the names of the days of the week.

7 Color the Sundays green and the Thursdays blue.

8 Write the days of the week in order.

_____ Sunday _____ , _____ Monday _____ ,

_____ , _____ ,

_____ , _____ , _____

May						
Sunday	Monday	Tuesday	Wednesday	Thursday	Friday	Saturday
						1
2	3	4	5	6	7	8
9	10	11	12	13	14	15
16	17	18	19	20	21	22
23 / 30	24 / 31	25	26	27	28	29

Problem Solving   Visual Thinking

Find the pattern.

Then write the day that comes next.

9 | Tuesday | | Wednesday | | Thursday | _____

10 | Saturday | | Sunday | | Monday | _____

Home Connection Your child learned about the calendar and named the days of the week. **Home Activity** Begin with Sunday and have your child name the days of the week in order. Look at the calendar for the current month. Talk about the dates on which your family has special plans.

Name_____

There are 12 months in one **year**.

January						
S	M	T	W	T	F	S
					1	2	3
4	5	6	7	8	9	10
11	12	13	14	15	16	17
18	19	20	21	22	23	24
25	26	27	28	29	30	31

February						
S	M	T	W	T	F	S
1	2	3	4	5	6	7
8	9	10	11	12	13	14
15	16	17	18	19	20	21
22	23	24	25	26	27	28

March						
S	M	T	W	T	F	S
1	2	3	4	5	6	7
8	9	10	11	12	13	14
15	16	17	18	19	20	21
22	23	24	25	26	27	28
29	30	31				

April						
S	M	T	W	T	F	S
			1	2	3	4
5	6	7	8	9	10	11
12	13	14	15	16	17	18
19	20	21	22	23	24	25
26	27	28	29	30		

May						
S	M	T	W	T	F	S
					1	2
3	4	5	6	7	8	9
10	11	12	13	14	15	16
17	18	19	20	21	22	23
24/31	25	26	27	28	29	30

June						
S	M	T	W	T	F	S
	1	2	3	4	5	6
7	8	9	10	11	12	13
14	15	16	17	18	19	20
21	22	23	24	25	26	27
28	29	30				

July						
S	M	T	W	T	F	S
			1	2	3	4
5	6	7	8	9	10	11
12	13	14	15	16	17	18
19	20	21	22	23	24	25
26	27	28	29	30	31	

August						
S	M	T	W	T	F	S
						1
2	3	4	5	6	7	8
9	10	11	12	13	14	15
16	17	18	19	20	21	22
23/30	24/31	25	26	27	28	29

September						
S	M	T	W	T	F	S
		1	2	3	4	5
6	7	8	9	10	11	12
13	14	15	16	17	18	19
20	21	22	23	24	25	26
27	28	29	30			

October						
S	M	T	W	T	F	S
				1	2	3
4	5	6	7	8	9	10
11	12	13	14	15	16	17
18	19	20	21	22	23	24
25	26	27	28	29	30	31

November						
S	M	T	W	T	F	S
1	2	3	4	5	6	7
8	9	10	11	12	13	14
15	16	17	18	19	20	21
22	23	24	25	26	27	28
29	30					

December						
S	M	T	W	T	F	S
		1	2	3	4	5
6	7	8	9	10	11	12
13	14	15	16	17	18	19
20	21	22	23	24	25	26
27	28	29	30	31		

Word Bank

year

Check ✓

Use the calendar above to answer the questions.

1. How many months are in one year? _____

2. Which month comes before May? _____

3. Which month comes between January and March? _____

4. How many months have 31 days? _____

Think About It   Number Sense

Are there more months with 30 days or 31 days?

January						
S	M	T	W	T	F	S
		1	2	3	4	5
6	7	8	9	10	11	12
13	14	15	16	17	18	19
20	21	22	23	24	25	26
27	28	29	30	31		

February						
S	M	T	W	T	F	S
					1	2
3	4	5	6	7	8	9
10	11	12	13	14	15	16
17	18	19	20	21	22	23
24	25	26	27	28		

March						
S	M	T	W	T	F	S
					1	2
3	4	5	6	7	8	9
10	11	12	13	14	15	16
17	18	19	20	21	22	23
24/31	25	26	27	28	29	30

April						
S	M	T	W	T	F	S
	1	2	3	4	5	6
7	8	9	10	11	12	13
14	15	16	17	18	19	20
21	22	23	24	25	26	27
28	29	30				

May						
S	M	T	W	T	F	S
				1	2	3	4
5	6	7	8	9	10	11
12	13	14	15	16	17	18
19	20	21	22	23	24	25
26	27	28	29	30	31	

June						
S	M	T	W	T	F	S
						1
2	3	4	5	6	7	8
9	10	11	12	13	14	15
16	17	18	19	20	21	22
23/30	24	25	26	27	28	29

July						
S	M	T	W	T	F	S
	1	2	3	4	5	6
7	8	9	10	11	12	13
14	15	16	17	18	19	20
21	22	23	24	25	26	27
28	29	30	31			

August						
S	M	T	W	T	F	S
					1	2	3
4	5	6	7	8	9	10
11	12	13	14	15	16	17
18	19	20	21	22	23	24
25	26	27	28	29	30	31

September						
S	M	T	W	T	F	S
1	2	3	4	5	6	7
8	9	10	11	12	13	14
15	16	17	18	19	20	21
22	23	24	25	26	27	28
29	30					

October						
S	M	T	W	T	F	S
		1	2	3	4	5
6	7	8	9	10	11	12
13	14	15	16	17	18	19
20	21	22	23	24	25	26
27	28	29	30	31		

November						
S	M	T	W	T	F	S
					1	2
3	4	5	6	7	8	9
10	11	12	13	14	15	16
17	18	19	20	21	22	23
24	25	26	27	28	29	30

December						
S	M	T	W	T	F	S
1	2	3	4	5	6	7
8	9	10	11	12	13	14
15	16	17	18	19	20	21
22	23	24	25	26	27	28
29	30	31				

5 Write the names of the missing months.

Then say the names of the months in order.

January, <u>February</u>, March, _____,

May, _____, July, _____,

September, _____, November, _____

Problem Solving   Number Sense

You can show the date two ways.

January 12, 2004 or **1/12/2004**

6 Draw lines to match the dates.

April 21, 2004   6/20/2004

June 20, 2004   4/21/2004

The 1 tells that January is the 1st month!

© Pearson Education, Inc.

Home Connection Your child used a calendar to find and name the months. **Home Activity** Look at a one-year calendar and take turns saying the names of the months in order. Ask your child to name the 5th month and the 7th month. *(May; July)*

Name _____

Dorling Kindersley

Do You Know...
that a mother tortoise digs a hole and lays her eggs in the warm soil?

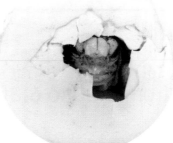

1 Before this egg began to hatch, it looked like a table tennis ball. What shape was the egg?

_____

Fun Fact!
Caterpillars hatch from eggs and become butterflies.

2 At 4:30 this baby tortoise began to bite the shell to make the hole bigger. Show 4:30 on both clocks.

3 The mother tortoise laid 12 eggs. 6 of the eggs have hatched. How many eggs have not hatched?

_____ − _____ = _____ eggs

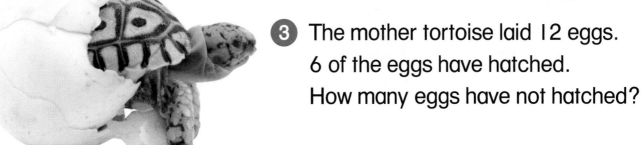

4 At 6:30 the baby tortoise walked out of the shell. Show 6:30 on both clocks.

5 How many hours passed from 4:30 to 6:30?

_____ hours

6 The baby tortoise started to hatch on Saturday. It walked out of the shell the next day. On which day did the baby tortoise walk out of the shell?

_____

7 **Writing in Math**

It takes 5 months for tortoise eggs to hatch. Use a calendar to show in which month the eggs will hatch if they are laid in March.

Name_____

When did this activity happen?
Draw a line to match.

1

- morning

- afternoon

- night

About how long does each activity take?
Draw lines to match.

2

about 1 minute   about 1 day   about 1 hour

Use the schedule to answer the question.

3 What class does Tim have after music?

_____

Tim's Schedule	
11:00	Music
11:30	Art
12:00	Lunch

Answer the questions.

4 What days are missing?

Sunday, _____,
Tuesday, Wednesday,
_____, Friday, Saturday

_____ and _____

5 What day of the week will June 6 be?

June				
Sunday	Monday	Tuesday	Wednesday	Thursday
1	2	3	4	5
8	9	10	11	12

_____

Name_____

1 What is the sum?

$$3 + 9 = \_\_$$

9	10	11	12
Ⓐ	Ⓑ	Ⓒ	Ⓓ

2 How many vertices does this shape have?

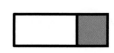

4	5	6	7
Ⓐ	Ⓑ	Ⓒ	Ⓓ

3 Which shape has one half shaded?

Ⓐ	Ⓑ	Ⓒ	Ⓓ

4 Which takes less than 1 minute?

Ⓐ	Ⓑ	Ⓒ	Ⓓ

5 What is the ending time?

4 o'clock ⟶ 2 hours ⟶ _____ o'clock

6 o'clock	7 o'clock	8 o'clock	9 o'clock
Ⓐ	Ⓑ	Ⓒ	Ⓓ

Hour or Half Hour

Our dance recital starts at 4:00. It will last about 1 hour.

The recital will end at about 5:00.

Decide whether the activity lasted about an hour or about a half hour.

Then show the ending time on the clock.

1 We started our lunch at 11:00.

2 We started dance practice at 2:00.

3 We started walking the dog at 6:30.

Home Connection Your child decided if activities lasted a half hour or an hour.
Home Activity Before you do an activity with your child, have him or her predict how long it will last. Time your activity to see if he or she was right.

Name _____

Create a Schedule Using a Computer

You can use a computer to show the times that you start your after-school activities.

1 Make a list of 5 things you do after school. Write the activities in order on a separate sheet of paper.

2 On a computer, go to the Time eTool.

3 Choose a start time for your first activity by setting the hands of the clock.

4 Check the digital clock to make sure that it shows the time you want your first activity to start. Write this time next to the first activity on your sheet of paper.

5 Repeat Steps 3 and 4 for your other after-school activities.

Think About It   Reasoning

On which activity do you spend the greatest amount of time? On which activity do you spend the least amount of time?

Home Connection Your child used a computer to show the starting times of different after-school activities and created a schedule for those activities.
Home Activity Ask your child questions about his or her weekday and weekend schedules.

© Pearson Education, Inc.

Get Information for the Answer

You can get information from a table to help you solve math problems.

Test-Taking Strategies

Understand the Question

Get Information for the Answer

Plan How to Find the Answer

Make Smart Choices

Use Writing in Math

1. Which activity will Megan miss if she comes to the fair at 1:30?

   Ⓐ Beanbag Toss

   Ⓑ Face Painting

   Ⓒ Cake Sale

   Ⓓ Musical Chairs

Find the activity that starts before 1:30. Fill in the answer bubble.

School Fun Fair	
Activity	**Time**
Beanbag Toss	1:00
Face Painting	1:30
Cake Sale	2:00
Musical Chairs	2:30

Your Turn

Use the table to solve this problem.
Fill in the answer bubble.

2. At what time should Frank come to the fair if he does not want to miss anything?

   Ⓐ 1:00

   Ⓑ 1:30

   Ⓒ 2:00

   Ⓓ 2:30

Home Connection Your child prepared for standardized tests by using information from a table to solve math problems. **Home Activity** Ask your child to explain how he or she used the table to solve the problem in Exercise 2.

Name _____

Time for Math!

Do you know at what time you wake up, have breakfast, and go to school?
Do you know at what time you get home from school?

Right now it's time to do some math!

What Time Is It?

1 Carlos wakes up at 7:00 each morning.
He arrives at school 1 hour later.
At what time does Carlos get to school?

_____

2 At school, lunch begins at noon.
It is now 10:00. In how many
hours will lunch begin?

_____ hours

3 Jennifer gets home from school
at the time shown on the clock.
She will play for 1 hour.
At what time will she finish playing?

_____

Take It to the NET
Video and Activities
www.scottforesman.com

Home Connection Your child solved problems about daily activities by telling time on analog (dial) and digital clocks. **Home Activity** Ask your child to tell at what time three daily activities begin or end, using both analog and digital clocks.

© Pearson Education, Inc.

Chapter Test

How long does this activity take?
Circle the correct answer.

less than 1 minute

more than 1 minute

Draw the hands on each clock face.
Then write the time on the other clock.

2   5 o'clock   **3**   11 o'clock

Write the same time.

4   **5**

Answer the questions.

6 What day comes after Tuesday?

Sunday, Monday,
Tuesday, _____

_____

7 Which month comes after June?

January	February	March
April	May	June

_____

When did this activity happen?

Draw a line to match.

8

- morning

- afternoon

- night

About how long does each activity take?

Draw lines to match.

9

about 2 minutes   about 2 hours   about 2 days

Use the schedule to answer the question.

10 At what time does Bill play soccer?

_____

Bill's Schedule	
10:00	Play Soccer
12:00	Visit Grandma

Write the starting time and the ending time.

Then draw the hands on the clock to show the ending time.

11

_____ o'clock   ⟶   1 hour   ⟶   _____ o'clock

Name _____

1 Which clock shows the same time?

Ⓐ   Ⓑ   Ⓒ   Ⓓ

2 Which shape has 2 flat surfaces and 0 vertices?

Ⓐ   Ⓑ   Ⓒ   Ⓓ

3 Which fraction tells how much is shaded?

$\frac{3}{4}$ $\frac{2}{4}$ $\frac{2}{3}$ $\frac{1}{3}$

Ⓐ   Ⓑ   Ⓒ   Ⓓ

4 Which number sentence answers the question?

**The girls packed 8 sandwiches.
They ate 4 of them.
How many sandwiches are left?**

$4 + 4 = 8$ $8 + 4 = 12$ $8 - 4 = 4$ $10 - 8 = 2$

Ⓐ   Ⓑ   Ⓒ   Ⓓ

Add. Use a number line if you like.

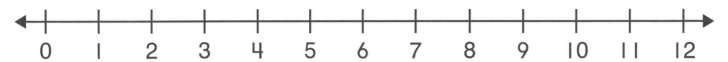

0 1 2 3 4 5 6 7 8 9 10 11 12

5 5 + 3 = ___   8 + 1 = ___   9 + 2 = ___

Look at the first shape.
Circle the shape that matches it.

6  |

About how long does each activity take?
Draw lines to match.

7

·   ·   ·

about 2 minutes   about 2 hours   about 2 days

Which day comes after Wednesday?

8

Sunday   Monday   Tuesday   Wednesday

_____

Four Little Chickens

A New Adaptation of An Old Rhyme About Ordinals

Illustrated by Amy Vangsguard

This Math Storybook belongs to

_____

Said the third little chicken
with an odd little tug,

I wish I could find
a fat little slug.

Dear Family,

Today my class started Chapter 7, **Counting to 100.** I will learn to count with groups of tens. I will also learn to recognize number patterns and to skip count. Here are some of the math words I will be learning and some things we can do to help me with my math.

Love,

_____

Math Activity to Do at Home

Gather about 30 small objects, such as pennies or buttons. First, ask your child to estimate, or guess, how many objects you collected. Then help him or her count out groups of 10. With your child, count the groups by 10s. Then *count on* any objects that are left over. Repeat this activity often with different-sized groups of objects. With practice, your child will get better at estimating.

Books to Read Together

Reading math stories reinforces concepts. Look for these titles in your local library:

Monster Math
By Anne Miranda
(Harcourt Brace, 1999)

A Fair Bear Share
By Stuart J. Murphy
(HarperCollins, 1998)

Take It to the NET
More Activities
www.scottforesman.com

My New Math Words

estimate Guess or predict. For example, estimate how many objects are in a group: "There are **about** 20 marbles in the bowl."

36 is **before** 37.

37 is **between** 36 and 38.

38 is **after** 37.

even 0, 2, 4, 6, and 8 are **even** numbers.

All multi-digit even numbers end in 0, 2, 4, 6, or 8.

odd 1, 3, 5, 7, and 9 are **odd** numbers.

All multi-digit odd numbers end in 1, 3, 5, 7, or 9.

Barnyard Concentration

What You Need

24 paper squares ■

How to Play

1. Place the squares on the gameboard.
2. Take turns. Pick up 2 squares.
3. If you find a match, keep both squares.
4. If you do not find a match, put the squares back.
5. Keep playing until you and your partner find all of the matches.

3rd	sixth	7th	twelfth	second	6th
fifth	4th	first	eighth	10th	fifteenth
12th	twentieth	15th	8th	third	2nd
tenth	1st	fourth	20th	5th	seventh

Name_____

16 is 10 and 6 left over.

Numbers from 11 to 19 can be made with one group of 10 and some left over.

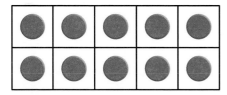

Check ✓

Use counters and Workmat 3.

Write each number as 10 and some left over.

1 | fifteen | 15 is __10__ and __5__.

2 | nineteen | 19 is ____ and ____.

3 | twelve | 12 is ____ and ____.

4 | fourteen | 14 is ____ and ____.

5 | seventeen | 17 is ____ and ____.

Think About It   Number Sense

If you have 2 toy cars, how many more do you need to have 12? Tell how you know.

Use counters and Workmat 3.

Write each number as 10 and some left over.

6 | eleven | 11 is ___10___ and ___1___.

7 | thirteen | 13 is _____ and _____.

8 | sixteen | 16 is _____ and _____.

9 | eighteen | 18 is _____ and _____.

10 | fifteen | 15 is _____ and _____.

I think of these numbers as 10 and some left over!

Problem Solving Algebra

Write each missing number.

11 ☐ and 10 is 16.

12 1 and ☐ is 11.

13 10 and ☐ is 17.

14 ☐ and 9 is 19.

15 ☐ and 10 is 18.

16 10 and ☐ is 14.

17 5 and ☐ is 15.

18 ☐ and 2 is 12.

Home Connection Your child used counters to show numbers as a group of 10 and some left over. **Home Activity** Tell your child a number between 11 and 19. Ask him or her to say the number as 10 and some left over. For example, 17 is 10 and 7.

Name_____

Learn!

Sometimes counting by 10s is easier than counting by 1s.

4 groups of 10 is 40 in all!

40

| 10, | 20, | 30, | 40 |
| ten, | twenty, | thirty, | forty |

Check ✓

Count by 10s. Then write the numbers.

1

_5_ groups of 10

_50_
fifty

2

____ groups of 10

____
sixty

Think About It Reasoning

When might it be better to count by 10s instead of counting by 1s?

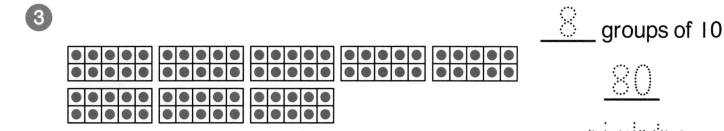

10,	20,	30,	40,	50,
ten,	twenty,	thirty,	forty,	fifty,
60,	70,	80,	90,	100
sixty,	seventy,	eighty,	ninety,	one hundred

Count by 10s. Then write the numbers.

3

_8_ groups of 10

_80_

eighty

4

_____ groups of 10

_____

_____

5

_____ groups of 10

_____

_____

Problem Solving Mental Math

6 Paul saves 10¢ each day. How much money has he saved after 8 days?

_____¢

Home Connection Your child counted by 10s. **Home Activity** Choose a multiple of 10 less than 100 (10, 20, 30, ..., 90) and ask your child to tell how many groups of 10 make up that number. For example, 40 is made up of 4 groups of 10.

Name_____

You can use the hundred chart to count on from any number.

If I start at 36, what number will I say next?

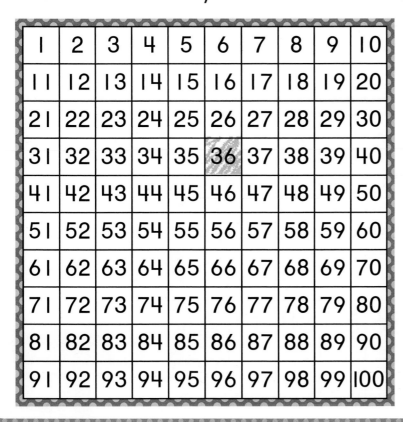

1	2	3	4	5	6	7	8	9	10
11	12	13	14	15	16	17	18	19	20
21	22	23	24	25	26	27	28	29	30
31	32	33	34	35	36	37	38	39	40
41	42	43	44	45	46	47	48	49	50
51	52	53	54	55	56	57	58	59	60
61	62	63	64	65	66	67	68	69	70
71	72	73	74	75	76	77	78	79	80
81	82	83	84	85	86	87	88	89	90
91	92	93	94	95	96	97	98	99	100

Check ✓

Use the hundred chart above to count on by 1s.

1. 21, _22_, _23_, ____, ____, ____, ____

2. 45, ____, ____, ____, ____, ____, ____

3. 74, ____, ____, ____, ____, ____, ____

4. 59, ____, ____, ____, ____, ____, ____

Think About It   Reasoning

How are the numbers in each row of the hundred chart alike? How are they different?

5 Write the missing numbers. Look for patterns.

1	2	3	4	5	6	7	8	9	10
11	12								
21	22	23	24	25	26	27	28	29	30
41	42	43	44	45	46	47	48	49	50
51	52	53	54	55					
					66	67	68	69	70
71	72	73	74	75					
					86	87	88	89	90
91	92								100

Use the hundred chart above to count back by 1s.

6 99, 98, 97, ____, ____, ____, ____

7 51, ____, ____, ____, ____, ____, ____

Problem Solving   Number Sense

Look at these parts of the hundred chart.

Write the missing numbers.

8

26		
	37		39

9

	52	
61			64

Home Connection Your child used a hundred chart to count forward to 100 and backward from 100. **Home Activity** Have your child choose a number on the hundred chart and show you how to count forward to 100 and backward to 1 from that number.

Learn!

I count 2 groups of 10 and 4 left over.

I count 24 ones.

10, 20, 21, 22, 23, **24**

Check ✓

Circle groups of 10.
Then write the numbers.

①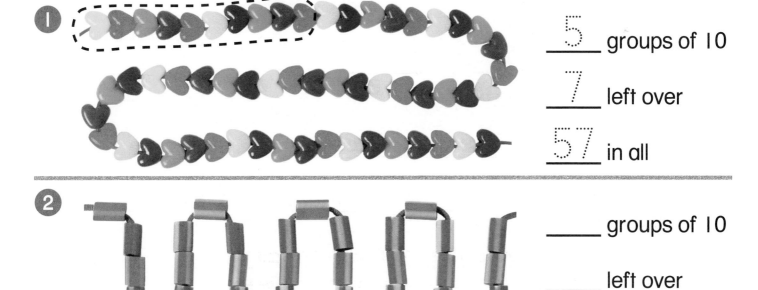

___5___ groups of 10

___7___ left over

__57__ in all

②

_____ groups of 10

_____ left over

_____ in all

Think About It   Number Sense

Sam counted 8 groups of 10 stamps and 3 left over.

If he counts all of the stamps by 1s, how many will he count?

Circle groups of 10.
Then write the numbers.

3

_4_ groups of 10

_5_ left over

_45_ in all

4

_____ groups of 10

_____ left over

_____ in all

5

_____ groups of 10

_____ left over

_____ in all

Problem Solving   Visual Thinking

Draw a picture to solve.

6 Sara has 26 beads.
10 beads fit on a necklace.

How many necklaces
can she make?   _____

How many beads will
be left over?   _____

Home Connection Your child circled groups of 10 to help name numbers as groups of 10 with some left over. **Home Activity** Draw between 20 and 30 dots. Have your child circle groups of 10 and then tell how many groups of 10 there are and how many dots are left over. Then ask your child to name the total.

Name_____

Estimate.
About how many balls are there?

This group has 10 balls, so there must be about 30 balls in all.

about

10 (30) 50

Check ✓

Use the group of 10 to estimate. Circle the best estimate for how many there are in all.

Word Bank

estimate
about

1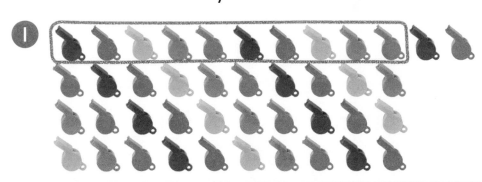

about

20 40 60

2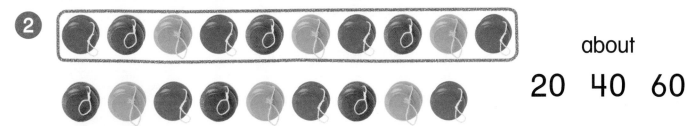

about

20 40 60

Think About It Number Sense

Travis has 55 fish. What would be a good estimate for about how many fish he has? Explain.

Circle a group of 10.
Then circle the best estimate for
how many there are in all.

3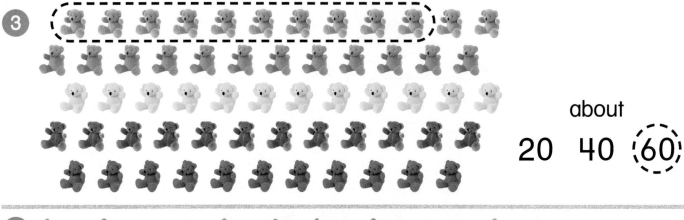

about

20 40 (60)

4

about

10 30 50

5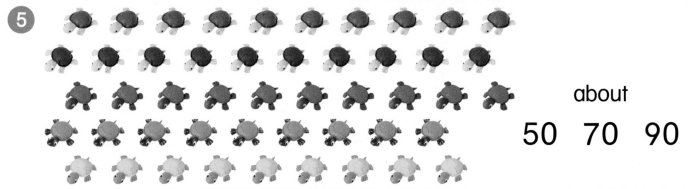

about

50 70 90

Problem Solving Estimation

Circle all of the numbers that answer the question.

6 Martin estimates that he has about 40 marbles.
If 40 is a good estimate, which numbers could
show how many marbles Martin really has?

11   23   38   42   56   61   70

Home Connection Your child used a group of 10 to estimate a larger
quantity. **Home Activity** Draw between 35 and 45 dots. Ask your child to
circle a group of 10 and then tell whether he or she thinks there are about 20
dots or about 40 dots in all. *(About 40)*

This **graph** shows how many of each
kind of sticker there are.

Count by 10s to
find how many
stickers there are.

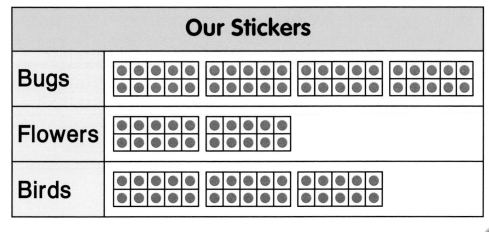

Our Stickers

Bugs	
Flowers	
Birds	

Word Bank

graph

Check ✔

Use the graph to answer each question.

1 How many bug stickers are there? _____

2 Of which kind of sticker are there the most? _____

3 Of which kind of sticker are there the fewest? _____

4 How many more bug stickers than
flower stickers are there? _____

5 How many more bird stickers do we
need to make 50? _____

Think About It   Reasoning

How do you use the graph to find out which group
of stickers has the most?

Practice

Our Stamp Collection		
Red Stamps	**Yellow Stamps**	**Green Stamps**
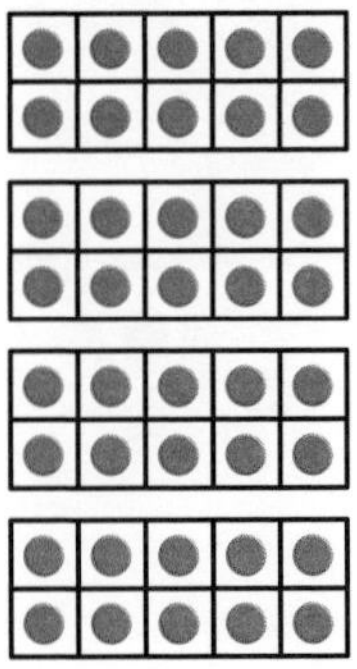	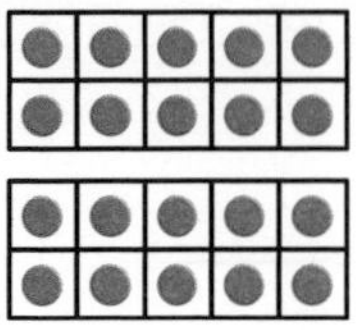	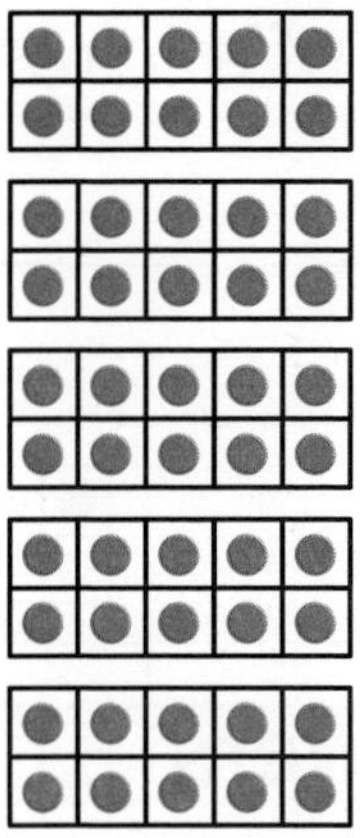

Use the graph to answer each question.

6. Of which color stamp are there the most? ____________

7. Of which color stamp are there the fewest? ____________

8. How many more green stamps than yellow stamps are there? ____________

9. How many red and yellow stamps are there altogether? ____________

Writing in Math

10. Write your own question about the graph.

____

____

Home Connection Your child read and interpreted graphs. **Home Activity** Ask your child to look at the graph on this page and to tell how many of each color stamp there are. *(Red: 40; Yellow: 20; Green: 50)*

Name _____

Write each number as 10 and some left over.

1 18 is 10 and _____.

2 13 is 10 and _____.

Count by 10s. Then write the numbers.

3 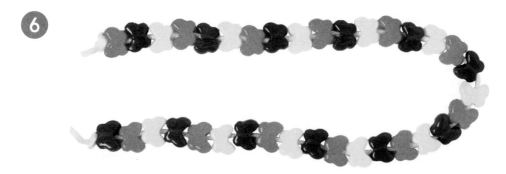   _____ groups of 10

_____

Count on or count back by 1s.
Use a hundred chart if you like.

4 47, 48, 49, _____, _____, _____, _____, _____, _____

5 65, 64, 63, _____, _____, _____, _____, _____, _____

Circle groups of 10. Then write the numbers.

6

_____ groups of 10

_____ left over

_____ in all

Circle a group of 10.
Then circle the best estimate for
how many there are in all.

7

about

20   40   60

Name_____

1 What is the difference?

9 − 4 = ___

Ⓐ 0
Ⓑ 4
Ⓒ 5
Ⓓ 7

$\begin{array}{r} 9 \\ -4 \\ \hline \end{array}$

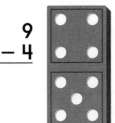

2 What fraction of the cherries is red?

$\frac{1}{4}$ $\frac{1}{2}$ $\frac{2}{3}$ $\frac{3}{4}$

Ⓐ   Ⓑ   Ⓒ   Ⓓ

Use the schedule for Exercises 3, 4, and 5.

Camp Daisy Schedule	
Time	**Activity**
9:00	Art
10:30	Swimming
12:00	Lunch
1:00	Gardening
2:30	Hiking

3 What do the campers do at 10:30?

Art   Swimming   Lunch   Hiking
Ⓐ   Ⓑ   Ⓒ   Ⓓ

4 At what time does lunch begin?

10:30   12:00   1:00   2:30
Ⓐ   Ⓑ   Ⓒ   Ⓓ

5 What do the campers do just after Gardening?

Hiking   Lunch   Art   Swimming
Ⓐ   Ⓑ   Ⓒ   Ⓓ

Learn! Algebra

There are lots of patterns on the hundred chart!
Write the numbers to continue the pattern.

I am beginning to see a pattern.

1	2	3	4	5	6	7	8	9	10
11	12	13	14	15	16	17	18	19	20
21	22	23	24	25	26	27	28	29	30
31	32	33	34	35	36	37	38	39	40
41	42	43	44	45	46	47	48	49	50
51	52	53	54	55	56	57	58	59	60

Check ✓

1 Skip count by 5s to continue the pattern.
Write the numbers.

1	2	3	4	5	6	7	8	9	10
11	12	13	14		16	17	18	19	
21	22	23	24		26	27	28	29	
31	32	33	34		36	37	38	39	

Think About It Reasoning

How is the pattern for counting by 5s like the
pattern for counting by 10s? How is it different?

2 Color the numbers you say when you count by 2s.

1	2	3	4	5	6	7	8	9	10
11	12	13	14	15	16	17	18	19	20
21	22	23	24	25	26	27	28	29	30
31	32	33	34	35	36	37	38	39	40
41	42	43	44	45	46	47	48	49	50
51	52	53	54	55	56	57	58	59	60
61	62	63	64	65	66	67	68	69	70
71	72	73	74	75	76	77	78	79	80
81	82	83	84	85	86	87	88	89	90
91	92	93	94	95	96	97	98	99	100

What pattern do you see?

3 Color the numbers you say when you count by 5s.

41	42	43	44	45	46	47	48	49	50
51	52	53	54	55	56	57	58	59	60
61	62	63	64	65	66	67	68	69	70
71	72	73	74	75	76	77	78	79	80

Problem Solving   Visual Thinking

Finish coloring the calendar. Then write **yes** or **no**.

4 Kendra has a soccer game every 3 days.

Does she have a game on April 21? _____

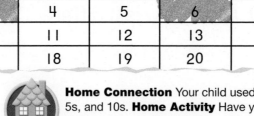

April						
Sunday	Monday	Tuesday	Wednesday	Thursday	Friday	Saturday
1	2	3	4	5	6	7
8	9	10	11	12	13	14
15	16	17	18	19	20	21

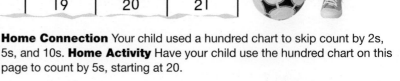

Home Connection Your child used a hundred chart to skip count by 2s, 5s, and 10s. **Home Activity** Have your child use the hundred chart on this page to count by 5s, starting at 20.

Skip counting is an easy way to count.
There are 5 windows in each car.

_5_, _10_, _15_, _20_

There are 20 windows on the train.

Check ✓

Skip count to find how many.

1 fingers

 _10_, _____, _____, _____, _____, _____

2 shoes

 _2_, _____, _____, _____, _____, _____

Think About It Reasoning

What are some other things that you could
count by 2s? What are some other things
that you could count by 5s?

How many blocks are there?
Count by 10s.

3

__10__, _____, _____, _____, _____, _____

How many star points are there?
Count by 5s.

4

_____, _____, _____, _____, _____, _____

How many eyes are there?
Count by 2s.

5

_____, _____, _____, _____, _____, _____

Problem Solving   Algebra

Find the pattern. Write the missing numbers.

6 10, ____, 30, 40, ____, ____, 70, ____, ____, 100

7 50, 45, 40, ____, 30, 25, ____, ____, 10, 5

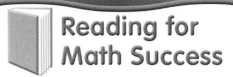
Predict

Read this beginning of a story.

**The sky is full of big, dark clouds.
Thunder booms, and lightning flashes.**

1 What do you think will happen next?

_____

_____

_____

_____

**The rain stops, so Isso, Alex, John,
and Marco want to play in the puddles.
They go to find their boots.**

2 How many boots do they
need to find altogether?

Complete the chart.

Number of Boys	1	2	3	4
Number of Boots	2	4		

The boys need to find _____ boots altogether.

Think About It   Reasoning

How did you complete the chart?

Read the beginning of another story.

**As the boys go outside,
the sun begins to shine.**

3 What do you think will happen
to the puddle?

_____

_____

_____

_____

**The boys decide to pick flowers.
Each boy picks 3 flowers.**

4 How many flowers do the
boys pick altogether?

Complete the chart.

Number of Boys	1	2	3	4
Number of Flowers	3			

The boys pick _____ flowers
altogether.

Name_____

Learn! Algebra

1 The horses need new shoes.

Each horse has 4 hooves.

How many shoes will be needed for all of the horses?

Read and Understand

You need to find how many hooves
there are on the horses altogether.

Plan and Solve

Find a pattern. Count the horses by 1s.

Count their hooves by 4s. Write the numbers.

Number of Horses	1	2			
Number of Hooves	4	8			

_____ shoes will be needed for all of the horses.

Look Back and Check

Does your answer make sense?

Think About It   Reasoning

How could you use the pattern to find how
many shoes would be needed for 8 horses?

Practice

Find a pattern. Then write the numbers.

2 There are 6 dogs.

Each dog has 2 ears.

How many ears are on the dogs altogether?

Number of Dogs	1					
Number of Ears	2					

There are _____ ears in all on the dogs.

3 There are 5 ladybugs.

Each ladybug has 6 legs.

How many legs are on the ladybugs altogether?

Number of Ladybugs					
Number of Legs					

There are _____ legs in all on the ladybugs.

4 There are 5 hens.

Each hen lays 3 eggs.

How many eggs do the hens lay altogether?

Number of Hens					
Number of Eggs					

The hens lay _____ eggs in all.

Home Connection Your child used number patterns to solve problems.
Home Activity Draw a blank chart like the one in Exercise 4. Have your child show how to find the number of eggs if each hen lays 2 eggs.

262   two hundred sixty-two

© Pearson Education, Inc.

Learn!

As we count, numbers
follow a pattern.

46 comes **before** 47.

48 and 49 come **between** 47 and 50.

51 comes **after** 50.

46
47
48
49
50
51

Word Bank

before
between
after

Check ✓

Use Workmat 6.

Write the number that comes before.

① __14__, 15   _____, 79   _____, 40

Write the number that comes after.

② 38, _____   81, _____   64, _____

Write the numbers that come between.

③ 52, _____, _____, 55   28, _____, _____, 31

Think About It   Number Sense

Which number is before 20?

Which number is after 20?

How did the numbers change?

Use Workmat 6 if you like.
Write the number that comes after.

72 comes after 71.

71
72

4 71, _72_   29, _____   60, _____

5 96, _____   49, _____   33, _____

Write the number that comes before.

6 _____, 21   _____, 82   _____, 70

7 _____, 91   _____, 56   _____, 19

Write the numbers that come between.

8 79, _____, _____, 82   47, _____, _____, 50

9 7, _____, _____, 10   34, _____, _____, 37

Problem Solving   Reasoning

Write the number that answers the riddle.

10 I am a number between 29 and 39.
You say my name when you count by 10s.

What number am I? _____

29   ?   39

Home Connection Your child found numbers that come before, after, or between other numbers. **Home Activity** Ask your child to tell the numbers that are before and after 36. *(35 and 37)* Then have your child tell the numbers that are between 24 and 27. *(25 and 26)*

© Pearson Education, Inc.

Name_____

Even numbers can make two equal rows.
Odd numbers have one extra.

What other numbers
are even?
What other numbers
are odd?

8 is even.

9 is odd.

Word Bank

even

odd

Check ✓

Draw circles to show each number.

Try to make equal rows.

Then circle **odd** or **even**.

1

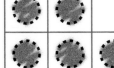

odd

even

2

odd

even

3

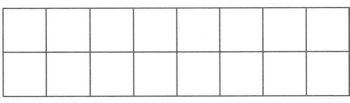

odd

even

Think About It Reasoning

Polly counted the number of birds in a tree by 2s.

There were none left over. Was there an even number

or an odd number of birds? Explain.

Draw circles to show each number.
Try to make equal rows.
Then circle **odd** or **even**.

4

odd

(even)

5 ③

odd

even

6 ⑪

odd

even

7 ⑭

odd

even

Problem Solving   Visual Thinking

Find the pattern.

Write **even** or **odd** to complete each sentence.

8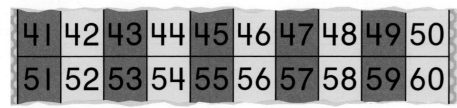

The red numbers are _____.

The yellow numbers are _____.

© Pearson Education, Inc.

 Home Connection Your child decided whether numbers are odd or even.
Home Activity Ask your child to draw circles, as he or she did above, to decide whether 7 is odd or even. *(Odd)*

Learn!

Numbers can tell position.
Which car is 10th in line?

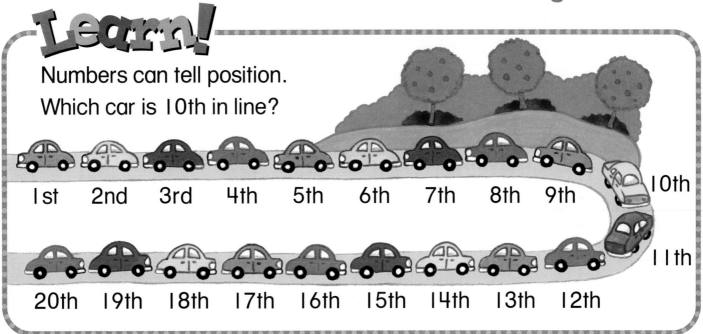

Check ✓

Color to show the positions of the boats.

1 2nd   5th   9th

12th   16th   19th

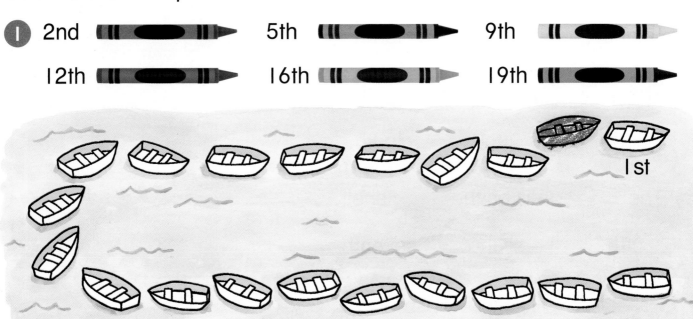

1st

Think About It   Reasoning

If Sunday is the 1st day of the week,
which is the 5th day? Explain.

Sunday	Monday	Tuesday	Wednesday	Thursday	Friday	Saturday

2 Circle the plane that is third in line.
Cross out the plane that is fifth in line.
Draw a box around the plane that is eighth in line.

| 10th | 9th | 8th | 7th | 6th | 5th | 4th | 3rd | 2nd | 1st |
| tenth | ninth | eighth | seventh | sixth | fifth | fourth | third | second | first |

Circle the word that completes each sentence.

3 The 🚂 is on the _____ shelf.

third   fourth   fifth

4 The 🚁 is on the _____ shelf.

eighth   ninth   tenth

5 The 🎎 is on the _____ shelf.

first   fifth   tenth

6 The 📕 is on the _____ shelf.

fifth   sixth   seventh

first
1st

Problem Solving   Reasoning

Solve.

7 How many dolls
are missing?

_____ dolls

  ?

first   second   sixth   seventh   eighth

Home Connection Your child used ordinal numbers 1st through 20th to show position. **Home Activity** Draw 20 circles in a row. Starting on the left, have your child cross out the 5th, 11th, and 19th circles.

Name _____

 Dorling Kindersley

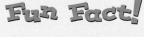

Do You Know...
that the sunflower starfish has about 20 arms?

1 Each starfish has 5 arms. If there are 5 starfish in all, skip count to find how many arms there are.

_____, _____, _____, _____, _____

Fun Fact!
The red and yellow colors seen in some shells make them stronger.

2 Is there an even or an odd number of starfish above?

even   odd

3 Circle the 5th fish.

4 Draw a box around the 8th fish.

5 If there were 2 more fish, how many fish would there be in all?

_____ fish

6 Circle the boat that comes next in the pattern.

7 There are 5 ships.
Each ship has 3 anchors.
How many anchors are there on the ships altogether?

Number of Ships					
Number of Anchors					

There are _____ anchors in all.

8 **Writing in Math**

Sylvia went to the beach at 11:00.
She stayed for 2 hours.
What time did Sylvia leave the
beach? Explain how you know.

270 two hundred seventy

Name_____

Color the numbers you say when you count by 2s.

1

51	52	53	54	55	56	57	58	59	60
61	62	63	64	65	66	67	68	69	70
71	72	73	74	75	76	77	78	79	80

How many cans of vegetables are there?
Count by 5s.

2

_____, _____, _____, _____, _____, _____

Find a pattern. Then write the numbers.

3 There are 5 sailboats.

Each boat has 3 sails.

How many sails are on the boats altogether?

Number of Boats					
Number of Sails					

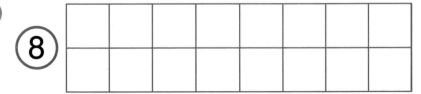

There are _____ sails in all on the sailboats.

Draw circles to show the number.
Try to make equal rows.
Then circle **odd** or **even**.

4 (8)

odd

even

Name_____

1 What is the sum?

$$\begin{array}{r} 6 \\ + 6 \\ \hline \end{array}$$

0	6	10	12
Ⓐ	Ⓑ	Ⓒ	Ⓓ

2 What is the missing number?

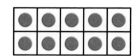 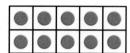

____ groups of 10

1	2	5	10
Ⓐ	Ⓑ	Ⓒ	Ⓓ

3 Use the group of 10 to estimate.
What is the best estimate for how many there are in all?

Ⓐ about 20

Ⓑ about 40

Ⓒ about 60

Ⓓ about 80

4 Which day of the week answers the question?

On Thursday a baby bird leaves the nest.
It hops and tries to fly.
It is strong enough to fly away 2 days later.
On what day can the baby bird fly away?

Thursday	Friday	Saturday	Sunday
Ⓐ	Ⓑ	Ⓒ	Ⓓ

Writing in Math

5 What is something you do in the morning?
What is something you do in the evening?

_____

_____

Name _____  **Enrichment**

Counting by 10s from Any Number

If you use a hundred chart, it is easy to count by 10s from any number.

1	2	3	4	5	6	7	8	9	10
11	12	13	14	15	16	17	18	19	20
21	22	23	24	25	26	27	28	29	30
31	32	33	34	35	36	37	38	39	40
41	42	43	44	45	46	47	48	49	50
51	52	53	54	55	56	57	58	59	60
61	62	63	64	65	66	67	68	69	70
71	72	73	74	75	76	77	78	79	80
81	82	83	84	85	86	87	88	89	90
91	92	93	94	95	96	97	98	99	100

6, _16_, _26_, _36_, _46_,

_56_, _66_, _76_, _86_, _96_

Start at the number given and count by 10s.
Use the hundred chart if you like.

1 3, ____, ____, ____, ____, ____, ____, ____, ____, ____

2 29, ____, ____, ____, ____, ____, ____, ____

3 14, ____, ____, ____, ____, ____, ____, ____, ____

4 38, ____, ____, ____, ____, ____

5 **Writing in Math**

 When you use a hundred chart to count by 10s, what pattern do you see?

 Home Connection Your child counted by 10s starting from different numbers. **Home Activity** Name a number and have your child count by 10s from that number.

Name_____

Skip Count Using a Calculator

You can use a calculator to skip count.

Press ON/C . Press the keys that are shown.

Write what the display shows each time you press = .

1  [2] [+] [2] [=] 4 [=] ___ [=] ___

The pattern is counting by _____2s_____.

2 [1] [0] [+] [1] [0] [=] ___ [=] ___ [=] ___

The pattern is counting by _____.

3 [4] [0] [+] [5] [=] ___ [=] ___ [=] ___

The pattern is counting by _____.

4 [8] [5] [+] [1] [0] [=] ___ [=] ___ [=] ___

The pattern is counting by _____.

Think About It   Number Sense

In Exercise 4, which calculator key would you press to find the next number in the pattern? Explain.

 Home Connection Your child used a calculator to skip count by 2s, 5s, and 10s. **Home Activity** Ask your child to explain how to use a calculator to skip count by 3s. *(Sample answer: I would press 3 + 3 = = = .)*

Plan How to Find the Answer

You can use problem-solving strategies
to help you find answers to math problems.

Test-Taking Strategies

Understand the Question

Get Information for the Answer

Plan How to Find the Answer

Make Smart Choices

Use Writing in Math

1 Liz learns 2 new songs every day.
How many new songs does she
learn in 5 days?

  Ⓐ 2 songs   Ⓑ 10 songs   Ⓒ 8 songs   Ⓓ 12 songs

Use problem-solving strategies. Make a table.
Look for a pattern. Count the songs by twos.

Number of Days	1	2	3	4	5
Number of Songs	2	4	6	8	10

In 5 days, Liz learns ___10___ new songs. Fill in the answer bubble.

Your Turn

Use problem-solving strategies to solve this problem.
Fill in the answer bubble.

2 Derrick plays the piano 3 hours a week.
How many hours does he play the piano in 6 weeks?

  Ⓐ 3 hours   Ⓑ 14 hours   Ⓒ 10 hours   Ⓓ 18 hours

Home Connection Your child prepared for standardized tests by using problem-
solving strategies to answer math questions. **Home Activity** Ask your child to
describe the strategies he or she used to solve Exercise 2. *(Possible answers: Make
a table; look for a pattern; use objects)*

Name _____

Animal Families

How big is your family? Some families are small.
Some families are big.

Many animals live in groups. These groups are a lot
like families. Some of them are small. Some of them
are big. You can count groups of 10 to find out how
many animals there are in an animal family.

Family Pride

1 A group of lions is called a **pride.**
   How many groups of 10 are in a pride of 30 lions?

   _____ groups of 10

   How many lions are left over? _____ lions

2 A group of sheep is called a **flock.**
   How many groups of 10 are in a flock of 93 sheep?

   _____ groups of ten

   How many sheep are left over? _____ sheep

3 A group of monkeys is called a **troop.**
   How many groups of 10 are in a troop of 11 monkeys?

   _____ group of ten

   How many monkeys are left over? _____ monkey

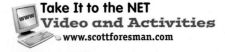

Take It to the NET
Video and Activities
www.scottforesman.com

Home Connection Your child solved problems about different kinds of
animal groups by counting groups of 10. **Home Activity** Show your
child a group of 20 to 60 small objects and ask him or her to count the
objects by groups of 10, to tell how many objects (if any) are left over,
and to write the total number of objects.

Write each number as 10 and some left over.

1 14 is 10 and _____.

2 19 is 10 and _____.

Count by 10s. Then write the numbers.

3 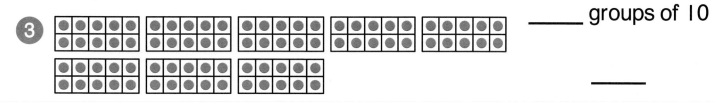 _____ groups of 10

_____

Count on or count back by 1s.
Use a hundred chart if you like.

4 21, 20, 19, _____, _____, _____, _____, _____, _____

5 91, 92, 93, _____, _____, _____, _____, _____, _____

Circle groups of 10. Then write the numbers.

6

_____ groups of 10

_____ left over

_____ in all

Use the graph to answer the question.

7 Of which color button are there the most?

_____

My Button Collection	
Gold	▦▦▦▦
Silver	▦▦
Black	▦▦▦

8 Color the numbers you say when you count by 5s.

31	32	33	34	35	36	37	38	39	40
41	42	43	44	45	46	47	48	49	50
51	52	53	54	55	56	57	58	59	60

How many socks are there? Count by 2s.

9

_____, _____, _____, _____, _____, _____

Find a pattern. Then write the numbers.

10 There are 5 fish tanks. Each tank contains 10 fish. How many fish are in the tanks altogether?

Number of Tanks					
Number of Fish					

There are _____ fish in all the tanks.

Draw circles to show the number. Try to make equal rows. Then circle **odd** or **even**.

11 (9)

odd

even

12 Write the number that comes after.

39, _____

13 Write the numbers that come between.

75, _____, _____, 78

Race to One Hundred

Written by Paul Jamison

Illustrated by Cameron Eagle

This Math Storybook belongs to

_____

Use cubes or clips in sets of tens
on a grid that's **10** by **10**.

Toss a number cube, please do.
Then take that many **tens** for you.

This is how you play the game.
Making **100** is your aim.

8B

8C

Dear Family,

Today my class started Chapter 8, **Place Value, Data, and Graphs.** I will learn about numbers made with tens and ones. I will also learn how to use data to make different kinds of graphs. Here are some of the math words I will be learning and some things we can do to help me with my math.

Love,

_____

Math Activity to Do at Home

Play a number guessing game with your child. Think of a number between 10 and 100. Give your child clues, using math words. For example, if your number is 37, you might say: "I am thinking of an *odd number* between 35 and 39."

Books to Read Together

Reading math stories reinforces concepts. Look for these titles in your local library:

100th Day Worries
By Margery Cuyler
(Simon and Schuster, 2000)

One Hundred Hungry Ants
By Elinor J. Pinczes
(Houghton Mifflin, 1993)

My New Math Words

The number **135** can be shown with these models:

| 1 **hundred** | 3 **tens** | 5 **ones** |

Symbols are used to compare numbers.

20 **<** 30   30 **>** 20   30 **=** 30

is less than   **is greater than**   **equals**

Graphs are used to display data.

bar graph

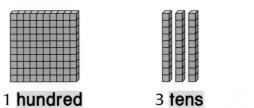

picture graph

Race to One Hundred

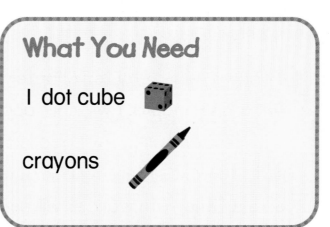

What You Need

I dot cube

crayons

How to Play

1. Play with a partner.

2. Take turns tossing the cube.

3. Color that many sets of ten on one of your grids. Say the number (for example, "6 tens is 60").

4. Keep playing until all of the grids have been colored in.

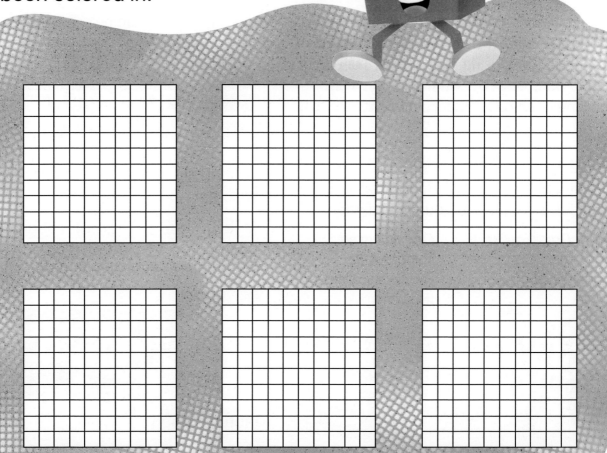

Name_____

You can count the **tens** to find
how many there are in all.

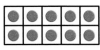 1 ten

 2 tens

 3 tens

4 tens

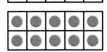 5 tens

The 5 in 50
stands for 5 tens.

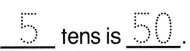 __5__ tens is __50__.

Word Bank

tens

Check ✓

Count the tens. Then write the numbers.

 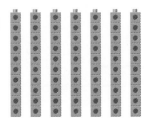

_____ tens is _____.

❷

_____ tens is _____.

❸

_____ tens is _____.

❹

_____ tens is _____.

Think About It   Reasoning

Without counting, how do you know
how many tens there are in 80?

Count the tens. Then write the numbers.

5

___3___ tens is __30__.

6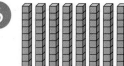

_____ tens is _____.

7

_____ tens is _____.

8

_____ tens is _____.

9

_____ tens is _____.

10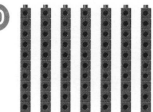

_____ tens is _____.

11

_____ tens is _____.

12

_____ tens is _____.

Problem Solving Mental Math

13 Mike has 90 blocks.

50 of the blocks are in the blue box.

The rest of the blocks are in the red box.

How many blocks are in the red box? _____ blocks

 Home Connection Your child counted the number of tens to find the total number. **Home Activity** Say a number of tens (between 2 tens and 9 tens) and ask your child to tell how many in all and write the number. For example, 2 tens is 20.

Name _____

The **3** in **3**5 is the tens **digit**.
The **5** in 3**5** is the **ones** digit.

35 stands for 3 tens and 5 ones.

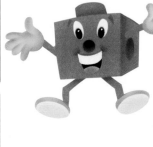

Tens	Ones

Tens	Ones
3	5

35

Word Bank

digit

ones

Check ✓

Count the tens and ones.
Then write the numbers.

1

Tens	Ones

Tens	Ones

___

2

Tens	Ones

Tens	Ones

___

Think About It   Reasoning

How are these numbers alike?
How are they different?

Count the tens and ones.
Then write the numbers.

Now try it sideways.

3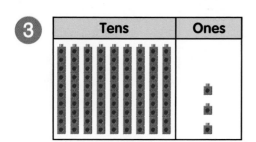

Tens	Ones
9	3

93

4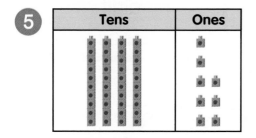

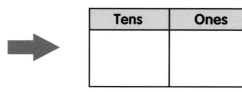

Tens	Ones

_____

5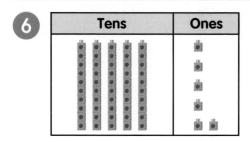

Tens	Ones

_____

6

Tens	Ones

_____

Problem Solving   Visual Thinking

Rosa wants to show 87 with models.

Draw the missing models to help Rosa show 87.

7

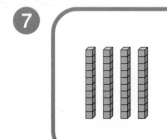

Home Connection Your child found how many tens and ones were in a number. **Home Activity** Choose a number between 21 and 99. Ask your child to draw the tens and ones and then to write the number.

26 stands for 2 tens and 6 ones. That is the same as 20 + 6.

Tens	Ones

2 tens + 6 ones = 26

20 + 6 = 26

Check ✓

Draw the tens and ones. Then write the numbers.

1 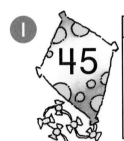 45

Tens	Ones

__4__ tens + __5__ ones = __45__

__40__ + __5__ = __45__

2  72

Tens	Ones

___ tens + ___ ones = ___

___ + ___ = ___

3  50

Tens	Ones

___ tens + ___ ones = ___

___ + ___ = ___

Think About It   Number Sense

In the number 38, which digit stands for the greater amount? Why?

Draw the tens and ones. Then write the numbers.

4

Tens	Ones
▯	▯ ▯ ▯ ▯

____1____ ten + ____4____ ones = ____14____

____10____ + ____4____ = ____14____

5

Tens	Ones

_____ tens + _____ ones = _____

_____ + _____ = _____

6

Tens	Ones

_____ tens + _____ ones = _____

_____ + _____ = _____

7

Tens	Ones

_____ tens + _____ ones = _____

_____ + _____ = _____

Problem Solving   Reasoning

Write the number that matches the clues.

8 The digit in the tens place is odd,
and it is greater than 7.

The digit in the ones place is even,
and it is between 2 and 6.

Tens	Ones

Home Connection Your child showed numbers in expanded form (the value of the tens plus the value of the ones). **Home Activity** Choose numbers between 21 and 99. Ask your child to write each number in expanded form. For example, 25 is 2 tens + 5 ones, or 20 + 5.

Name_____

You can show 32 in different ways.

You can break apart a ten to make 10 ones.

Tens	Ones

$32 = 30 + 2$

Tens	Ones

$32 = 20 + 12$

Check ✓

Use cubes and Workmat 4.
Follow the directions to show a different way to make the number.

1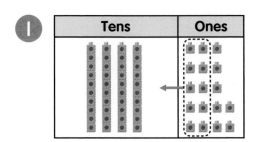

Tens	Ones

$57 = 40 + 17$

Make a ten with 10 ones:

$57 = \underline{50} + \underline{7}$

2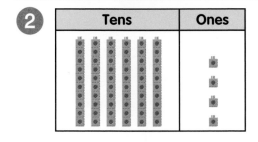

Tens	Ones

$64 = 60 + 4$

Break apart a ten into 10 ones:

$64 = \underline{} + \underline{}$

Think About It   Number Sense

Why is 2 tens and 7 ones the same as 1 ten and 17 ones?

Use cubes and Workmat 4.
Follow the directions to show a different
way to make the number.

3

Tens	Ones

$43 = 40 + 3$

Break apart a ten into 10 ones:

$43 = \underline{30} + \underline{13}$

4

Tens	Ones

$26 = 10 + 16$

Make a ten with 10 ones:

$26 = \underline{} + \underline{}$

5

Tens	Ones

$78 = 70 + 8$

Break apart a ten into 10 ones:

$78 = \underline{} + \underline{}$

Problem Solving   Number Sense

Use cubes to solve.
Circle **yes** or **no**.

6 On Lori's workmat there are 2 tens and 11 ones.
On Beth's workmat there are 3 tens and 2 ones.

Are the girls showing the same number
on each of their workmats?

yes

no

Home Connection Your child showed numbers in different ways.
Home Activity Choose a number between 21 and 99. Ask your
child to tell you two different ways to make that number. For example,
$53 = 50 + 3$ and $53 = 40 + 13$.

Name_____

Understand Graphic Sources: Pictures

Read this story problem.
Use the picture to help you.

Mateo and Emily are selling wrapping paper.
Mateo has 24 rolls.
Emily has 22 rolls.
How many rolls do they have in all?

1 How many tens and ones are in
Mateo's group of rolls?

There are _____ tens and _____ ones.

2 How many tens and ones are in
Emily's group of rolls?

There are _____ tens and _____ ones.

3 How many tens and ones are there in all?

There are _____ tens and _____ ones in all.

4 How many rolls do Mateo and Emily have in all?

_____ rolls

Think About It Reasoning

If you didn't have the picture, how could you find
how many rolls there are in all?

Read another story problem.
Use the picture to help you.

Amy and her mom went to a used-book sale.
Amy bought 27 books.
Her mom bought 32 books.
How many books did they buy in all?

5 Find the number of tens and ones
in each group.

Amy has _____ tens and _____ ones.

Amy's mom has _____ tens and _____ ones.

6 Find the number of tens and ones in all.

There are _____ tens and _____ ones in all.

7 How many books did Amy and her mom
buy in all?

_____ books

Home Connection Your child used pictures to find the total number of objects
in two groups. **Home Activity** Ask your child to explain how he or she found the
total number of books in the picture on this page.

Lars collects pine cones.
He has 15 big pine cones
and 23 small pine cones.
How many pine cones
does Lars have in all?

Read and Understand

You need to find how many
pine cones Lars has altogether.

Plan and Solve

Make each number with cubes.
Join the two groups of cubes.
Find how many there are in all.

There are ___3___ tens and ___8___ ones in all.

Lars has ___38___ pine cones.

Look Back and Check

How can you check that your answer is correct?

Check ✓

Use cubes to find how many there are in all.

1 Katie has 42 small walnuts
and 14 large walnuts.
How many walnuts does she have in all?

42 walnuts   14 walnuts

_____ walnuts

Think About It Reasoning

How could you use cubes to find how
many walnuts there are in both baskets?

Use cubes to find how many there are in all.

2 How many beets are there in all?

_59_ beets

 35 beets
 24 beets

3 How many turnips are there in all?

_____ turnips

 43 turnips
 12 turnips

4 How many mushrooms are there in all?

_____ mushrooms

 40 mushrooms
 41 mushrooms

5 How many berries are there in all?

_____ berries

 57 berries
 21 berries

6 How many carrots are there in all?

_____ carrots

 26 carrots
 11 carrots

Problem Solving Algebra

Use cubes. Write the number of rice cakes below the basket.

7 There are 43 rice cakes in all.
31 rice cakes are in one basket.
How many rice cakes are in the other basket?

31 rice cakes   _____ rice cakes

 Home Connection Your child put two groups of cubes together to find the total. **Home Activity** Give your child two groups of small objects, such as pennies or beans. Ask him or her to show each group as tens and ones and then to explain how to put the two groups together to find the total.

Count the tens. Then write the numbers.

  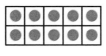

_____ tens is _____.   _____ tens is _____.

Count the tens and ones. Then write the numbers.

 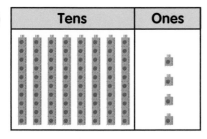

Tens	Ones

 _____

Draw the tens and ones. Then write the numbers.

4 27

Tens	Ones

_____ tens + _____ ones = _____

_____ + _____ = _____

Use cubes and Workmat 4 to show a different way to make the number.

5 58

Tens	Ones

58 = 50 + 8

Break apart a ten into 10 ones:

58 = _____ + _____

Use cubes to find how many there are in all.

 6 How many pecans are there in all?

_____ pecans

23 pecans   36 pecans

Name_____

Use the hundred chart to answer the questions.

71	72	73	74	75	76	77	78	79	80
81	82	83		85	86	87	88	89	
91	92	93	94		96	97	98	99	100

1 What number is between 83 and 85?

84   86   88   90
Ⓐ   Ⓑ   Ⓒ   Ⓓ

2 What number is just before 91?

81   89   90   91
Ⓐ   Ⓑ   Ⓒ   Ⓓ

3 What number comes just after 94?

94   95   96   97
Ⓐ   Ⓑ   Ⓒ   Ⓓ

4 Which fraction tells how much is shaded?

$\frac{1}{4}$ $\frac{1}{3}$ $\frac{2}{3}$ $\frac{3}{4}$
Ⓐ   Ⓑ   Ⓒ   Ⓓ

Writing in Math

5 Write two number sentences that have a sum of 10.

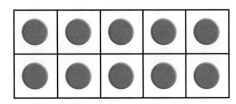

___ + ___ = 10

___ + ___ = 10

Learn!

Take one cube away to show 1 less.

Add a ten to show 10 more.

55   56   66

I less than 56 is _55_ .   10 more than 56 is _66_ .

Check ✓

Use cubes. Write the numbers.

1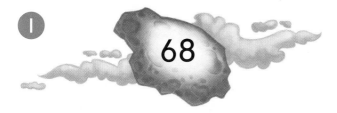

68

10 less than 68 is _____ .

I more than 68 is _____ .

2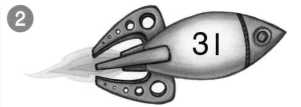

31

10 more than 31 is _____ .

I less than 31 is _____ .

3

45

10 less than 45 is _____ .

I more than 45 is _____ .

4

17

I less than 17 is _____ .

10 more than 17 is _____ .

Think About It   Reasoning

Without using cubes, how can you find
I less than 70? Explain.

Use cubes. Write the numbers.

5

I more than 22 is __23__ .

I0 less than 22 is __12__ .

6

I0 more than 50 is _____ .

I less than 50 is _____ .

7

I0 less than 89 is _____ .

I more than 89 is _____ .

8

I less than 60 is _____ .

I0 more than 60 is _____ .

9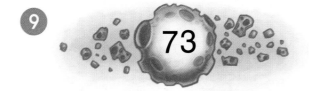

I0 more than 73 is _____ .

I less than 73 is _____ .

10

I more than 34 is _____ .

I0 less than 34 is _____ .

Problem Solving   Reasoning

Sari, Chris, and Lin are playing a game. Use the clues to tell how many points each child has.

11 Sari has 10 points more than Chris.
Chris has 1 point less than Lin.
Lin has 24 points.

_____   _____   _____
Sari   Chris   Lin

 Home Connection Your child found 1 less and 1 more than a number and 10 less and 10 more than a number. **Home Activity** Say a number between 21 and 89. Ask your child to write the numbers that are 1 less, 1 more, 10 less, and 10 more.

© Pearson Education, Inc.

**Algebra**

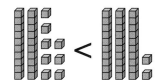 <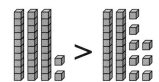

28 is **less than** 32.

28 < 32

32 is **greater than** 28.

32 > 28

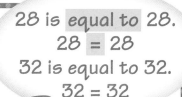
28 is equal to 28.
28 = 28
32 is equal to 32.
32 = 32

Word Bank

less than (<)
greater than (>)
equal to (=)

Check ✓

Write **less than, greater than,** or **equal to.**
Then write <, >, or =.

1

72 is _greater than_ 27.

72 (>) 27

2

18 is _____ 38.

18 ( ) 38

3

39 is _____ 50.

39 ( ) 50

4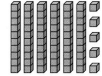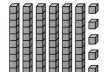

65 is _____ 65.

65 ( ) 65

Think About It   Number Sense

How do you know that 57 is greater than 50?

< less than	> greater than	= equal to

Write <, >, or =.

5   58 (<) 70   **6**   13 ( ) 31

7   23 ( ) 23   **8**   86 ( ) 68

9   45 ( ) 54   **10**   29 ( ) 33

11   41 ( ) 39   **12**   93 ( ) 93

13   52 ( ) 25   **14**   77 ( ) 81

15   97 ( ) 79   **16**   15 ( ) 50

Problem Solving   Visual Thinking

17 Draw different models in the empty box.
Make both sides equal.

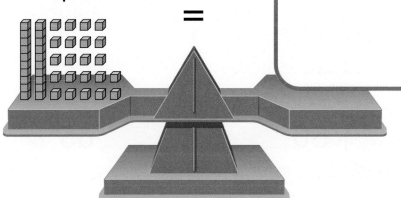

Home Connection Your child compared two numbers. **Home Activity** Say two numbers between 21 and 99. Ask your child to tell which number is less, which number is greater, or if they are equal.

Name_____

Draw lines to show where the
numbers go on the number line.

Each number has its own
place on the number line.

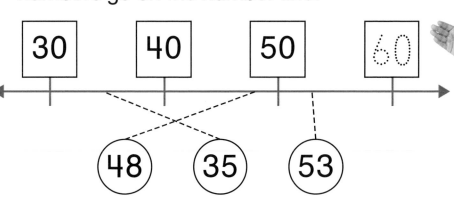

Check ✓

Complete the number line.
Then draw lines to show where the numbers go.

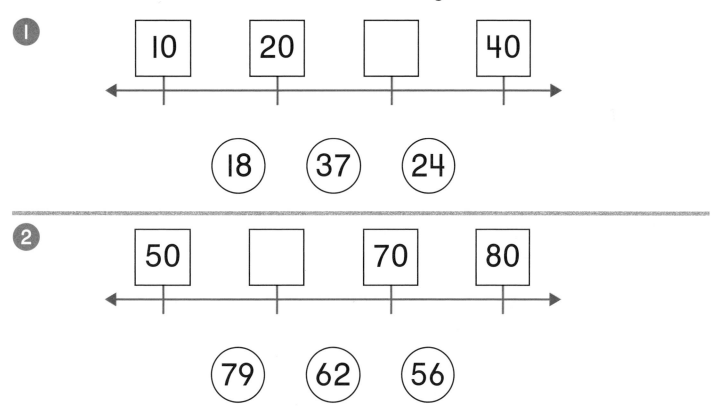

1

| 10 | 20 | | 40 |

18   37   24

2

| 50 | | 70 | 80 |

79   62   56

Think About It   Number Sense

Is 75 closer to 70 or to 80? Explain.

Complete the number line.

Then draw lines to show where the numbers go.

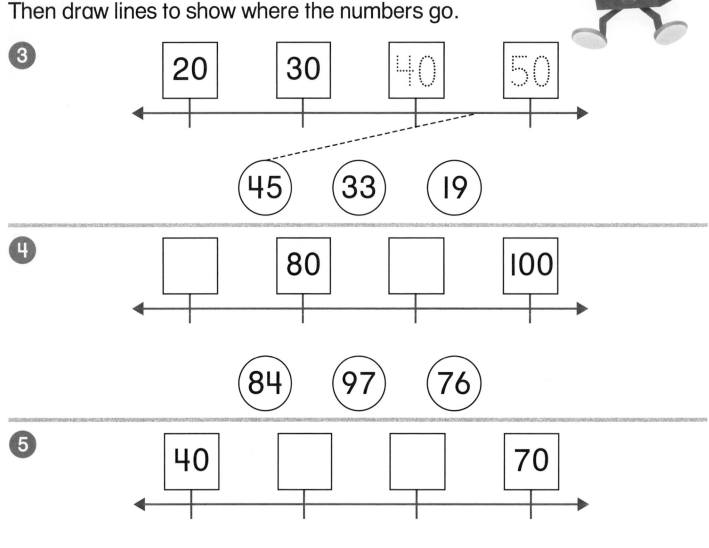

3

| 20 | 30 | 40 | 50 |

45 33 19

4

| | 80 | | 100 |

84 97 76

5

| 40 | | | 70 |

48 61 52

Problem Solving Estimation

6 Draw lines to show where the numbers go.

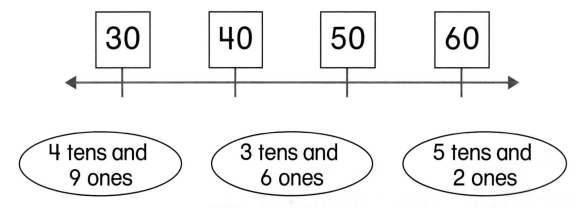

| 30 | 40 | 50 | 60 |

4 tens and 9 ones   3 tens and 6 ones   5 tens and 2 ones

Home Connection Your child estimated the positions of numbers on a number line. **Home Activity** Draw a number line from 20 to 50 as in Exercise 3. Have your child show you where 25, 39, and 47 go.

Name _____

least   greatest

Word Bank

least

greatest

Check ✓

Write the numbers in order from **least** to **greatest**.
Use Workmat 6 if you like.

1
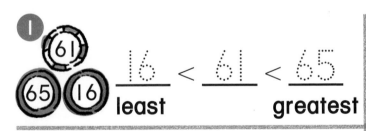
$\underline{16} < \underline{61} < \underline{65}$
least   greatest

2
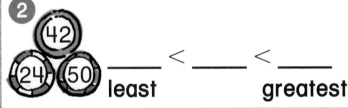
___ < ___ < ___
least   greatest

3
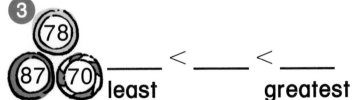
___ < ___ < ___
least   greatest

4
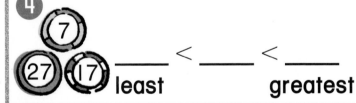
___ < ___ < ___
least   greatest

5
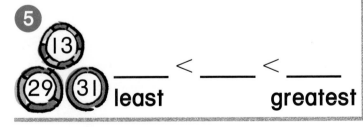
___ < ___ < ___
least   greatest

6
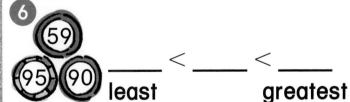
___ < ___ < ___
least   greatest

Think About It Number Sense

How can you tell which of these
numbers is the greatest?

41
43 14

Write the numbers in order
from **greatest** to **least**.

This time start with
the greatest number!

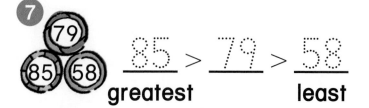

7

$85 > 79 > 58$

greatest   least

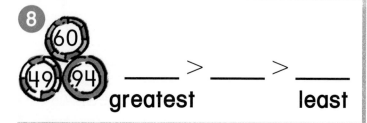

8   ____ > ____ > ____
greatest   least

9   ____ > ____ > ____
greatest   least

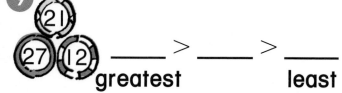

10   ____ > ____ > ____
greatest   least

11   ____ > ____ > ____
greatest   least

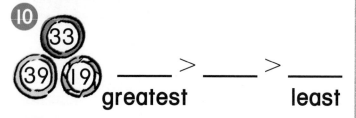
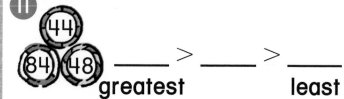

12   ____ > ____ > ____
greatest   least

13   ____ > ____ > ____
greatest   least

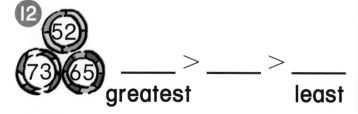
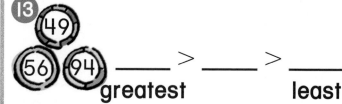

14   ____ > ____ > ____
greatest   least

15   ____ > ____ > ____
greatest   least

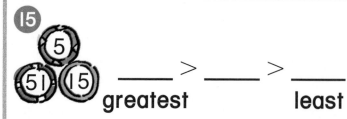

Problem Solving   Algebra

Find the pattern. Write the numbers that come next.

16   60, 64, 68, 72, 76, ____, ____, ____

17   42, 40, 38, 36, 34, ____, ____, ____

Home Connection Your child put three numbers in order. **Home Activity**
Say three numbers between 21 and 99. Ask your child to write them in order
from least to greatest. Repeat with three new numbers, but this time ask
your child to write them in order from greatest to least.

Name_____

 **Learn!**

A number can have
hundreds , tens, and ones.

A group of 10 tens
equals 1 hundred.

__2__ hundreds __2__ tens __6__ ones

__226__

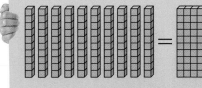

Word Bank

hundreds

Check ✓

Write how many hundreds, tens, and ones.
Then write the number.

1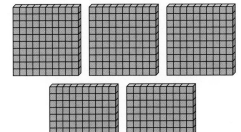

____ hundreds ____ tens ____ ones = _____

2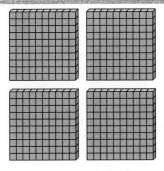

____ hundreds ____ ten ____ ones = _____

Think About It Number Sense

What number is 100 more than 625?

What number is 10 less than 625?

625

Write how many hundreds, tens, and ones.
Then write the number.

3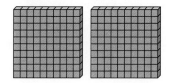

___2___ hundreds ___7___ tens ___0___ ones = ___270___

4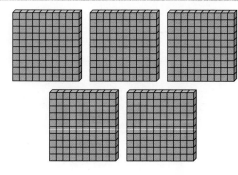

_____ hundreds _____ tens _____ ones = _____

5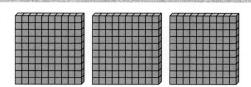

_____ hundreds _____ tens _____ ones = _____

Problem Solving   Visual Thinking

Write the missing numbers in the chart.

6

191	192			195			198	199	
	202	203				207			210
211			214					219	
221		223		225				229	230

Home Connection Your child found how many hundreds, tens, and ones were in a number. **Home Activity** Say a three-digit number, such as 257. Ask your child to tell how many hundreds, how many tens, and how many ones are in the number. *(2 hundreds, 5 tens, 7 ones)*

Name_____

Use cubes.
Write the numbers.

1

89

10 less than 89 is _____.

1 more than 89 is _____.

Write **less than**, **greater than**, or **equal to**. Write **<**, **>**, or **=**.

2

52 is _____ 25.

52 ◯ 25

Write the numbers in order from **least** to **greatest**.

3

_____ < _____ < _____
least   greatest

4

_____ < _____ < _____
least   greatest

Complete the number line.
Draw lines to show where the numbers go.

5

| 20 | 30 | ☐ | ☐ |

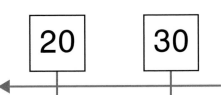

43   21   39

Write how many hundreds, tens, and ones.
Write the number.

6

_____ hundreds   _____ tens   _____ ones = _____

What is the missing number?

1

10 is 6 and _____.

0	4	5	6
Ⓐ	Ⓑ	Ⓒ	Ⓓ

2

13 is 10 and _____.

0	2	3	4
Ⓐ	Ⓑ	Ⓒ	Ⓓ

3 What time is it?

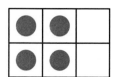

Ⓐ 1 o'clock

Ⓑ 2 o'clock

Ⓒ 11 o'clock

Ⓓ 12 o'clock

4 Which group shows an even number?

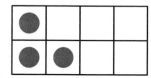

   Ⓐ   Ⓑ   Ⓒ   Ⓓ

5 What is the missing number?

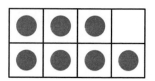

Tens	Ones
2	7

20	27	70	72
Ⓐ	Ⓑ	Ⓒ	Ⓓ

Name_____

How are these fish sorted?

In what other ways could you **sort** them?

Word Bank

sort

Check ✔

1 Cut apart the butterflies.

Sort them in different ways.

Glue the butterflies to show one way.

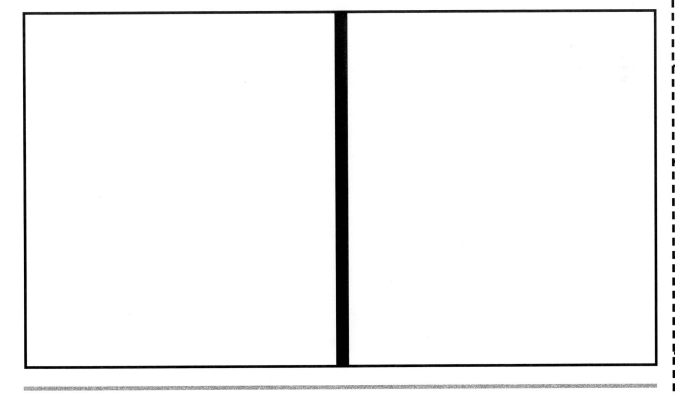

Think About It   Reasoning

In what different ways could you sort the butterflies?

2 How could you sort these shapes?
Draw and color to show two groups
you could make.

Problem Solving   Reasoning

3 Circle the shape that does not belong
in the group.

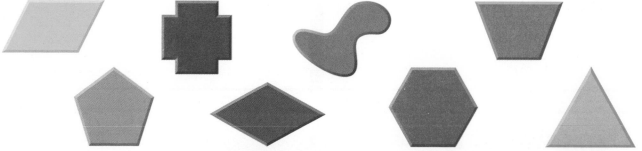

© Pearson Education, Inc.

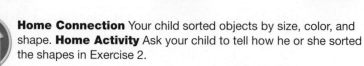

Home Connection Your child sorted objects by size, color, and
shape. **Home Activity** Ask your child to tell how he or she sorted
the shapes in Exercise 2.

308   three hundred eight

Name_____

You can show information in a **picture graph**.

Which toy is the favorite?

Check ✓

1. Ask your classmates to choose their favorite lunches.
Draw to make a picture graph.

Our Favorite Lunches									
Soup									
Sandwich									
Pizza									

Now use your graph to answer the questions.

2. Which lunch is the favorite? _____

3. Which lunch is the least favorite? _____

Think About It   Reasoning

How does the picture graph help
you keep track of the choices?

Practice

4. Ask your classmates to choose their favorite fruits. Draw to make a picture graph. Then answer the questions.

Our Favorite Fruits		
Apples	Bananas	Oranges

5. Which fruit is the favorite of the class?

____

6. Which fruit is the least favorite?

____

7. How many children would have selected oranges if 1 more child had selected oranges?

____

Problem Solving Writing in Math

8. Write a question about the picture graph above.

____

____

Home Connection Your child made picture graphs to show information about the preferences of his or her classmates. **Home Activity** Have your child explain the information in the graph on this page.

Name_____

Read the **bar graph**.

Which sport is the favorite?

I chose soccer.

Our Favorite Sports									
🏃 Soccer									
🏊 Swimming									
⚾ Baseball									

0 1 2 3 4 5 6 7 8 9

Word Bank

bar graph

Check ✓

1 Ask your classmates to choose their favorite places.

Color to make a bar graph.

Our Favorite Places to Go									
🛝 Park									
📕 Library									
🦒 Zoo									

0 1 2 3 4 5 6 7 8 9

Use the bar graph to answer the question.

2 Which place is the favorite of your class? _____

Think About It Reasoning

How is a bar graph like a picture graph?

How is it different?

3 Ask your classmates to choose their favorite pets.
Color to make a bar graph.
Then answer the questions.

4 Which pet is the favorite
of the class?

_____

5 Which pet is the least
favorite?

_____

6 How many children
would have selected cats
if 2 more children
had selected them?

_____

Our Favorite Pets

	Cats	Dogs	Fish
10			
9			
8			
7			
6			
5			
4			
3			
2			
1			
0			

Problem Solving Number Sense

Put the pets in order from **least** to **greatest**
according to the number of spaces colored.
Write the words **Dogs, Cats,** and **Fish.**

7 _____, _____, _____
   least   **greatest**

Home Connection Your child made bar graphs to show information about
the preferences of his or her classmates. **Home Activity** Ask your child
how the bar graphs in this lesson are the same as and different from the
picture graphs in the previous lesson.

Name _____

 **Learn!**

You can use **tally marks** to record information.

I made one tally mark for each spin.

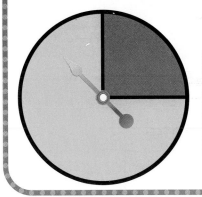

		Total
Green	||||	4
Yellow	₵₵₵ ₵₵₵ ₵₵₵ |	16

Word Bank

tally mark

Check ✓

1 Spin the spinner 20 times using a pencil and a paper clip.
Make a tally mark for each spin.
Then write the totals.

		Total
Blue		
Red		
Yellow		

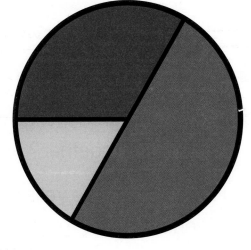

Use the tally chart to answer the questions.

2 Which color did you spin the most often? _____

3 Predict: If you spin one more time, on which
color do you think the spinner will land? _____

Think About It Reasoning

How did you use the tally marks to help
you predict the next color?

Make tally marks to show how many frogs
of each color there are. Then write the totals.

4

		Total
Green		
Yellow		
Orange		

Use the tally chart to answer the questions.

5 Of which color frogs are there the fewest? _____

6 How many green frogs and orange frogs
are there altogether? _____

7 How many more yellow frogs than
green frogs are there? _____

Problem Solving   Writing in Math

8 Write your own question about the tally chart above.

_____

_____

Home Connection Your child made tally marks to record and count
information. **Home Activity** Have your child make tally marks to record the
number of males and females living in your house.

Name _____

 **Algebra**

This is a map of Tory's town.

How would you get from Tory's house to the school?

Go 3 blocks right and 2 blocks up.

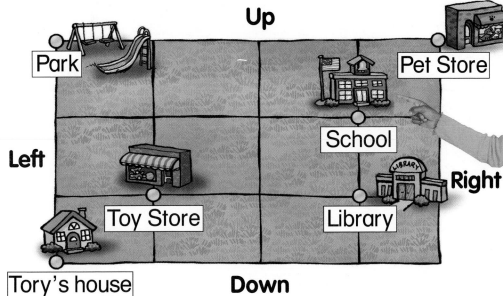

Up

Park

Pet Store

School

Left

Right

Toy Store

Library

Tory's house

Down

Check ✓

Read the map. Then complete each sentence.

1 To go from the  to the 🏪 ,

go __3__ blocks left and __2__ blocks down.

2 To go from the 🏛 to the 🛝 ,

go _____ blocks left and _____ blocks up.

3 To go from the 🛝 to the 🏫 ,

go _____ blocks right and _____ block down.

Think About It Reasoning

In what different ways could you go from

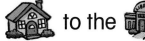 to the 🏛 ? Explain.

This is a map of Bryan's town.

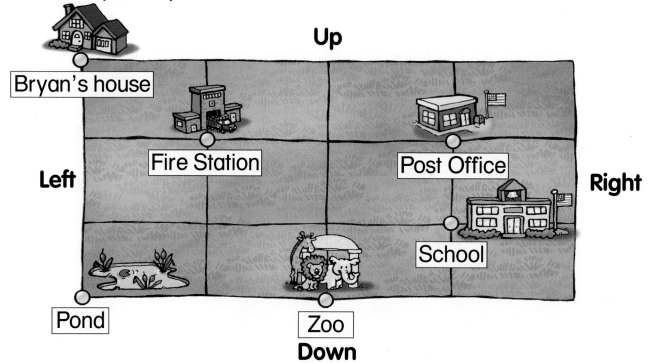

Read the map. Then complete each sentence.

4 To go from to the ,

go __2__ blocks right and __3__ blocks down.

5 To go from the to the ,

go _____ blocks left and _____ block up.

6 To go from the to the ,

go _____ blocks left and _____ blocks down.

Problem Solving   Visual Thinking

7 Start at the ☆.
Move 4 spaces to the right
and 2 spaces up.
Draw a circle.

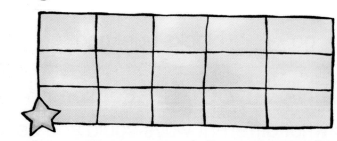

Home Connection Your child gave directions for finding places on maps.
Home Activity Have your child tell how to get from the pond to the fire station on the map on this page. *(Sample response: Go 1 block right and 2 blocks up.)*

This is a map of Lori's neighborhood. How many blocks is it from Lori's house to the ball field?

You can write an addition sentence to find out!

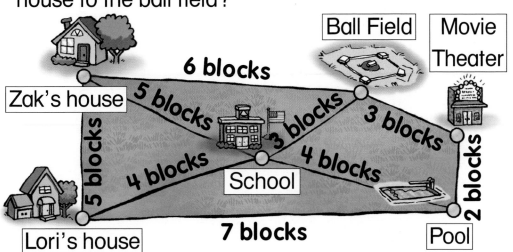
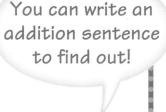

Ball Field

Movie Theater

6 blocks

Zak's house

5 blocks

5 blocks

3 blocks

3 blocks

4 blocks

School

4 blocks

2 blocks

Lori's house

7 blocks

Pool

It is 4 blocks from Lori's house to the school and 3 blocks from the school to the ball field.

__4__ + __3__ = __7__ blocks

Check ✔

Find the shortest path.
Then write an addition sentence.

1. From to the   ___ + ___ = ___ blocks

2. From to the   ___ + ___ = ___ blocks

3. From the to the   ___ + ___ = ___ blocks

Think About It   Reasoning

What are some of the different ways you could get from 🏠 to the 🎬? Explain.

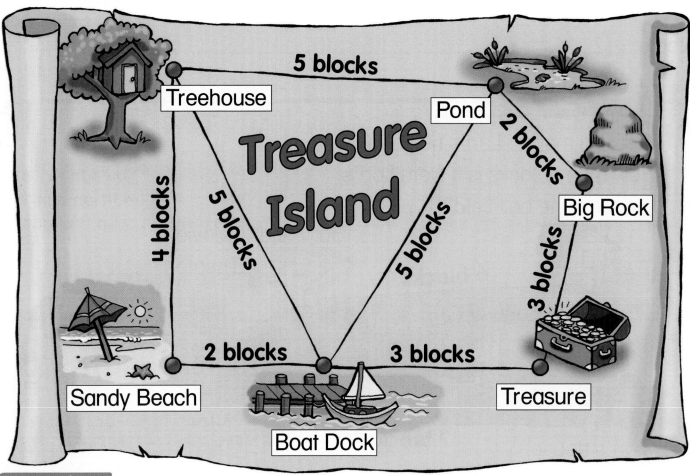

Treasure Island

5 blocks — Treehouse to Pond
2 blocks — Pond to Big Rock
4 blocks — Treehouse to Sandy Beach
5 blocks — Treehouse to Boat Dock
5 blocks — Pond to Boat Dock
3 blocks — Big Rock to Treasure
2 blocks — Sandy Beach to Boat Dock
3 blocks — Boat Dock to Treasure

Practice

Find the shortest path.

Then write an addition sentence.

4 From the to the   _2_ + _5_ = _7_ blocks

5 From the to the   ___ + ___ = ___ blocks

6 From the to the   ___ + ___ = ___ blocks

7 From the  to the   ___ + ___ = ___ blocks

8 From the  to the   ___ + ___ = ___ blocks

9 From the to the   ___ + ___ = ___ blocks

Home Connection Your child found total distances between places on a map. **Home Activity** Ask your child to explain how to find the distance from the boat dock to the big rock on the map on this page.

Let's Make Soup!

Name _____

Dorling Kindersley

Daryl is making soup.
He needs 10 carrots and 10 peppers.

Do You Know...
that early Americans used dried asparagus for medicine?

1 How many carrots will be left over?

_____ carrots

2 How many peppers does Daryl still need?

_____ peppers

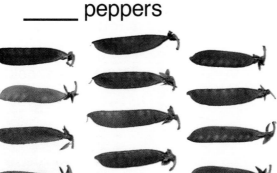

3 How many snow peas are there in all?

_____ snow peas

4 Make tally marks to show how many vegetables.
Then write the totals.

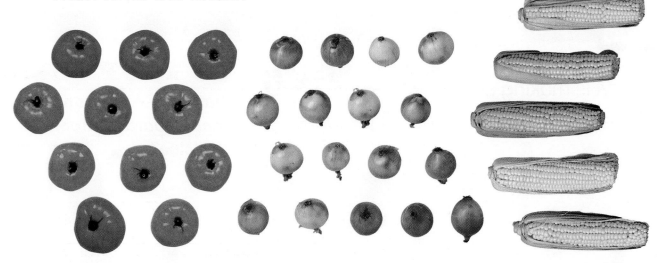

		Total
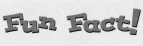		

5 Write the numbers of vegetables
in order from **least** to **greatest**.

____ < ____ < ____
least   greatest

6 **Writing in Math**

Make a picture graph that shows how
many of each vegetable are on this page.

Name_____

1 Sort the shapes.
Make a tally mark for each shape.

		Total
Circles		
Squares		
Triangles		

Use the picture graph to answer the question.

2 Which snack is the favorite?

_____

Our Favorite Snacks						
Pretzels	🥨	🥨	🥨	🥨	🥨	🥨
Muffins	🧁	🧁	🧁			
Celery	🥬	🥬	🥬	🥬		

Use the bar graph to answer the question.

3 Which color is the least favorite?

_____

Our Favorite Colors						
Green						
Blue						
Red						
	0	1	2	3	4	5	6

Read the map and complete the sentence.

4 To go from 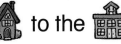 to the ,

go _____ blocks right

and _____ blocks down.

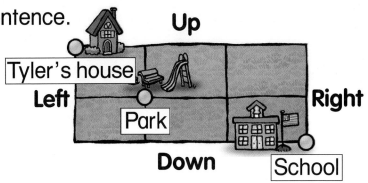

Up
Tyler's house
Left **Right**
Park
Down School

Name_____

What is the missing number?

1

3 − 3 = ___

0	I	2	3
Ⓐ	Ⓑ	Ⓒ	Ⓓ

2

2 tens is _____.

10	20	30	40
Ⓐ	Ⓑ	Ⓒ	Ⓓ

---

3 Which clock shows the same time?

1:00	5:00	6:00	12:00
Ⓐ	Ⓑ	Ⓒ	Ⓓ

---

4 What is the missing number?

Tens	Ones
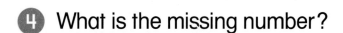	

3 tens + 6 ones = _____

30 + 6 = _____

9	36	63	90
Ⓐ	Ⓑ	Ⓒ	Ⓓ

---

5 What number is less than 29?

29	92	30	18
Ⓐ	Ⓑ	Ⓒ	Ⓓ

Rounding Numbers

Is 30 closer to 0 or to 100?
You can use the number line to find out.

30 is 70 away from 100, but only 30 away from 0.

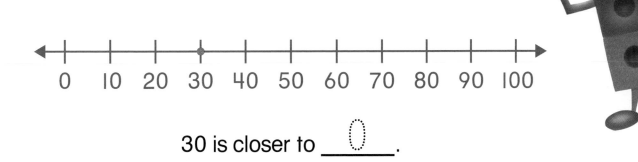

30 is closer to ___0___.

Find each number on the number line.
Is it closer to 0 or closer to 100?

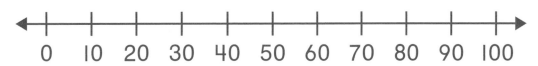

1 90 is closer to _____.

2 40 is closer to _____.

3 20 is closer to _____.

4 60 is closer to _____.

5 15 is closer to _____.

6 75 is closer to _____.

7 **Writing in Math**

Which digit of 25 is more helpful to use in deciding if it is closer to 0 or to 100?
Explain.

Home Connection Your child described two-digit numbers as closer to 0 or closer to 100. **Home Activity** Ask your child to tell whether these numbers are closer to 0 or closer to 100: 70, 10, 25, 95. *(100; 0; 0; 100)*

Name_____

Make a Bar Graph on a Computer

You can make a graph that shows
your class's favorite seasons of the year.

1 On a sheet of paper, write the words **summer,
spring, winter,** and **fall.**

2 Put a tally mark next to your favorite season.

3 Ask each person which season is his or
her favorite. Put a tally mark next to it.

4 On a computer, go to the
Primary Spreadsheet in the
Spreadsheet/Data/Grapher eTool.

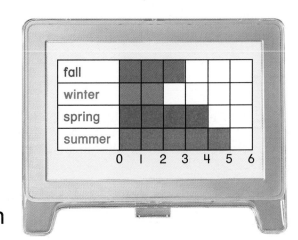

5 In the first box, type **summer.** Underneath
summer, type **spring, winter,** and **fall.**

6 Count the tallies on your paper and record the numbers
in the boxes next to each season's name on the computer.

7 Make a horizontal bar graph of your data.

Think About It   Reasoning

Which season is your class's favorite?
Which season is your class's least favorite?

I like all of them!

Home Connection Your child used a computer to record information and
make a bar graph. **Home Activity** Ask your child questions about the bar
graph he or she made about the class's favorite seasons. For example, ask how
many more children chose summer rather than winter as their favorite season.

Name _____

Make Smart Choices

First, find the **wrong** answers.
Then, choose the **correct** answer.

Test-Taking Strategies

Understand the Question

Get Information for the Answer

Plan How to Find the Answer

Make Smart Choices

Use Writing in Math

1 Which number is 10 less than 65?

- Ⓐ 50
- Ⓑ 70
- Ⓒ 55
- Ⓓ 75

You know that the correct answer
should have a **5** in the ones place.

You know that the correct answer
should be 10 **less** than 65.

Fill in the correct answer bubble.

Your Turn

First, find the wrong answers.
Then, fill in the correct answer bubble.

2 Which number is 10 more than 84?

- Ⓐ 74
- Ⓑ 94
- Ⓒ 83
- Ⓓ 85

You can
do it!

 Home Connection Your child prepared for standardized tests by
eliminating wrong answer choices to help find the correct answer
choice. **Home Activity** Ask your child to explain why three of the
answer choices are wrong in Exercise 2.

three hundred twenty-five **325**

Discover Math in Your World

Discovery CHANNEL SCHOOL™

An Important Part of History

For hundreds of years, Native Americans lived in parts of what is now called the United States of America.

Native American Families

1 In an Iroquois tribe, each family lived in a building called a longhouse. One longhouse had 42 people living in it. Another longhouse had 54 people living in it. Make cube trains to find out how many people lived in the two longhouses.

_____ people

2 There were about 53 Cherokee families living in 35 towns. Which number is greater, 53 or 35? Tell how you know.

_____

_____

_____

Take It to the NET
Video and Activities
www.scottforesman.com

Home Connection Your child solved math problems about Native American families by using tens and ones to find how many in all and to compare two numbers. **Home Activity** Write two numbers that are less than 100. Ask your child to tell which number is greater and to explain how he or she compared the two numbers.

Chapter Test

Count the tens. Then write the numbers.

①

_____ tens is _____.

②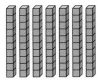

_____ tens is _____.

---

③ Write >, <, or =.

79 ◯ 81

④ Write the numbers in order from **least** to **greatest**.

13
31 23

_____ < _____ < _____
least   greatest

Count the tens and ones. Then write the numbers.

⑤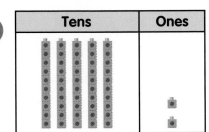

Tens	Ones

➡ _____

Draw the tens and ones. Then write the numbers.

⑥  45

Tens	Ones

_____ tens + _____ ones = _____

_____ + _____ = _____

Use cubes and Workmat 4 to show a different way to make the number.

⑦  36

Tens	Ones

36 = 20 + 16

Make a ten with 10 ones:

36 = _____ + _____

Complete the number line.
Then draw lines to show where the numbers go.

8

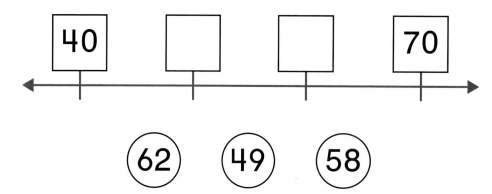

62   49   58

Write how many hundreds, tens, and ones.
Then write the number.

9

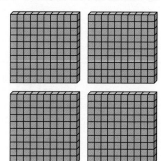

_____ hundreds   _____ tens   _____ ones = _____

Use the bar graph to answer the question.

10 How many more children
chose milk than water?

_____ more children

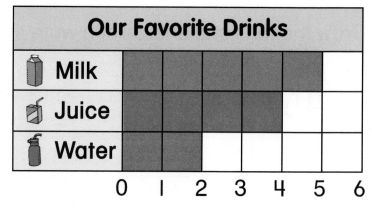

Find the shortest path.
Then write an addition sentence.

11 From  to

_____ + _____ = _____ blocks

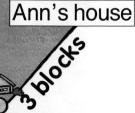

328   three hundred twenty-eight

What is the missing number?

1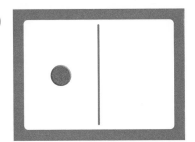

9 is 1 and _____.

7	8	9	10
Ⓐ	Ⓑ	Ⓒ	Ⓓ

2

5 tens is _____.

50	5	500	40
Ⓐ	Ⓑ	Ⓒ	Ⓓ

3 27 < _____

27	20	17	45
Ⓐ	Ⓑ	Ⓒ	Ⓓ

4 17 is 10 and _____.

3	5	7	9
Ⓐ	Ⓑ	Ⓒ	Ⓓ

5 What is the ending time?

5 o'clock ⟶ 1 hour ⟶ _____ o'clock

8 o'clock	6 o'clock	5 o'clock	7 o'clock
Ⓐ	Ⓑ	Ⓒ	Ⓓ

6 Which fish is seventh?

1st	Ⓐ	Ⓑ	Ⓒ	Ⓓ

Add or subtract.

 7
+ 3

4
+ 8

11
− 2

6
+ 0

7
− 1

4
− 4

Divide the group in half.

Circle groups of 10. How many groups of 10, and
how many left over?

_____ groups of 10

_____ left over

Draw the tens and ones.
Then write the numbers.

62

Tens	Ones

_____ tens + _____ ones = _____

_____ + _____ = _____

Writing in Math

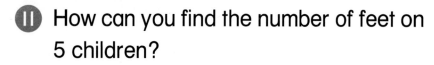

How can you find the number of feet on
5 children?

_____

_____

328B

Rhyme Time

Written by Evie Lester   Illustrated by Laura Ovresat

This Math Storybook belongs to

_____

9A

Penny, nickel, dollar, dime.
We can make change all the time.

9B

I had **5** pennies that I changed for a nickel.
Either will buy me a sweet, green pickle.

I had **10** pennies that I changed for a dime.
Either will buy me a bright green lime.

I had **2** nickels that I changed for a dime.
Either will buy me some gooey, green slime.

I had **4** quarters that I changed for a dollar.
Either will buy Rex a brand-new collar!

Dear Family,

Today my class started Chapter 9, **Money**. I will learn the value of a penny, nickel, dime, quarter, half-dollar, and dollar. I will also learn to count by 10s, 5s, and 1s to find the value of a group of coins. Here are some of the math words I will be learning and some things we can do to help me with my math.

Love,

Math Activity to Do at Home

Practice counting money with your child. Lay out a group of coins. Then help him or her count the coins, beginning with the coin or coins of greatest value. Challenge your child to make small purchases at the store for you.

Books to Read Together

Reading math stories reinforces concepts. Look for these titles in your local library:

Bunny Money
By Rosemary Wells
(Dial, 1997)

Deena's Lucky Penny
By Barbara deRubertis
(The Kane Press, 1999)

My New Math Words

penny 1 **cent** 1¢

nickel 5 **cents** 5¢

dime 10 **cents** 10¢

quarter 25 **cents** 25¢

half-dollar  50 **cents** 50¢

dollar  $1.00 or 100¢

Take It to the NET
More Activities
www.scottforesman.com

Name _____

Make Some Cents!

What You Need

20 paper squares ■

How to Play

1. Place the squares on the gameboard.
2. Take turns. Remove 2 squares.
3. If you find a match, keep the paper squares.
4. If you do not find a match, put the squares back.
5. Keep playing until you find every match.

Name_____

Learn!

Count by 1s to count pennies.
Count by 5s to count nickels.

or

penny
I ¢
I **cent**

or

nickel
5¢
5 cents

In All

___5___¢ ___10___¢ ___11___¢ ___12___¢

In All
___12___¢

Word Bank

penny
cent (¢)
nickel

Check ✓

Count on. Then write how much money in all.

1

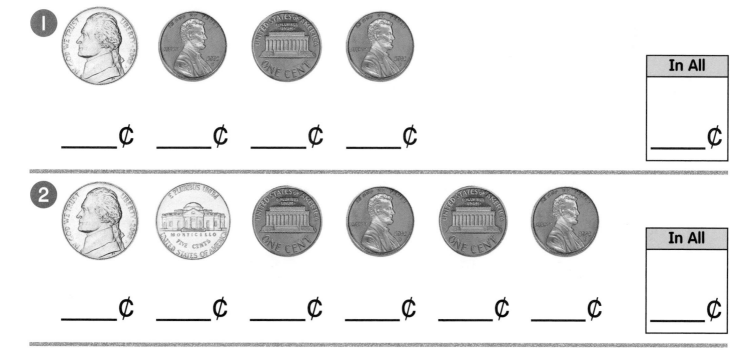

_____¢ _____¢ _____¢ _____¢

In All
_____¢

2

_____¢ _____¢ _____¢ _____¢ _____¢ _____¢

In All
_____¢

Think About It   Number Sense

Would you rather have 3 pennies or
I penny and I nickel? Explain.

Circle the coins that match each price.

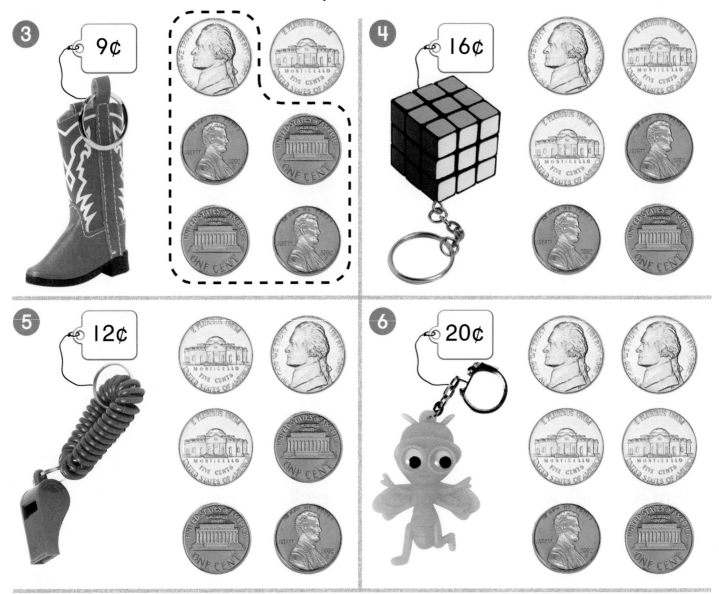

3 9¢

4 16¢

5 12¢

6 20¢

Problem Solving Algebra

Write the price for each toy.

Remember, the price of the purple fish must stay the same.

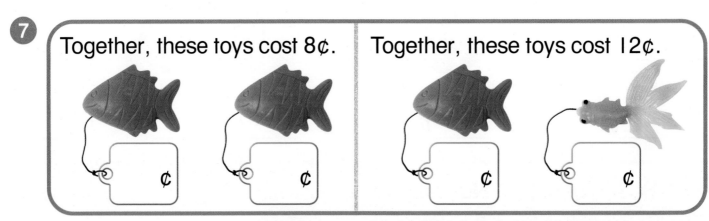

7 Together, these toys cost 8¢.   Together, these toys cost 12¢.

_____ ¢   _____ ¢   _____ ¢   _____ ¢

You can count by 10s to count dimes.

__10__¢ __20__¢ __21__¢

In All
__21__¢

 or **dime**
10¢
10 cents

Word Bank

dime

Check ✓

Count on.

Then write how much money in all.

❶

_____¢ _____¢ _____¢ _____¢

In All
_____¢

❷

_____¢ _____¢ _____¢ _____¢

In All
_____¢

❸

_____¢ _____¢ _____¢ _____¢

In All
_____¢

Think About It   Reasoning

Which coin is bigger?

Which coin is worth more?

Circle the coins that match each price.

4 81¢

5 31¢

6 42¢

7 51¢

Problem Solving   Number Sense

Color each bank to make the sentences true.

8 The blue bank has the most money.

The red bank has more money than the green bank.

 Home Connection Your child found the values of groups of dimes and pennies. **Home Activity** Ask your child to tell or show different ways to make 32¢ using dimes and pennies.

Name _____

Count the dimes first.
Then count the nickels.

						In All
10 ¢	20 ¢	30 ¢	35 ¢	40 ¢	45 ¢	45 ¢

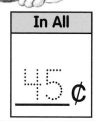

Check ✓

Count on. Then write how much money in all.

1

____¢ ____¢ ____¢ ____¢ ____¢ ____¢

In All
____¢

2

____¢ ____¢ ____¢ ____¢ ____¢

In All
____¢

3

____¢ ____¢ ____¢ ____¢ ____¢ ____¢

In All
____¢

Think About It   Number Sense

Name the different ways you can show 15¢.

Write how much money in all.
Then circle the toy that you can buy.

I have 3 dimes and 1 nickel.
Which toy can I buy?

4

In All
35 ¢

 35¢

 45¢

5

In All
____ ¢

 50¢

 55¢

6

In All
____ ¢

 55¢

45¢

Problem Solving   Number Sense

Solve the riddles.

7 Dave has 7 coins.
He has 1 dime.
The rest are nickels.
How much money does
Dave have?

____ ¢

8 Carla has 7 coins.
She has 1 nickel.
The rest are dimes.
How much money does
Carla have?

____ ¢

Home Connection Your child found the values of groups of dimes and nickels. **Home Activity** Ask your child to draw the dimes and nickels to show one way he or she could buy a toy that costs 65¢.

336   three hundred thirty-six

Name _____

Start counting with the coins of greatest value.

Which of these coins is worth the most?

							In All
__10__¢	__20__¢	__25__¢	__30__¢	__35__¢	__36__¢	__37__¢	__37__¢

Check ✓

Count on. Then write how much money in all.

1

_____¢   _____¢   _____¢   _____¢   _____¢   _____¢

In All
_____¢

2

_____¢   _____¢   _____¢   _____¢   _____¢   _____¢

In All
_____¢

3

_____¢   _____¢   _____¢   _____¢   _____¢   _____¢

In All
_____¢

Think About It   Number Sense

In Exercise 3, if you started counting with the penny, would the group of coins still be worth 46¢? Explain.

Count on.

Then write how much money in all.

Remember, count by 10s, 5s, and then by 1s.

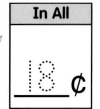

4

In All
18 ¢

5

In All
____ ¢

6

In All
____ ¢

7

In All
____ ¢

Problem Solving   Algebra

8 There are four coins in Tina's pocket.
She has at least one dime and at least one nickel.

What is the greatest amount
of money Tina could have? _____¢

What is the least amount of
of money Tina could have? _____¢

Home Connection Your child found the values of groups of dimes, nickels, and pennies up to 99¢. **Home Activity** Ask your child to tell or show two ways to use dimes, nickels, and pennies to make 23¢.

Name _____

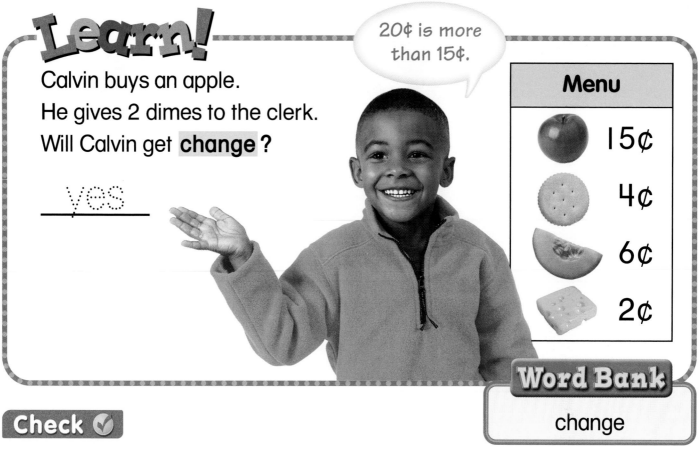

Learn!

Calvin buys an apple.
He gives 2 dimes to the clerk.
Will Calvin get **change**?

_____yes_____

20¢ is more than 15¢.

Menu

apple	15¢
cracker	4¢
melon	6¢
cracker	2¢

Word Bank

change

Check ✓

Use the menu above.
Write **yes** or **no**.

You buy:	You use:	Will you get change?
❶		
❷		

Think About It Reasoning

How can you decide if you will get change?

Use the menu.
Write **yes** or **no**.

Did you pay more than the price?

Menu	
🍊	12¢
🍓	3¢
🧃	7¢
🥝🥝	13¢

	You buy:	You use:	Will you get change?
3	🍓	penny penny	
4	🧃	nickel nickel	
5	🥝🥝	dime nickel	

Writing in Math

6 Write a story problem using the information from the menu.

_____

_____

_____

Home Connection Your child figured out if he or she would receive change when buying items from a menu. **Home Activity** Ask your child questions similar to the following: If you bought the orange from the menu and gave the clerk three nickels, would you get change?

Count on.

Then write how much money in all.

1

____¢ ____¢ ____¢ ____¢ ____¢

In All
____¢

2

____¢ ____¢ ____¢ ____¢ ____¢

In All
____¢

3

In All
____¢

4

In All
____¢

Use the menu.

5 You buy .

You use   .

Will you get change?

_____

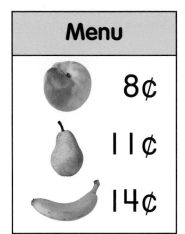

Menu	
	8¢
	11¢
	14¢

What is the missing number?

1

5 and 4 is _____.

1	4	8	9
Ⓐ	Ⓑ	Ⓒ	Ⓓ

2

10 more than 45 is _____.

35	44	54	55
Ⓐ	Ⓑ	Ⓒ	Ⓓ

3 Which fact completes this fact family?

$$6 + 4 = 10$$
$$4 + 6 = 10$$
$$10 - 4 = 6$$

Ⓐ $4 + 4 = 8$

Ⓑ $10 - 6 = 4$

Ⓒ $6 + 6 = 12$

Ⓓ $6 - 4 = 2$

4 Circle groups of 10. Count how many beads are left over. How many beads are there in all?

8 in all	18 in all	28 in all	82 in all
Ⓐ	Ⓑ	Ⓒ	Ⓓ

5 Which shows the numbers in order from **greatest** to **least**?

$14 > 34 > 43$	$34 > 43 > 14$	$43 > 34 > 14$	$43 > 14 > 34$
Ⓐ	Ⓑ	Ⓒ	Ⓓ

Name _____

You can make 25¢ in different ways!

I can make 25¢ with 25 pennies.

I can make 25¢ with 5 nickels.

quarter
25¢
25 cents

Word Bank

quarter

 Check ✔

Use coins. Show two ways to make 25¢.

Then draw the coins.

1

2

Think About It Number Sense

Can you show 25¢ using only nickels? Explain.

Can you show 25¢ using only dimes? Explain.

Circle the coins that equal 25¢.

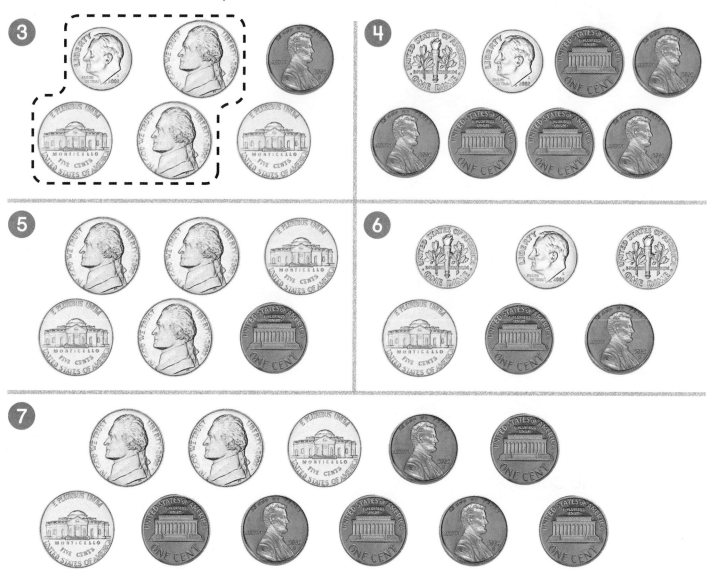

Problem Solving Visual Thinking

8 Maya has three coins in her bank.
They are worth 25¢ in all.
Draw and label Maya's coins.

Home Connection Your child identified and discussed the value of a quarter. **Home Activity** Ask your child to tell which different groups of coins equal 25¢, the value of a quarter.

Name_____

Remember to start counting with the coin that has the greatest value.

The quarter is worth the most!

						In All
25¢	35¢	45¢	50¢	55¢	56¢	56¢

Check ✓

Count on. Then write how much money in all.

1

_____¢ _____¢ _____¢ _____¢ _____¢ _____¢   In All
_____¢

2

_____¢ _____¢ _____¢ _____¢ _____¢ _____¢   In All
_____¢

3

_____¢ _____¢ _____¢ _____¢ _____¢ _____¢ _____¢   In All
_____¢

Think About It   Number Sense

Name some ways to show 30¢ without using pennies.

Circle the coins that match each amount.

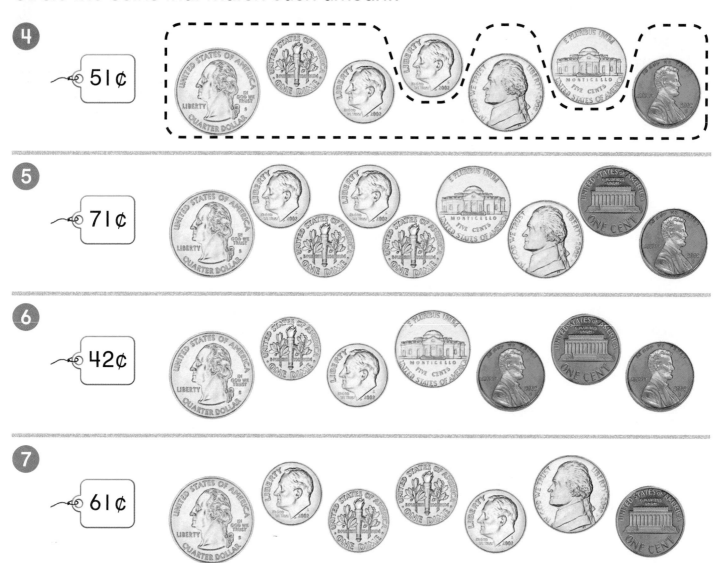

4 51¢

5 71¢

6 42¢

7 61¢

Problem Solving Reasoning

8 How can you show the same amount using fewer coins?
Draw and label the coins in the empty coin purse.

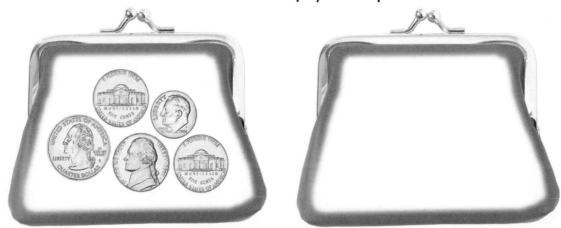

Home Connection Your child found the values of groups of quarters, dimes, nickels, and pennies. **Home Activity** Ask your child how much money there would be if he or she had one of each kind of coin: a quarter, a dime, a nickel, and a penny. *(41¢)*

Name _____

Learn!

One dollar is worth the same as two half-dollars!

or

half-dollar
50¢
50 cents

or

dollar
100¢ = **$**1.00
100 cents

Word Bank

half-dollar
dollar ($)

Check ✓

Use coins. Show two ways to make $1.00.
Then draw the coins.

 1   2

Think About It   Number Sense

Does it take more dimes or more nickels
to make $1.00? Explain.

50 cents equals a half-dollar.
100 cents equals a dollar.

Write how much money in all.

3

In All
$1.00

4

In All

5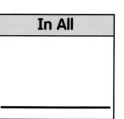

In All

Problem Solving Reasoning

6 How can you show the same amount using only 3 coins?
Draw and label the coins in the empty bank.

Home Connection Your child identified and discussed the value of a half-dollar, a dollar bill, and a dollar coin. **Home Activity** Ask your child to show amounts that equal a dollar using coins or pictures of coins.

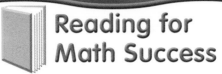

Reading for Math Success

Predict and Verify

Read this story problem.

Erin has 12¢. She wants to spend all of her money at a yard sale. Which toys do you think Erin will buy? Why do you think so?

1 What do you think will happen?

_____

_____

_____

2 Write a number sentence that shows the prices of the toys you guessed.

___ + ___ = 12¢

3 Was your guess correct?

_____

4 If your guess was not correct, try again.

___ + ___ = 12¢

Think About It   Reasoning

Explain why you chose the toys you did.

Read another story problem.

Grade 1 is having a sale.
Sam's job is to sell crayons.
Each crayon is 5¢.
A girl from preschool gives Sam 10¢.

crayons 5¢
books 9¢
pencils 4¢

5 Predict what the girl bought.
Why do you think so?

_____

_____

6 Write a number sentence that shows the prices of what the girl bought. Was your guess correct?

___ + ___ = 10¢

7 A little boy has 13¢ to spend at the sale.
Which two things can he buy for exactly 13¢?

_____

8 Write a number sentence to check your guess.

___ + ___ = 13¢

Home Connection Your child made predictions about items that might be purchased for a given amount and then checked his or her answer by writing a number sentence. **Home Activity** Ask your child to explain how he or she completed the problems on this page.

1 Manolo bought 2 toys at a yard sale.
Together the toys cost 13¢.
Which toys did he buy?

5¢

6¢

Read and Understand

Choose 2 toys.

Find the sum of the prices.

Plan and Solve

Try  and .

Test: ___5___ + ___6___ = __11__ ¢

8¢

11¢ is less than 13¢.
Try again.

9¢

Try  and .

Test: ___5___ + ___8___ = __13__ ¢

Look Back and Check

How can you check your guess?

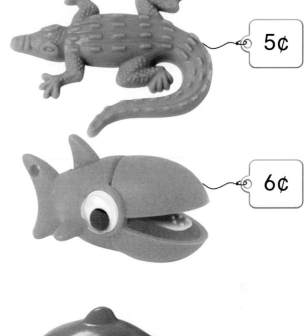

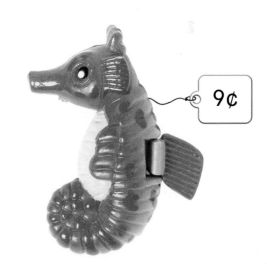

Think About It   Reasoning

When your first try is too much, how do you
decide what to try next?

Circle the toys each child bought.

Then write an addition sentence to check your guess.

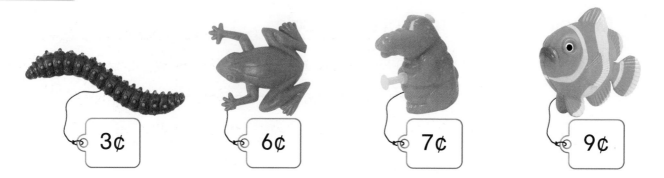

3¢   6¢   7¢   9¢

---

2 Wendy bought 2 different toys.
Together they cost 12¢.
What did Wendy buy?

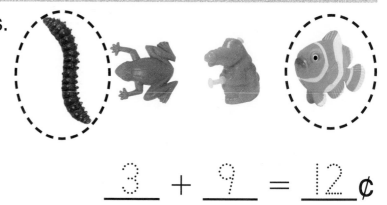

$\underline{3} + \underline{9} = \underline{12}$ ¢

---

3 Kendra bought 2 different toys.
Together they cost 15¢.
What did Kendra buy?

___ + ___ = ___¢

---

4 Tran bought 2 different toys.
Together they cost 13¢.
What did Tran buy?

___ + ___ = ___¢

---

352   three hundred fifty-two

Home Connection Your child solved problems using the try, check, and revise strategy. **Home Activity** Ask your child to use the try, check, and revise strategy to tell which two toys on this page cost exactly 10¢ when purchased together. *(The worm and the alligator)*

What Can You Buy?

Name_____

 Dorling Kindersley

Do You Know...

that all coins must show the year that they were made?

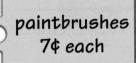

paintbrushes
7¢ each

1 Circle the coins you need to buy 1 paintbrush.

Fun Fact!

One side of a coin is called its head. President Abraham Lincoln's head is shown on a penny's head.

2 Circle the coins you need to buy 2 paintbrushes.

3 Circle the coins you need to buy 1 whistle.

whistles
20¢ each

Magnet Prices	
apple	10¢
pear	15¢
strawberry	17¢
lemon	20¢
grapes	25¢

Find the information you need in the list of magnet prices.

4 You buy a lemon magnet. You give the clerk a quarter. Will you get change? Circle **yes** or **no**.

yes   no

5 The price of a pear magnet is _____. Is the price an even number or an odd number? _____

Write **less than** or **greater than**.

6 The price of a grapes magnet is _____ the price of an apple magnet.

7 The price of a strawberry magnet is _____ the price of a lemon magnet.

8 **Writing in Math**

Each toy penguin costs 10 cents. You have 2 quarters to spend on penguins. What is the greatest number of penguins that you can buy? Explain.

Home Connection Your child learned to solve problems by applying his or her math skills. **Home Activity** Talk to your child about how he or she solved the problems on these two pages.

© Pearson Education, Inc.

Name_____

Circle the coins that equal 25¢.

Count on. Then write how much money in all.

____¢ ____¢ ____¢ ____¢ ____¢

In All
_____¢

Circle coins that match the amount.

53¢

Write how much money in all.

In All
_____¢

Circle the toys Kerry bought.

Then write an addition sentence to check your guess.

5 Kerry bought 2 different toys.
   Together they cost 14¢.

____ + ____ = ____¢

6¢   8¢   5¢   7¢

Use the graph to answer the questions.

Our Favorite Insects									
🦋 Butterflies	🦋	🦋	🦋	🦋	🦋				
🐞 Ladybugs	🐞	🐞	🐞	🐞	🐞	🐞	🐞	🐞	
🐜 Ants	🐜	🐜	🐜						

1 How many more children chose ladybugs than butterflies?

2 more
Ⓐ

3 more
Ⓑ

4 more
Ⓒ

5 more
Ⓓ

2 How many children chose ants and ladybugs in all?

9 children
Ⓐ

10 children
Ⓑ

11 children
Ⓒ

12 children
Ⓓ

3 Count on. How much money is there in all?

30¢
Ⓐ

40¢
Ⓑ

45¢
Ⓒ

60¢
Ⓓ

Writing in Math

4 About how long does it take to eat lunch?
Use **minutes** or **hours** in your answer. Explain.

_____

_____

Counting Dollars, Dimes, and Pennies

Counting dollars, dimes, and pennies is just like counting hundreds, tens, and ones.

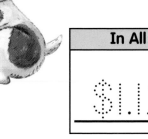

112¢ is the same as $1.12.

100 ¢   110 ¢   111 ¢   112 ¢

In All
$1.12

Count the money. Then write how much money in all.

1

_____¢ _____¢ _____¢ _____¢ _____¢

In All

2

_____¢ _____¢ _____¢ _____¢ _____¢

In All

3

_____¢ _____¢ _____¢ _____¢ _____¢

In All

 Home Connection Your child counted beyond $1.00.
Home Activity Using real money, have your child count dollars, dimes, and pennies.

Name_____

Count Sets of Coins Using a Calculator

You can use a calculator to find how much money in all.

Press ON/C each time you begin. Add the values of the coins.

Press 2 5 for a quarter. Press 1 0 for a dime.

Press 5 for a nickel. Press 1 for a penny.

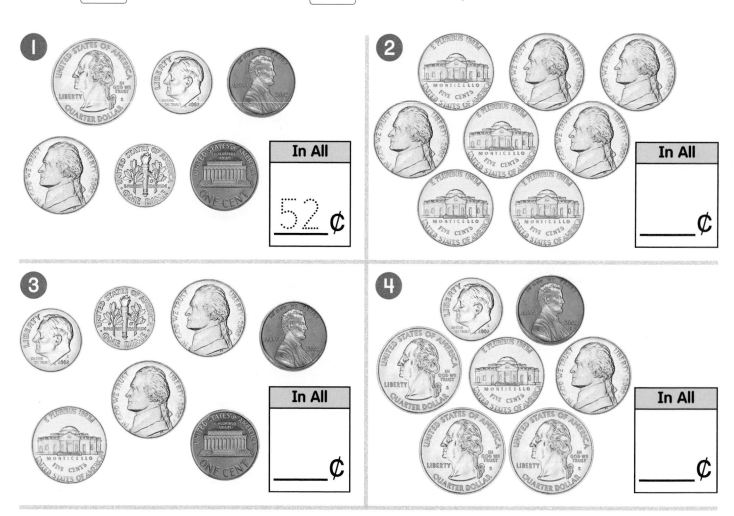

1 In All

52 ¢

2 In All

_____ ¢

3 In All

_____ ¢

4 In All

_____ ¢

Think About It   Number Sense

In Exercise 2, what are two ways you could
use a calculator to check your addition?

Home Connection Your child used a calculator to find the total value of
each of four different groups of quarters, dimes, nickels, and pennies. **Home
Activity** Ask your child to explain how he or she used a calculator to check
his or her addition in Exercise 2. (Note that some, but not all calculators have a
constant function that allows you to repeat an operation with one keystroke.)

Name_____

 **Get Information
for the Answer**

Looking at pictures can help you
solve math problems.

Test-Taking Strategies

Understand the Question

Get Information for the Answer

Plan How to Find the Answer

Make Smart Choices

Use Writing in Math

① How much money in all is in this
picture? Count on to add the coins.
Then fill in the answer bubble.

Ⓐ 42¢   Ⓑ 50¢   Ⓒ 52¢   Ⓓ 62¢

Your Turn

Read the question. Look at all four of the pictures.
Count on to add the coins in each picture.
Then fill in the answer bubble.

② Which group of coins has a total value of 25¢?

Ⓐ

Ⓑ

Ⓒ

Ⓓ

 Home Connection Your child prepared for standardized tests by learning to
get information from pictures. **Home Activity** Ask your child to count on to find
the total value of the coins in each set in Exercise 2, beginning with the coin or
coins of greatest value and then proceeding sequentially to the coin
or coins of least value. Use real coins, if possible.

Name _____

Discover Math in Your World

Saving Makes Cents!

Your class has been saving money in three piggy banks. How much money has your class saved so far?

Counting Coins

1 Max, Jackie, and Rachel opened each bank and counted the coins. Write how much money was in each bank.

_____¢   was in the red bank.

_____¢   was in the blue bank.

_____¢   was in the green bank.

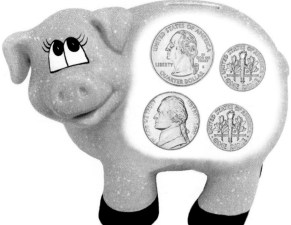

2 Which bank contained the most money?

_____

3 How much money has your class saved so far?

_____¢ or $_____

4 Can your class think of other combinations of coins that add up to this amount of money?

 **Take It to the NET**
Video and Activities
www.scottforesman.com

Home Connection Your child solved problems about saving money by finding the total value of each group of coins and the combined value of the three groups. **Home Activity** Ask your child to explain how he or she found the answers in Exercise 3. Also, help your child read both answers: "119 cents" and "1 dollar and 19 cents."

© Pearson Educ.

Circle the coins that match the price.

1.  43¢

Count on. Then write how much money in all.

2.

_____¢ _____¢ _____¢ _____¢ _____¢

In All
_____¢

3.

_____¢ _____¢ _____¢ _____¢ _____¢ _____¢ _____¢

In All
_____¢

4.

_____¢ _____¢ _____¢ _____¢ _____¢ _____¢ _____¢

In All
_____¢

Use the menu.

5. You buy .

You use   .

Will you get change?

_____

Menu
12¢
16¢
14¢

Circle the coins that equal 25¢.

6

Count on. Then write how much money in all.

7

| | | | | | | | In All |

____¢ ____¢ ____¢ ____¢ ____¢ ____¢ ____¢   ____¢

Circle coins that match the amount.

8

62¢

Write how much money in all.

9

In All

Circle the toys Adam bought.

Then write an addition sentence to check your guess.

10 Adam bought 2 different toys.
Together they cost 13¢.

____ + ____ = ____¢

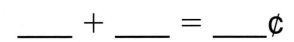  5¢ 7¢  6¢  9¢

Read Together

One Very Smart Chicken

By Anne Miranda

Illustrated by Bridget Starr Taylor

SPEED 25 LIMIT

This Math Storybook belongs to

_____

10A

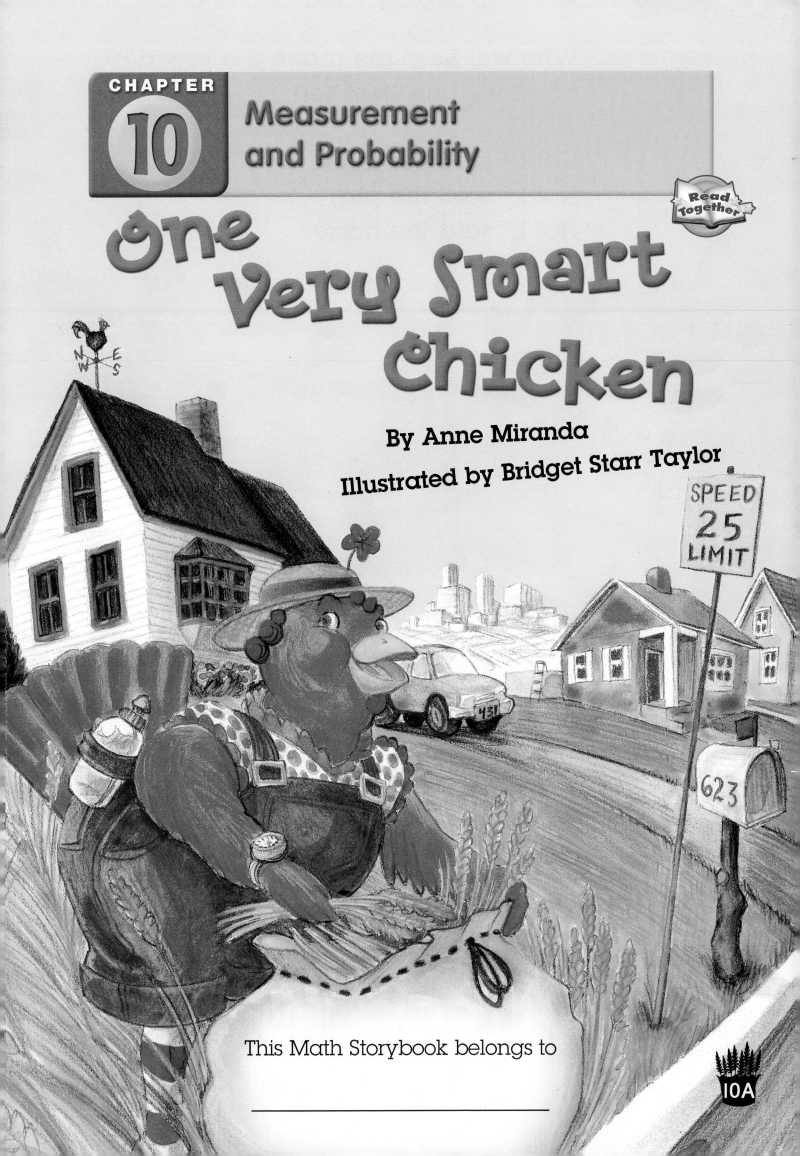

"Who will help me make the bread?"
asked the little red hen.

"Not I," said the duck.
"Not I," said the pig.
"Not I," said the horse.

WORK TO DO:
Duck–Grind
Pig–Mix
Horse–Bake

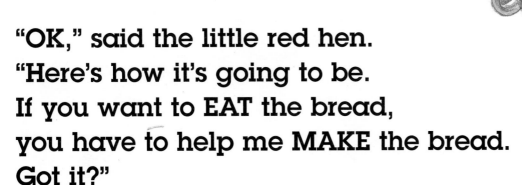

"OK," said the little red hen.
"Here's how it's going to be.
If you want to EAT the bread,
you have to help me MAKE the bread.
Got it?"

"Got it," sighed the duck, the pig,
and the horse.

"OK, that's more like it,"
said the little red hen.
"Now, here's a chart
that tells you what to do."

10C

So the duck helped grind the wheat.
It was hard work,
but when she was done
there were **5** cups of flour.

The pig helped make the dough.
That was hard work too.
He added about **2** cups of water
to the flour.
Then he put in some
sugar and some yeast.

And the horse put the bread
into the oven.
That was hard work too.
Each loaf weighed about 1 pound,
and this horse had not been
getting much exercise.
(Too much TV.)

10E

Everybody ate the bread.
Everybody enjoyed the bread.

"Now, who will help me do the dishes?"
asked the little red hen.

What do YOU think will happen next?

Are the duck, the pig, and the horse
likely or unlikely to jump up and
help the little red hen with the dishes?

Home-School Connection

Dear Family,

Today my class started Chapter 10, **Measurement and Probability.** I will learn to estimate and measure length, capacity, weight, and temperature. I will also learn to predict how likely or unlikely it is for an event to happen. Here are some of the math words I will be learning and some things we can do to help me with my math.

Love,

_____

Math Activity to Do at Home

Have some fun measuring with pieces of cereal! Try measuring the length of a spoon by laying the cereal pieces end to end beside the spoon. Then fill a cup with cereal and count the cereal pieces to see how many pieces it took to fill the cup.

Books to Read Together

Reading math stories reinforces concepts. Look for these titles in your local library:

Me and the Measure of Things
By Joan Sweeney
(Crown, 2001)

Measuring Penny
By Loreen Leedy
(Holt, 2000)

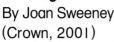

Take It to the NET
More Activities
www.scottforesman.com

My New Math Words

We measure length in inches, feet, and centimeters.

inch

There are 12 inches in 1 **foot** .

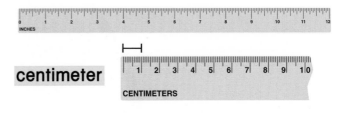

centimeter

We measure capacity in cups, pints, quarts, and liters.

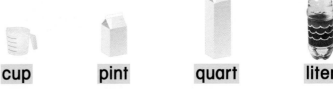

cup   **pint**   **quart**   **liter**

We measure weight in **pounds** , **grams** , and **kilograms** .

thermometer A thermometer measures **temperature** .

More likely or less likely?

What You Need

paper clip

pencil

How to Play

1. When you spin the spinner, which animal do you think you will land on the most?

2. Spin 10 times.

3. On the Tally Chart, put a tally mark next to the animal you land on.

4. Find the animal you landed on **most often.**

5. Find the animal you landed on **least often.**

6. Tell someone why it is **more likely** that you will land on the hen than that you will land on the duck, the pig, or the horse.

Tally Chart		
Duck		
Pig		
Horse		
Hen		

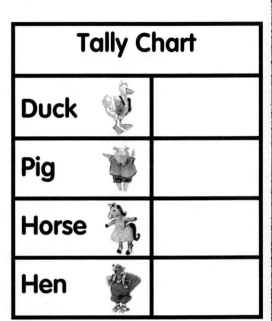

 **Learn!**

About how long is the bug?

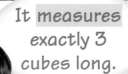

It **measures** exactly 3 cubes long.

It looks about 4 cubes long. 4 is a good **estimate**.

Estimate.
about __4__

Measure.
__3__ 🔲

Word Bank

estimate

measure

Check ✔

Estimate the length in cubes.
Then measure using cubes.

	Estimate.	Measure.
① 	about _____ 🔲	_____ 🔲
② 	about _____ 🔲	_____ 🔲
③ 	about _____ 🔲	_____ 🔲

Think About It Number Sense

Which is the longest object you measured?
How do you know?

Find each object in your classroom.
Estimate the length in cubes.
Then measure using cubes.

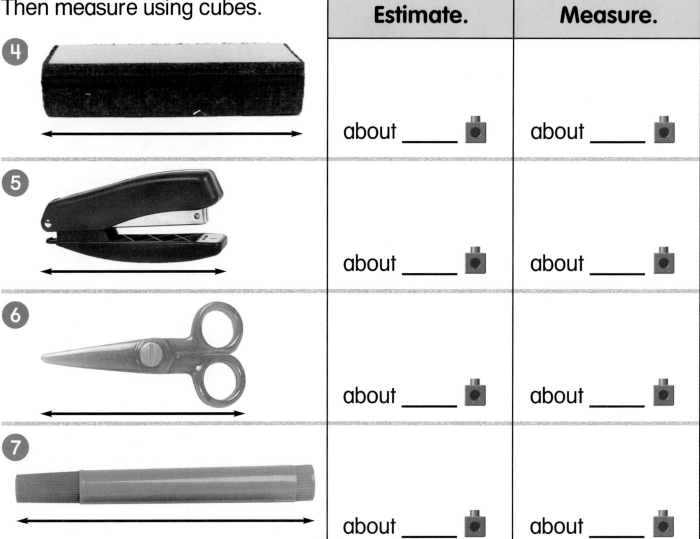

	Estimate.	Measure.
4	about _____ ◻	about _____ ◻
5	about _____ ◻	about _____ ◻
6	about _____ ◻	about _____ ◻
7	about _____ ◻	about _____ ◻

Problem Solving   Visual Thinking

8 Measure each turtle using cubes. Circle the
longest turtle. Mark an **X** on the shortest turtle.

_____ cubes   _____ cube   _____ cubes

 Home Connection Your child estimated and measured the lengths of
items using cubes. **Home Activity** Ask your child to use pieces of cereal
or pasta to measure the lengths of several small objects at home.

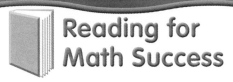
Name_____

Draw Conclusions

Sharon measured 3 objects using 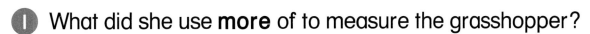 and ▪.
Here is what each object measured.

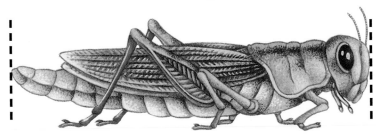

about 3 ⬭

about 5 ▪

① What did she use **more** of to measure the grasshopper?

Circle your answer.   more ⬭   or   (more ▪)

about 2 ⬭

about 3 ▪

② What did she use **more** of to measure the twig?

Circle your answer.   more ⬭   or   more ▪

about 4 ⬭

about 7 ▪

③ What did she use **more** of to measure the feather?

Circle your answer.   more ⬭   or   more ▪

Think About It   Reasoning

Why do you think it took more ▪ than ⬭ to
measure every object?

What do you need **fewer** of to measure each object?
Circle your answer.

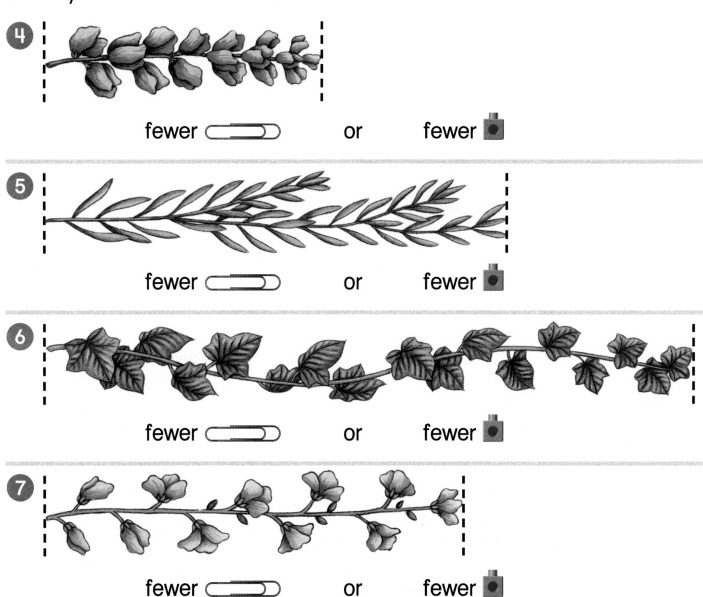

4 fewer ⊂══⊃ or fewer 🔲

5 fewer ⊂══⊃ or fewer 🔲

6 fewer ⊂══⊃ or fewer 🔲

7 fewer ⊂══⊃ or fewer 🔲

Writing in Math

8 Why do you think it took **fewer** ⊂══⊃
than 🔲 to measure every object?

_____

_____

368 three hundred sixty-eight

Home Connection Your child drew conclusions about whether it would take more paper clips or more cubes to measure the lengths of objects and then whether it would take fewer paper clips or cubes to measure the lengths of other objects. **Home Activity** Ask your child to explain his or her answer to Exercise 8.

1 **Predict**: Will you need more  or more ▪
to measure the shoe?

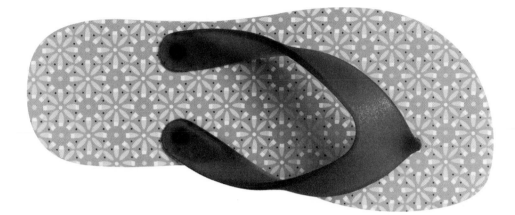

Read and Understand

You must find out if you
need more ⬭ or
more ▪.

You can measure with the ⬭ and the ▪ to check your prediction.

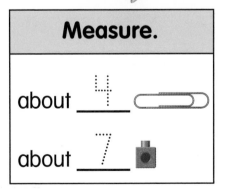

Plan and Solve

You can use reasoning to help
you predict. The cubes are shorter,
so you will need more cubes.

more ⬭   (more ▪)

Look Back and Check

Measure to check your prediction.
Was your prediction correct?

Measure.
about __4__ ⬭
about __7__ ▪

Think About It   Reasoning

Would you need more drinking straws or
more paper clips to measure a table? Why?

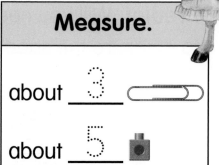

Will it take fewer  or fewer 🔲 to measure the objects below? Circle your prediction. Then measure.

2 (fewer ▭) fewer 🔲

Measure.

about __3__ ▭

about __5__ 🔲

---

3 fewer ▭ fewer 🔲

Measure.

about _____ ▭

about _____ 🔲

Will it take more  or more 🔲 to measure the objects below? Circle your prediction. Then measure.

4 more ▭ more 🔲

Measure.

about _____ ▭

about _____ 🔲

---

5 more ▭ more 🔲

Measure.

about _____ ▭

about _____ 🔲

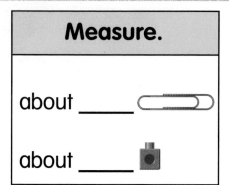

Home Connection Your child used logical reasoning to predict a measurement. **Home Activity** Ask your child if it would take more crayons or more paper clips to measure the length of a table. Have your child use crayons and paper clips to check the prediction. If you do not have crayons or paper clips, use other available items.

Learn!

The ribbon is about 1 **inch** long.

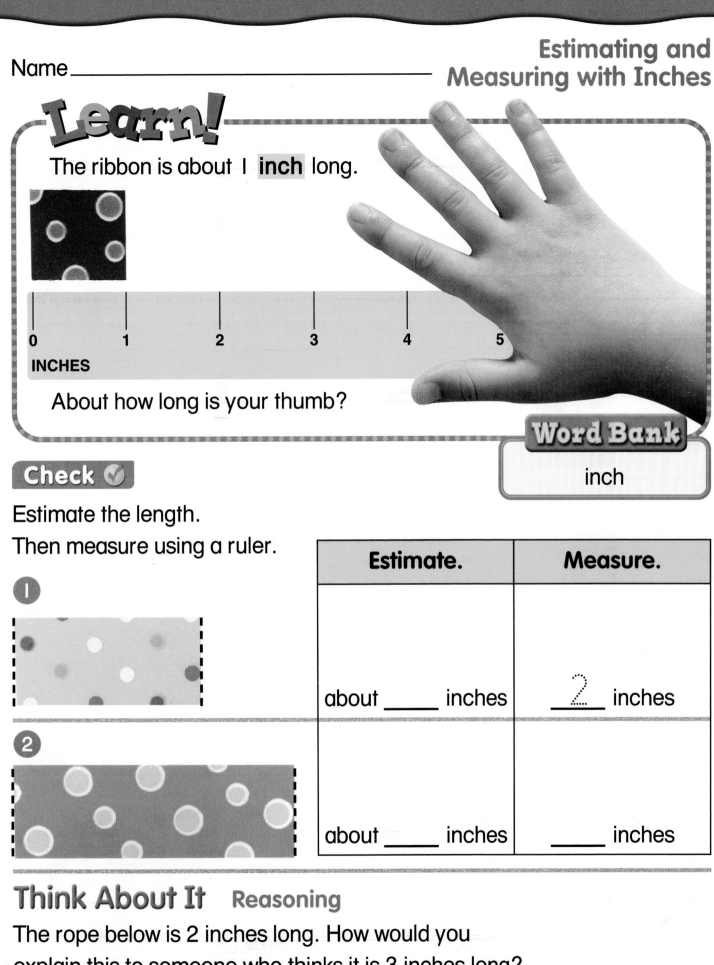

INCHES

About how long is your thumb?

Word Bank

inch

Check ✓

Estimate the length.
Then measure using a ruler.

	Estimate.	Measure.
1	about _____ inches	_2_ inches
2	about _____ inches	_____ inches

Think About It   Reasoning

The rope below is 2 inches long. How would you explain this to someone who thinks it is 3 inches long?

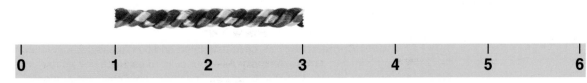

0	1	2	3	4	5	6

Find each object in your classroom. Estimate the
length or height. Then measure using a ruler.

	Estimate.	Measure.
3 about ____ inches	about ____ inches
4 about ____ inches	about ____ inches
5 about ____ inches	about ____ inches
6 about ____ inches	about ____ inches

Problem Solving Mental Math

7 Answer the questions.

This  is 1 inch long.

How long are 3  ? ____ inches

How long are 5  ? ____ inches

Home Connection Your child estimated and then measured objects
using inches. **Home Activity** Ask your child to estimate how many
inches his or her shoe will measure. Then have your child check the
estimate by measuring with a ruler.

372 three hundred seventy-two

Learn!

A **foot** is 12 inches long.

These things each measure about 1 foot.

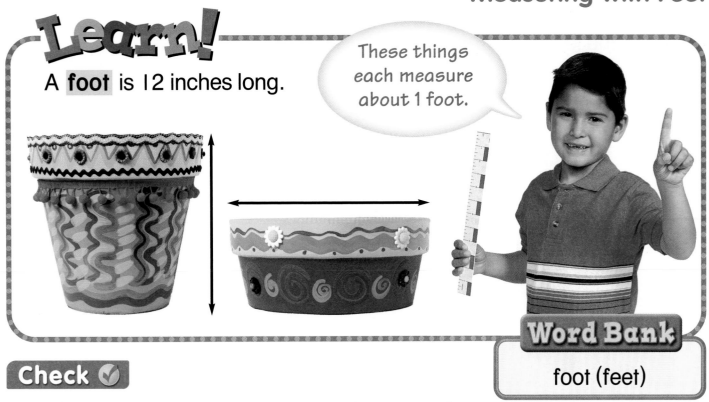

Word Bank

foot (feet)

Check ✓

Find each object in your classroom. Estimate the length or height. Then measure using a ruler.

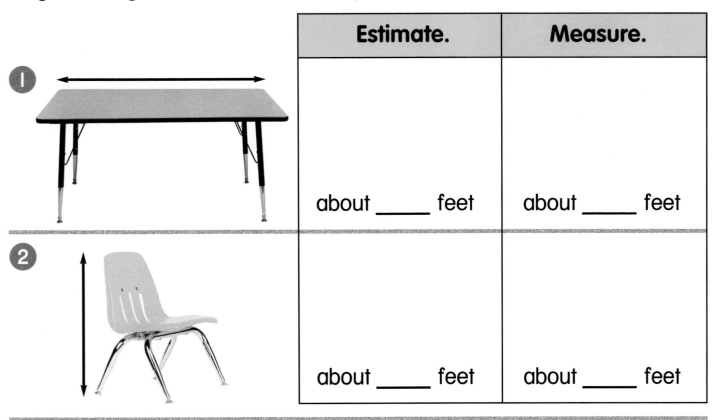

	Estimate.	Measure.
1	about ____ feet	about ____ feet
2	about ____ feet	about ____ feet

Think About It   Reasoning

Should you measure the length of your classroom in inches or in feet? Explain.

Find each object in your classroom.
Estimate the length or height.
Then measure using a ruler.

	Estimate.	Measure.
③	about _____ feet	about _____ feet
④	about _____ feet	about _____ feet
⑤	about _____ feet	about _____ feet

Problem Solving   Reasonableness

About how tall might each object be?

⑥ Circle the better estimate.

about 4 feet

about 4 inches

about 5 inches

about 5 feet

⑦ Draw a box around the taller object.

Home Connection Your child estimated and then measured items using a ruler. **Home Activity** Ask your child to find an item in the house that is about 4 feet long. Together, measure the item.

About how long is the blueberry?

About how long is the orange slice?

My fingernail is about 1 **centimeter** long.

| 1 | 2 | 3 | 4 | 5 | 6 | 7 | 8 |

CENTIMETERS

Word Bank

centimeter

Check ✓

Estimate the length. Then measure using a centimeter ruler.

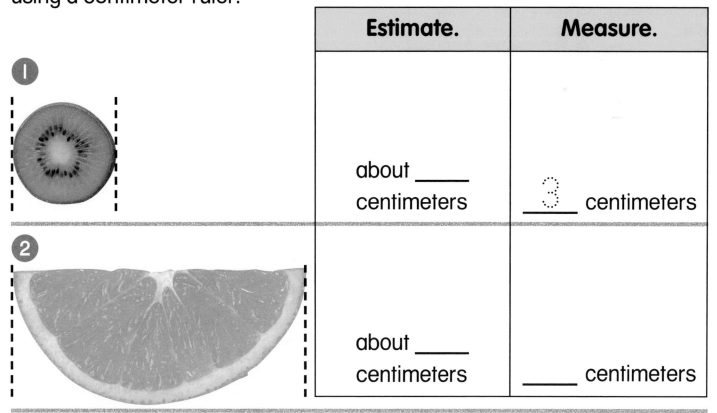

	Estimate.	**Measure.**
1	about _____ centimeters	3 centimeters
2	about _____ centimeters	_____ centimeters

Think About It   Reasoning

What are some things that are about 1 centimeter long?

Find each object in your classroom. Estimate the length.
Then measure using a centimeter ruler.

	Estimate.	Measure.
3	about ____ centimeters	about ____ centimeters
4	about ____ centimeters	about ____ centimeters
5	about ____ centimeters	about ____ centimeters
6	about ____ centimeters	about ____ centimeters

Problem Solving   Reasonableness

Are these objects taller or shorter than 10 centimeters?
Circle the better choice.

7

taller than
10 centimeters

shorter than
10 centimeters

8

taller than
10 centimeters

shorter than
10 centimeters

Home Connection Your child estimated and then measured objects using
a centimeter ruler. **Home Activity** Have your child collect small objects
and then ask him or her to measure the objects using a centimeter ruler.

Name_____

 **Learn!**

How many inches around this shape?

If I count the inches all the way around, I count 10 inches altogether.

___10___ inches

 Check ✓

Count how many inches around each shape.

1

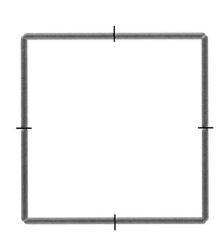

_____ inches

2

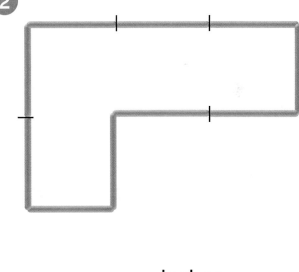

_____ inches

Think About It   Reasoning

How can you decide how many centimeters around each shape?

Count how many inches around each shape.

3

_____ inches

4

_____ inches

Problem Solving Mental Math

5 Ali measured 10 inches around this shape.
How many inches long is each side?

3 inches

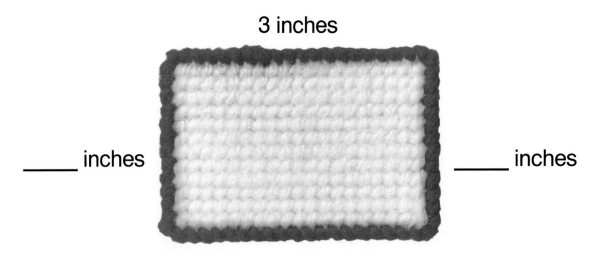

_____ inches

_____ inches

_____ inches

Home Connection Your child counted how many inches around some shapes. **Home Activity** Ask your child to find out how many footsteps it is around a table. Have your child place one foot in front of the other, heel to toe, and walk around the table as you count the footsteps together.

© Pearson Education, Inc.

Name _____

Learn!

How many cubes can you use to cover the shape?

3 are not enough. 5 cubes will cover the shape!

3 cubes

(5 cubes)

Does it make sense?

Check ✓

How many cubes will cover each shape?
Circle the answer that makes sense.

1

4 cubes

8 cubes

2

12 cubes

3 cubes

Think About It   Reasoning

Could you use pennies instead of cubes to cover the shapes above? Explain.

How many cubes will cover each shape?
Circle the answer that makes sense.

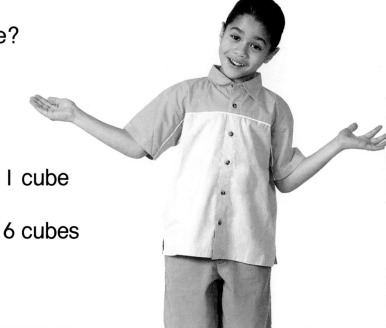

3

I cube

6 cubes

4

3 cubes

9 cubes

Problem Solving   Visual Thinking

5 Draw a different shape with the same number of square units.

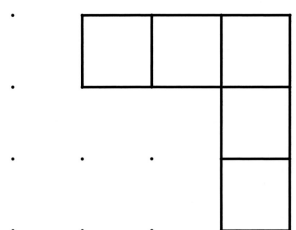

Home Connection Your child estimated how many cubes would cover a shape. Then he or she chose an answer that made sense. **Home Activity** Draw 20 dots like the ones shown in Exercise 5. Have your child draw and color in a shape made up of 6 square units.

Name_____

Estimate the length. Then measure using cubes.

1

Estimate.	**Measure.**
about _____	_____

Estimate the length. Then measure using an inch ruler.

2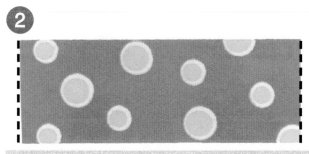

Estimate.	**Measure.**
about _____ inches	_____ inches

Estimate the length. Then measure using a centimeter ruler.

3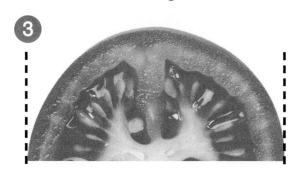

Estimate.	**Measure.**
about _____ centimeters	_____ centimeters

Count how many inches around this shape.

4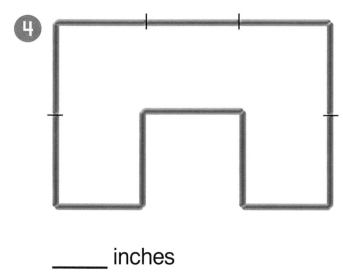

_____ inches

Write how many cubes will cover this shape.

5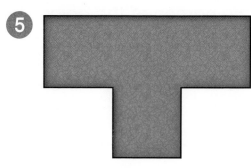

_____ cubes

How much money is there in all?

4¢	8¢	12¢	20¢
Ⓐ	Ⓑ	Ⓒ	Ⓓ

4¢	22¢	31¢	40¢
Ⓐ	Ⓑ	Ⓒ	Ⓓ

3 Which shape has parts that match when you fold on the line?

 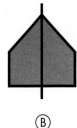 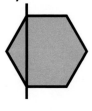 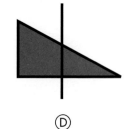

Ⓐ	Ⓑ	Ⓒ	Ⓓ

4

1st

Which position in line is the  ?

third	fourth	fifth	sixth
Ⓐ	Ⓑ	Ⓒ	Ⓓ

Writing in Math

5 Martha used some of these coins to buy the pen.
Write the names of the coins she used.

41¢

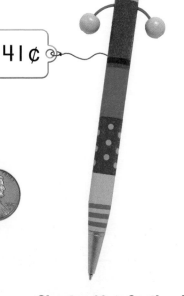

_____

_____

_____

_____

About how many cups of rice will fill the bowl?

I think about 3 cups of rice will fill the bowl.

Estimate.
about ___3___ cups

I can fill the bowl and count how many cups it takes.

Measure.
about ___5___ cups

Word Bank

cup

Check ✓

Estimate how many cups of rice will fill each item.
Then measure.

		Estimate.	Measure.
1		about _____ cups	about _____ cups
2		about _____ cups	about _____ cups

Think About It Number Sense

How would you put the bowl, the jar, and
the pitcher in order from the one that holds the
least to the one that holds the most?

Estimate how many cups of rice will fill each item.
Then measure.

	Estimate.	Measure.
③ 	about _____ cups	about _____ cups
④ 	about _____ cups	about _____ cups
⑤ 	about _____ cups	about _____ cups
⑥ 	about _____ cups	about _____ cups

Problem Solving   Estimation

⑦ Circle the container that holds about 1 cup.

Home Connection Your child estimated and then measured how many cups of rice various containers hold. **Home Activity** Have your child measure the capacities of containers at home using cups of beans, cereal pieces, or water.

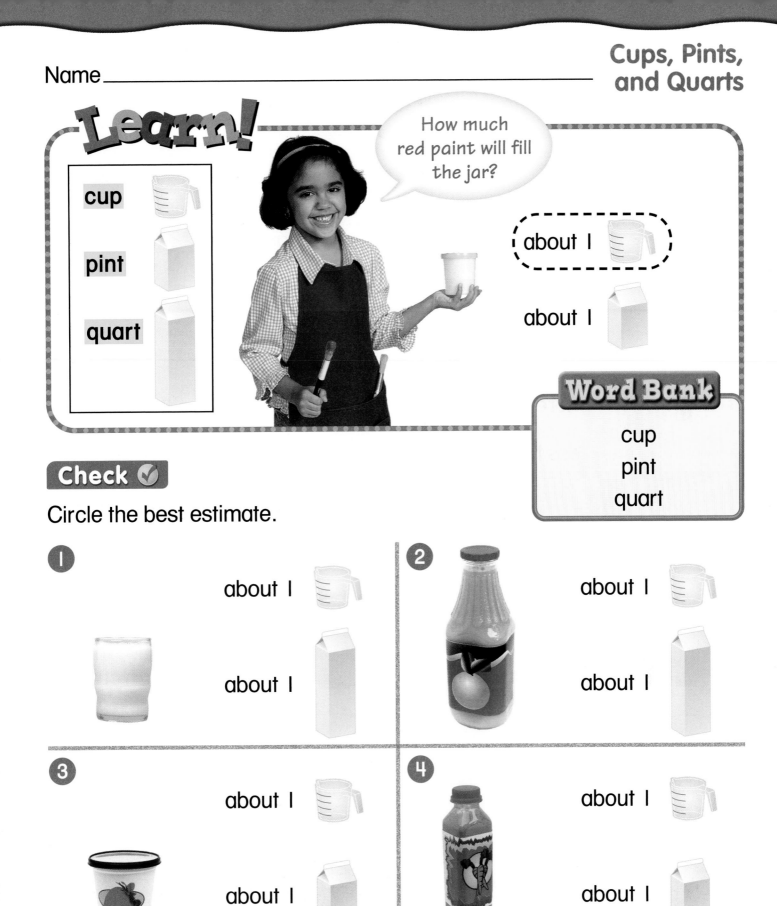

Learn!

cup

pint

quart

How much red paint will fill the jar?

about 1

about 1

Word Bank

cup

pint

quart

Check ✓

Circle the best estimate.

1

about 1

about 1

2

about 1

about 1

3

about 1

about 1

4

about 1

about 1

Think About It   Reasoning

Would you use cups, pints, or quarts to tell how much water is in a fish tank? Explain.

Circle the best estimate.

How much water will I need to fill the bathtub?

5

less than I quart

(more than I quart)

6

more than I cup

less than I cup

7

more than I quart

less than I quart

8

more than I pint

less than I pint

9

more than I cup

less than I cup

Problem Solving   Reasoning

Fill in each blank.

10 2 = I

4 = _____

11 2 = I

4 = _____

Home Connection Your child discussed the relative sizes of cups, pints, and quarts. Then your child compared containers to a cup, a pint, and a quart and estimated how much each would hold. **Home Activity** Set out different-sized containers. Together with your child, estimate whether each would hold about a cup, a pint, or a quart when filled.

Name _____

> Does this glass hold more or less than 1 liter?

less than 1 liter

about 1 liter

more than 1 liter

Word Bank

liter

Check ✓

Circle the best estimate.

1

(less than 1 liter)

more than 1 liter

2

less than 1 liter

more than 1 liter

3

less than 1 liter

more than 1 liter

4

less than 1 liter

more than 1 liter

Think About It   Number Sense

If a bottle of juice holds 2 liters, how much juice
will you have if you buy 2 bottles?

Practice

Circle the best estimate.

5  less than 1 liter

(more than 1 liter)

6  less than 1 liter

more than 1 liter

7  less than 1 liter

more than 1 liter

8  less than 1 liter

more than 1 liter

9  less than 1 liter

more than 1 liter

10  less than 1 liter

more than 1 liter

Problem Solving Estimation

Circle the best estimate.

11  30 liters

3 liters

12  10 liters

1 liter

 Home Connection Your child compared the capacities of various containers to the capacity of a liter. **Home Activity** Ask your child to identify items on the page that hold about 1 liter, less than 1 liter, and more than 1 liter.

About how many cubes will it take to balance?

I used 11 cubes.

Check ✓

Estimate how many cubes it will take to balance.
Then measure.

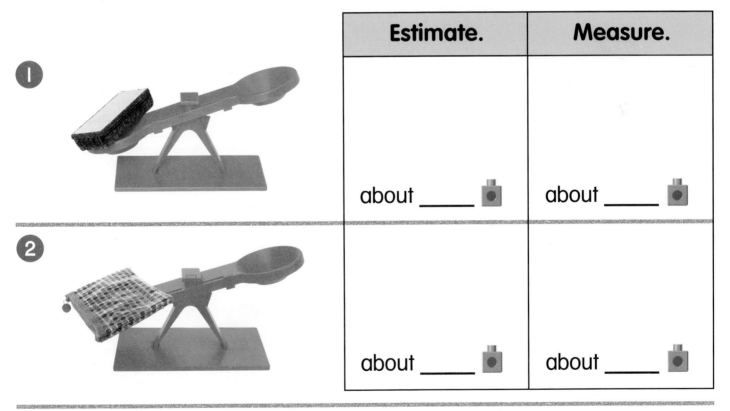

	Estimate.	Measure.
❶	about _____ 🔲	about _____ 🔲
❷	about _____ 🔲	about _____ 🔲

Think About It   Number Sense

Which is heavier, the eraser or the pencil case?
How do you know?

Estimate how many cubes it will take to balance.
Then measure.

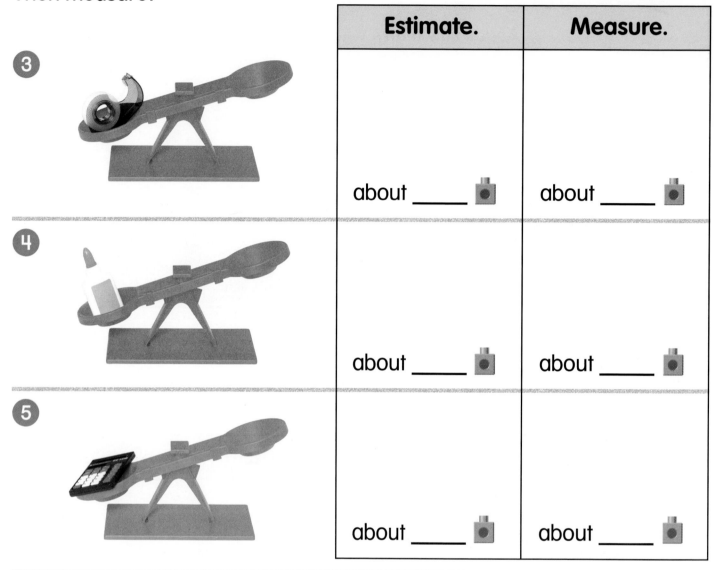

	Estimate.	Measure.
3	about _____ 🔲	about _____ 🔲
4	about _____ 🔲	about _____ 🔲
5	about _____ 🔲	about _____ 🔲

Problem Solving   Number Sense

6 Number the animals from lightest to heaviest.
Use **1** for the lightest and **4** for the heaviest.

———   ———   ———   ———

Home Connection Your child estimated and measured how many cubes it takes to balance an object on a balance scale. **Home Activity** Show your child an item in your home. Have your child find one item that is lighter and one item that is heavier.

Name_____

Learn!

An apple weighs less than I **pound** .

A loaf of bread weighs about I pound.

A brick weighs more than I pound.

Word Bank

pound

Check ✓

Circle the best estimate.

1

less than I pound

(more than I pound)

2

less than I pound

more than I pound

3

less than I pound

more than I pound

4

less than I pound

more than I pound

Think About It Reasoning

Imagine two bags that are exactly the same size.
One is filled with popped popcorn. The other is
filled with marbles. Which bag weighs more? Why?

Circle the best estimate.

5

(less than 1 pound)

more than 1 pound

6

less than 1 pound

more than 1 pound

7

less than 1 pound

more than 1 pound

8

less than 1 pound

more than 1 pound

9

less than 1 pound

more than 1 pound

10

less than 1 pound

more than 1 pound

11

less than 1 pound

more than 1 pound

12

less than 1 pound

more than 1 pound

Problem Solving   Mental Math

Count by 10s to solve.

13 Alicia's class is making tamales.
The students need 9 pounds of cornmeal.
Cornmeal costs 10¢ per pound.
How much will the class pay?   _____¢

Home Connection Your child estimated whether objects weighed more or less than 1 pound. **Home Activity** Have your child find an object in your home that weighs more than 1 pound and another that weighs less than 1 pound.

Learn!

We can use a **thermometer** to measure the **temperature**.

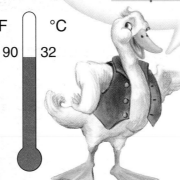

°F 90 °C 32

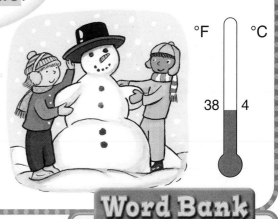

°F 38 °C 4

Word Bank

thermometer

temperature

Check ✓

Circle the thermometer that shows the temperature.

1

°F 38   °F 75

2

°C 6   °C 34

3

°F 85   °F 40

4

°C 32   °C 0

Think About It   Reasoning

If this were the temperature outside today, would you need to wear a coat? Explain.

°F 95

Draw lines to match each picture to a temperature.

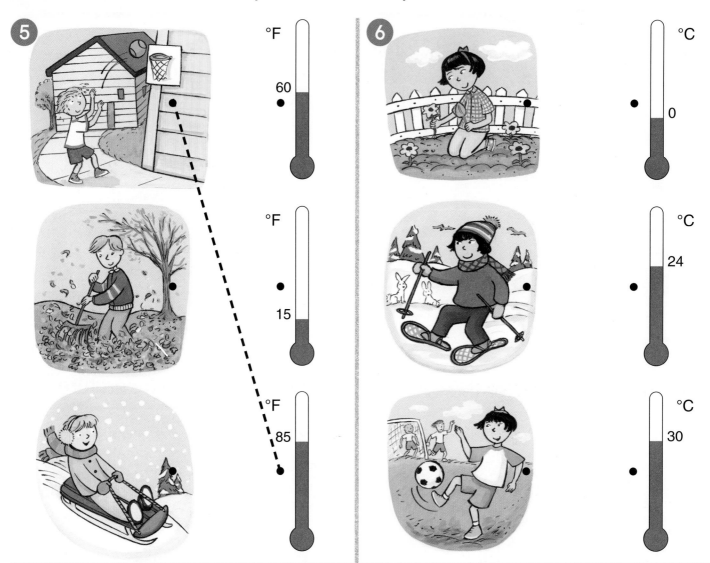

Problem Solving Number Sense

7 Number the thermometers from coldest to hottest.
Use **1** for the coldest and **3** for the hottest.

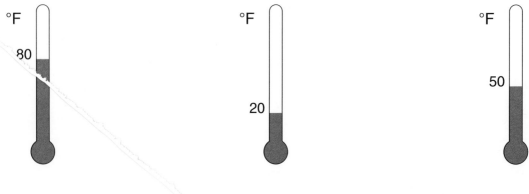

_____ _____ _____

Home Connection Your child used a thermometer to tell the temperature in various pictures. **Home Activity** Watch a weather report on TV with your child. Talk about the temperature and determine whether it will be hot or cold.

Learn!

How would you use a tool to measure?

I can use a ruler to measure how tall it is.

I can use a cup to find out how much it will hold.

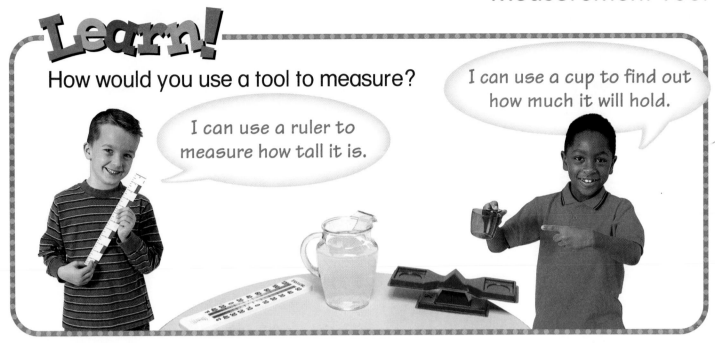

Check ✓

Circle the best tool to use for the measurement.

1 How heavy is it?

 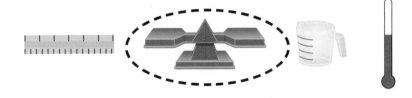

2 How hot is it outside?

3 How long is it?

  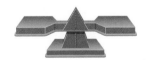

Think About It   Reasoning

What different ways can you measure
a pumpkin? Which tools can you use?

Circle the best tool to use for the measurement.

4 How much does it hold?

5 How cold is it?

6 How tall is it?

7 How heavy is it?

8 How wide is it?

Problem Solving Reasoning

Draw something you could measure with each tool.

9

10

 Home Connection Your child decided which measurement tool to use to answer questions. **Home Activity** Have your child tell you one thing that can be measured using each measuring tool shown in Exercise 4.

Name_____

Circle the best estimate.

1

about I

about I

2

less than I cup

more than I cup

3

less than I liter

more than I liter

4

grams

kilograms

Number these things from lightest to heaviest.
Use I for the lightest and **4** for the heaviest.

5

_____   _____   _____   _____

Circle the thermometer that shows the temperature.

6

°F 20 85 °F

Name_____

Use the map to answer the questions.

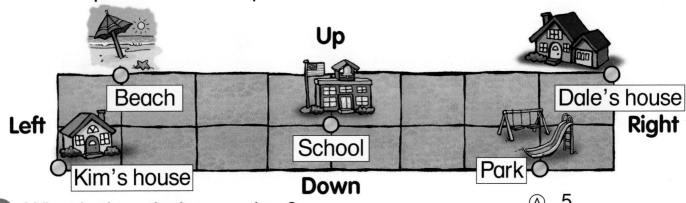

1 What is the missing number?

To go from to 🏠,
go ___ blocks left and 2 blocks down.

Ⓐ 5
Ⓑ 6
Ⓒ 7
Ⓓ 8

2 Which addition sentence tells how many blocks it is
from 🏠 to the ⛱️?

1 + 2 = 3	4 + 1 = 5	6 + 0 = 6	6 + 2 = 8
Ⓐ	Ⓑ	Ⓒ	Ⓓ

3 Count how many inches around this shape.

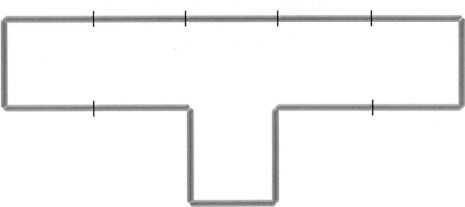

Ⓐ 11 inches
Ⓑ 12 inches
Ⓒ 13 inches
Ⓓ 14 inches

4 About how long is the flower?
Measure using a ruler.

Ⓐ 1 inch
Ⓑ 2 inches
Ⓒ 3 inches
Ⓓ 4 inches

5 What time is it?

Ⓐ 11:00
Ⓑ 11:30
Ⓒ 12:00
Ⓓ 12:30

I am **certain** to pick a green cube.

It is **impossible** for me to pick a green cube.

Word Bank

certain

impossible

Check ✓

Are you certain to pick a blue cube,
or is it impossible? Circle your answer.

1

certain

(impossible)

2

certain

impossible

3

certain

impossible

Think About It Reasoning

Are you certain to pick a red cube from the bowl
in Exercise 3? Explain.

Color the cubes so that each sentence is true.

4 You are certain to
pick an orange cube.

5 It is impossible to
pick a yellow cube.

6 It is impossible to
pick a blue cube.

7 You are certain to
pick a purple cube.

Problem Solving   Visual Thinking

8 Draw 5 cubes in the bag.
Color the cubes so that
it is impossible to pick
a red cube **and** you
are certain to pick
a green cube.

Home Connection Your child decided whether events were certain or
impossible to happen. **Home Activity** Ask your child to place 3 objects in a
bag so that it is impossible to pick a spoon.

It is more likely that the spinner will land on green.

It is less likely that the spinner will land on purple.

Color	Tally
Green	‖‖‖ ‖‖‖
Purple	‖‖‖

Word Bank

more likely
less likely

Check ✓

Use a pencil and a paper clip to make a spinner.
Spin the spinner 10 times.
Mark a tally for each spin.

①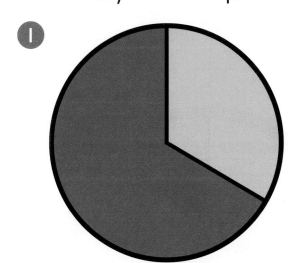

Color	Tally
Yellow	
Red	

② **Predict:** On which color is the spinner more
likely to land next? _____

Think About It   Reasoning

How did you use the tally chart to
help you predict?

Use each tally chart to answer the questions.

Color	Tally
Green	ЖЖ ЖЖ
Orange	ЖЖ

③ **Predict:** On which color is the spinner **more likely** to land next?

_____

Color	Tally
Blue	||||
Yellow	ЖЖ ||||

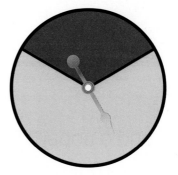

④ **Predict:** On which color is the spinner **less likely** to land next?

_____

Problem Solving   Algebra

Solve.

⑤ Liz spun this spinner 11 times. She landed on blue 8 times. How many times did she land on red?

_____ times

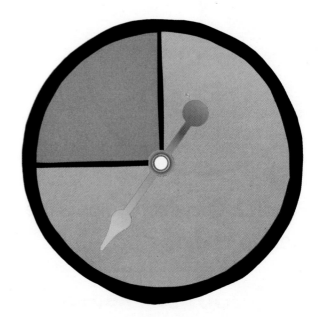

Home Connection Your child spun a spinner and predicted which color it would land on next. **Home Activity** Ask your child to explain how he or she made the predictions in Exercises 3 and 4.

Name_____

 Dorling Kindersley

Chow mein is made by combining noodles and stir-fried vegetables.

Do You Know...
that more people have soy sauce in their homes than have milk?

1. Lin is making chow mein. He needs 1 cup of dry noodles. Is 1 cup more than 1 quart or less than 1 quart?

_____

2. A chopstick measures about 10 inches long. Is 10 inches more than 1 centimeter or less than 1 centimeter?

_____

3. Is 10 inches more than 1 foot or less than 1 foot?

_____

Fun Fact!
People started using chopsticks in China over 4,000 years ago.

4 The carrots cost 20¢.
If Lin gave the clerk a quarter,
did he get change?

_____

5 Circle the thermometer that
shows the temperature at which
the chow mein will probably be
after Lin stir-fries it.

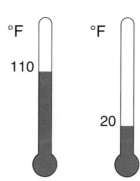

6 Lin started making chow mein at 5:00.
It takes a half hour to make chow mein.
At what time did Lin finish?

_____

7 **Writing in Math**

Ask 10 children in your class if
they have ever eaten chow mein.
Make a tally chart to show their answers.

Name _____

Are you certain to pick a purple crayon, or is it impossible?
Circle your answer.

certain

impossible

2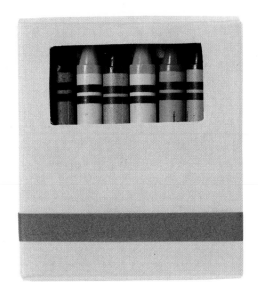

certain

impossible

Use the spinner and the tally chart to answer
each question.

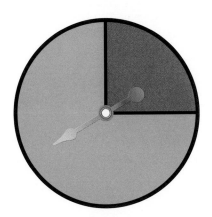

Color	Tally
Green	|||||
Orange	卌 卌

3 **Predict:** On which color is the spinner more likely
to land on the next spin? _____

4 On which color is it less likely to land? _____

1 How long is the watch?

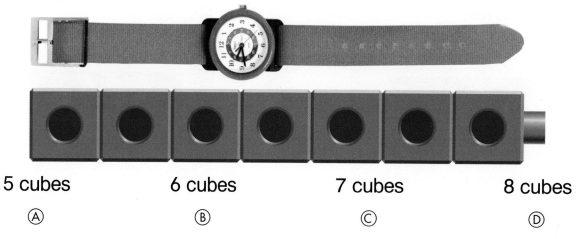

5 cubes	6 cubes	7 cubes	8 cubes
Ⓐ	Ⓑ	Ⓒ	Ⓓ

2 Which object holds more than 1 quart?

Ⓐ   Ⓑ   Ⓒ   Ⓓ

3 Which food would you weigh in kilograms?

Ⓐ   Ⓑ   Ⓒ   Ⓓ

Which number goes in the circle?

4

53 < ◯

31	35	50	63
Ⓐ	Ⓑ	Ⓒ	Ⓓ

5

94 > 49 > ◯
greatest   least

44	54	79	99
Ⓐ	Ⓑ	Ⓒ	Ⓓ

Standard and Nonstandard Units

Tim and Anna measured with paper clips.

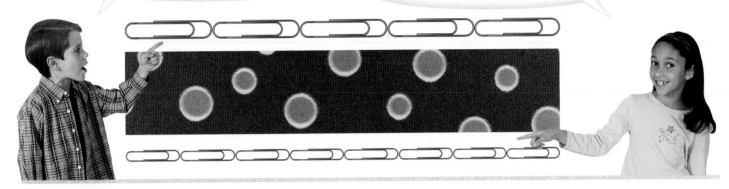

This ribbon is 5 clips long.

No, it is 8 clips long.

Use paper clips and an inch ruler
to measure the ribbons.

1 about _____  _____ inches

2 about _____ ⬭ _____ inches

3 about _____ ⬭ _____ inches

4 **Writing in Math**

Why did the children get different answers
when they measured with paper clips?

Home Connection Your child measured length with various sizes of paper
clips. **Home Activity** Use your child's thumb and then your own thumb to
measure a cookie sheet. Discuss the results.

Make Predictions Using a Computer

1 Go to the Geometry Shapes eTool.
Place 10 squares and 5 triangles in the workspace.

2 Color 5 squares red and 5 squares blue.
Color 3 triangles red and 2 triangles yellow.

3 Which **shape** do you think you will pick
more often with your eyes closed? _____

4 Try it. Close your eyes and touch the screen.
Use tally marks. Do this 20 times.

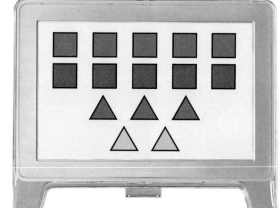

Shapes I Chose	
Square	
Triangle	

5 Which **color** do you think you will pick
most often with your eyes closed? _____

6 Try it 20 times.

Colors I Chose	
Red	
Blue	
Yellow	

Think About It   Reasoning

How did you make your predictions?

 Home Connection Your child predicted which of two shapes and which of
three colors he or she would most likely choose and then completed tally charts
to show the results. **Home Activity** Ask your child to explain one of the tally
charts to you.

Name_____

Plan How to Find the Answer

Choosing the correct measurement
tools can help you solve math problems.

Test-Taking Strategies

Understand the Question

Get Information for the Answer

Plan How to Find the Answer

Make Smart Choices

Use Writing in Math

1 Which tool would you use to find
the length of your math book?

Ⓐ a balance scale

Ⓑ an inch ruler

Ⓒ a thermometer

Ⓓ a cup

Choose the tool that measures length.
Fill in the answer bubble.

Your Turn

Choose the correct tool. Fill in the answer bubble.

2 Which tool would you use to find
the temperature in your classroom?

Ⓐ a thermometer

Ⓑ a centimeter ruler

Ⓒ a balance scale

Ⓓ a one-liter container

I know the
answer!

Home Connection Your child prepared for standardized tests by determining
which measurement tools he or she would use to solve different kinds of problems.
Home Activity Ask your child to identify the word in Exercise 2 that tells what
needs to be measured. *(Temperature)* Then ask your child to explain how he or she
chose the correct measurement tool.

four hundred eleven **411**

Name _____

Discover Math in Your World

Light as a Feather?

Can you pick up an elephant? No way!
Some things are very heavy.
Others are very light.
How would you weigh a feather?

Measuring Weight

1 Work in a group. Choose something light to weigh.

2 Put your object on one side of a balance scale.

3 On the other side of the scale, add seeds
or beans one at a time until the scale balances.

4 Record the weight of your object on a separate
sheet of paper.

5 Repeat Steps 1–4 using two other light objects.

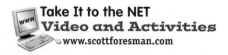
Take It to the NET
Video and Activities
www.scottforesman.com

Home Connection Your child weighed light objects by using
a balance scale and seeds or beans. **Home Activity** Ask your
child to explain how he or she found the weight of one of the
objects.

Estimate the length. Then measure using an inch ruler.

1

Estimate.	Measure.
about _____ inches	_____ inches

Estimate the length. Then measure using a centimeter ruler.

2

Estimate.	Measure.
about _____ centimeters	_____ centimeters

3 Circle the best estimate for the height of the butterfly.

1 inch

1 foot

4 Count how many inches around this shape.

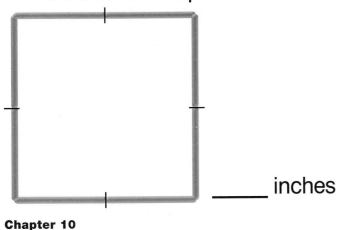

_____ inches

5 Write how many cubes will cover this shape.

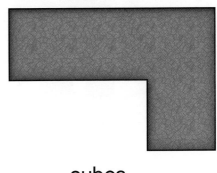

_____ cubes

Circle the best estimate.

 6

about 1 cup

about 1 quart

 **7**

less than 1 liter

more than 1 liter

 8

Jose Vasquez
125 Rio Sabinal
San Antonio, TX 78201

less than 1 pound

more than 1 pound

Would you measure this in grams or kilograms?
Circle your answer.

 9

grams

kilograms

Circle the thermometer that shows the temperature.

 10

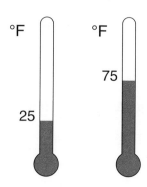

°F   °F

75

25

1 Which addition sentence matches the picture?

4 + 5 = 9   5 + 6 = 11   5 + 5 = 10   5 + 3 = 8
Ⓐ   Ⓑ   Ⓒ   Ⓓ

Use the picture graph to answer the question.

2 How many more children chose tacos than chose pizza?

Favorite Food							

3   6   9   12
Ⓐ   Ⓑ   Ⓒ   Ⓓ

3 How much money is there in all?

24¢   36¢   42¢   60¢
Ⓐ   Ⓑ   Ⓒ   Ⓓ

4 Count how many inches around the shape.

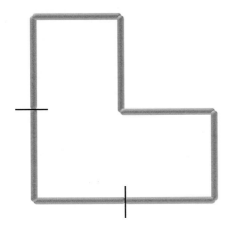

Ⓐ 4 inches

Ⓑ 8 inches

Ⓒ 10 inches

Ⓓ 12 inches

Circle the best estimate.

about 1 cup
about 1 quart

about 1 gram
about 1 kilogram

Draw a line of symmetry on each shape.

   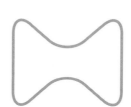 

Circle the coins that equal $1.00.

Writing in Math

 What must be in the bag if you are certain to pick an apple from it?

_____

_____

_____

Read Together

Fuzzy Wuzzy

By Anne Miranda

Illustrated by Diane Greenseid

This Math Storybook belongs to

_____

11A

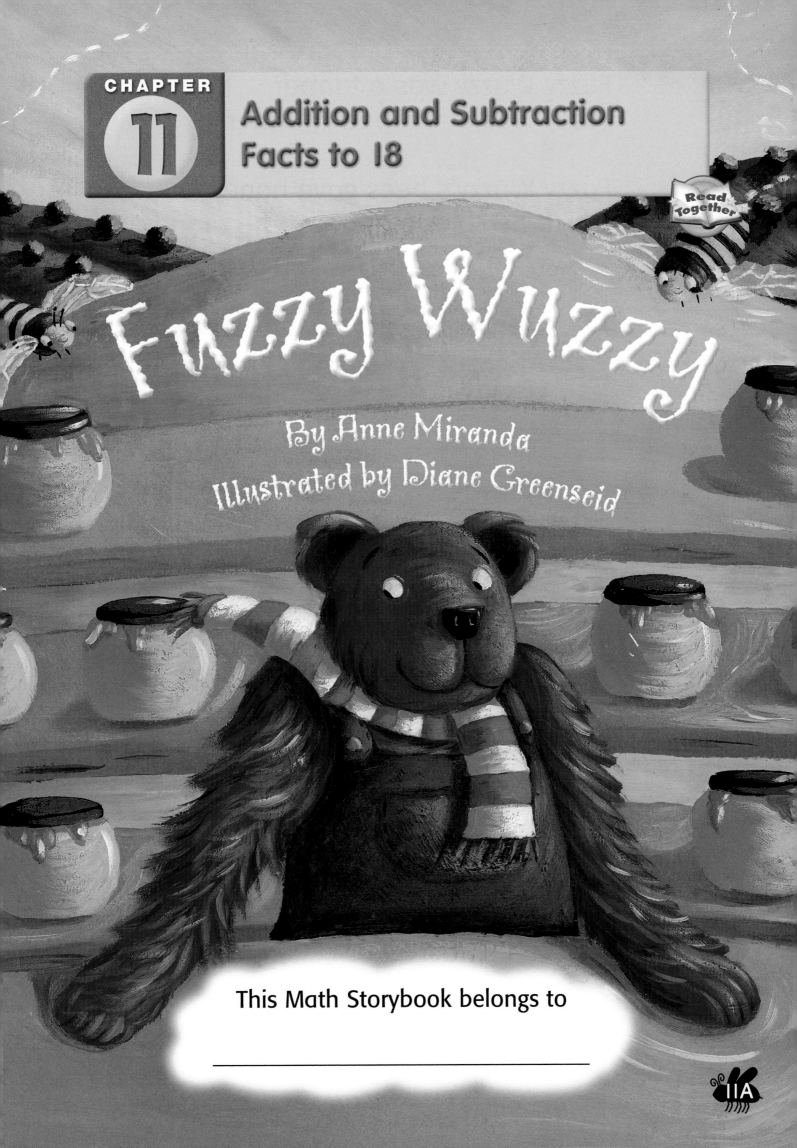

In came Mac and Benny Rabbit.
Buying honey was their habit.

Mac gave Fuzzy **7** pennies,
plus the **6** cents that were Benny's.

Fuzzy Wuzzy sure could count.
He saw it was the wrong amount.

Fuzzy Wuzzy looked at Mac,
and then he gave him **3** cents back.

Mac and Benny smiled because they saw how clever Fuzzy was!

The pair of honey-loving bunnies took their change and jars of honey.

With a wink they gave a hop,
thanked Fuzzy twice, and left his shop.

Fuzzy Wuzzy was a bear
who treated all his buyers fair.

His business grew, and grew, and grew.
That shows what being fair can do.

(Of course there was one other fact:
That bear knew how to add and subtract!)

Dear Family,

Today my class started Chapter 11, **Addition and Subtraction Facts to 18.** I will learn about addition fact strategies and subtraction fact strategies. Here are some of the math words I will be learning and some things we can do to help me with my math.

Love,

_____

Math Activity to Do at Home

Write 10 on a card. Then ask your child to write a doubles fact that has the sum of 10. Next, on the back of that card, together decide on a related subtraction fact to write. Continue with sums of 8, 6, and 4.

Books to Read Together

Reading math stories reinforces concepts. Look for these titles in your local library:

Mission: Addition
By Loreen Leedy
(Holiday House, 1997)

Two of Everything:
A Chinese Folktale
By Lily T. Hong
(Albert Whitman, 1993)

My New Math Words

related facts Addition and subtraction facts are related if they use the same numbers.

For example:

$$9 + 8 = 17$$
$$17 - 9 = 8$$

Related facts use the same numbers.

fact family A fact family is a group of related addition and subtraction facts. For example:

$7 + 6 = 13$
$6 + 7 = 13$
$13 - 6 = 7$
$13 - 7 = 6$

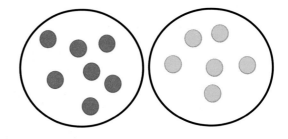

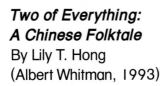
Take It to the NET
More Activities
www.scottforesman.com

Name _____

Get That Honey!

How to Play

1. Play with a partner. Put your markers on START.
2. Take turns tossing the cube. Move that number of spaces.
3. Read what it says on the space you land on.
   Do what it says on the space you land on.
4. Keep playing until both of you reach Fuzzy Wuzzy and his honey!

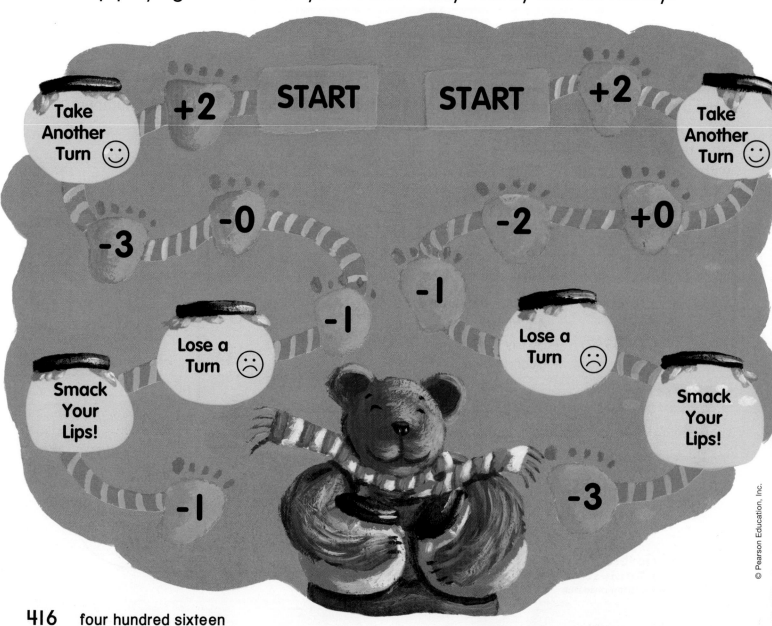

Name_____

You can use the pattern to learn more doubles facts.

__1__ + __1__ = __2__

__2__ + __2__ = __4__

__3__ + __3__ = __6__

__4__ + __4__ = __8__

__5__ + __5__ = __10__

__6__ + __6__ = __12__

__7__ + __7__ = __14__

Word Bank

double

Check ✓

Write the addition sentence for each double.

1  ___ + ___ = ___

2  ___ + ___ = ___

3  ___ + ___ = ___

Think About It   Reasoning

Can you use doubles to make 15? Explain.

Circle the doubles. Then add.

4 (5)   7   0   2   3   6
     +5   + 3   + 6   + 7   + 8   + 6
     10

5   5   9   1   4   8   9
     + 7   + 0   + 1   + 4   + 2   + 9

6   5   3   2   6   7   1
     + 1   + 3   + 9   + 3   + 7   + 8

7   8   3   6   7   2   9
     + 8   + 5   + 2   + 0   + 2   + 3

Problem Solving   Visual Thinking

For each picture write an addition sentence
that tells how many legs there are in all.

8    **9**

___ + ___ = ___   ___ + ___ = ___

 Home Connection Your child used doubles to add. **Home Activity** Hold up some fingers. Have your child hold up the same number of fingers and then ask him or her to say the doubles fact that tells how many fingers in all.

You can use doubles to solve other problems.

Think 3 + 3
and 1 more.

Think 3 + 3
and 1 less.

3 + 3 = _6_   3 + 4 = _7_   3 + 2 = _5_

Check ✓

Add the doubles.
Then use the doubles to help you add.

5 + 5 = ___   5 + 6 = ___   5 + 4 = ___

7 + 7 = ___   7 + 8 = ___   7 + 6 = ___

Think About It   Number Sense

Which two doubles facts could you use
to find the sum for 8 + 7? Explain.

Add the doubles.

Then use the doubles to help you add.

Think 8 + 8 = 16

so 8 + 9 = 17

and 8 + 7 = 15

Think 9 + 9 = ___

so 9 + 10 = ___

and 9 + 8 = ___

Think 4 + 4 = ___

so 4 + 5 = ___

and 4 + 3 = ___

Think 6 + 6 = ___

so 6 + 7 = ___

and 6 + 5 = ___

Problem Solving Mental Math

Answer each question.

7 Carrie has 7 red balloons and 8 yellow balloons. How many balloons does Carrie have in all?

_____ balloons

8 Pepe has 6 baseball cards. Dad gives him 7 more cards. How many cards does Pepe have in all?

_____ baseball cards

Home Connection Your child used a doubles fact to solve other addition problems. **Home Activity** Ask your child to show a doubles fact using crayons or other small objects. Then ask him or her to show you a doubles-plus-1 fact and a doubles-minus-1 fact.

Name_____

Learn! Algebra

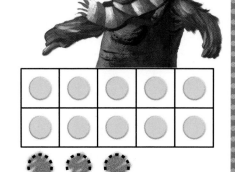

You can use a pattern when adding 10.

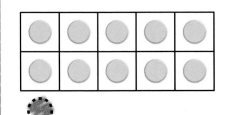 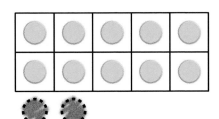

$10 + 1 = \underline{11}$ $10 + 2 = \underline{12}$ $10 + 3 = \underline{13}$

Check ✓

Draw the counters. Then find the sum.

①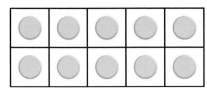

$10 + 5 = \underline{}$

②

$10 + 8 = \underline{}$

③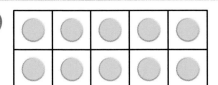

$10 + 4 = \underline{}$

④

$10 + 6 = \underline{}$

Think About It   Reasoning

Which addition fact can help you find the sum for $4 + 10$?

How can you show the addition fact with a ten-frame?

Write the addition sentence for each ten-frame.

5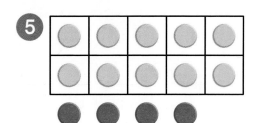

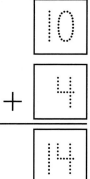

There are 10 counters in the ten-frame plus 4 more counters.
10 + 4 = 14

6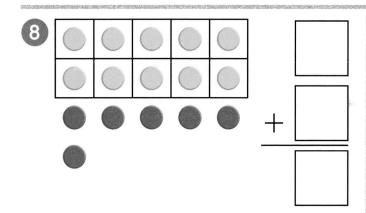

7

8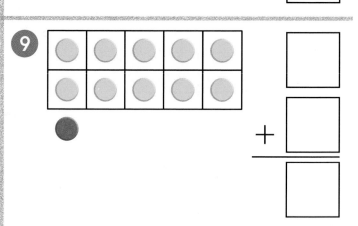

9

Problem Solving Algebra

Find the pattern. Then write the missing numbers.

10

3	4	☐	6	☐	8
+ 10	+ ☐	+ 10	+ 10	+ 10	+ ☐
☐	14	15	☐	17	18

Home Connection Your child found sums by adding 10 to numbers less than 10. **Home Activity** Have your child hold up 10 fingers. Then hold up 6 of your fingers. Ask your child to tell how many fingers in all. Repeat with 10 and other numbers.

Name_____

Learn!

You can make a 10 to add other numbers.

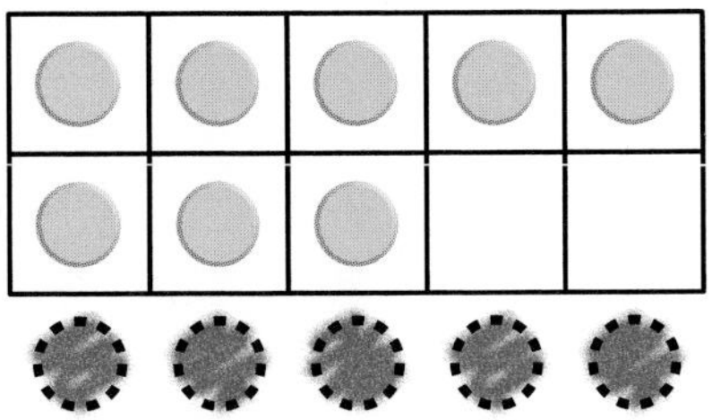

8
+ 5
13

8 + 5 is the same as 10 + 3.

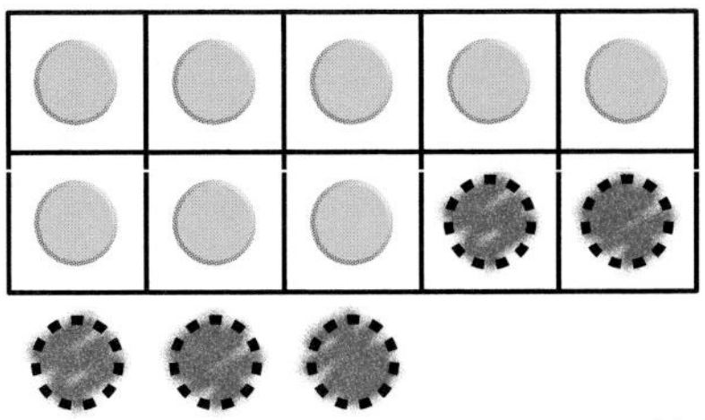

10
+ 3
13

Check ✓

Use counters and Workmat 2.

Draw the counters. Then write the sums.

1

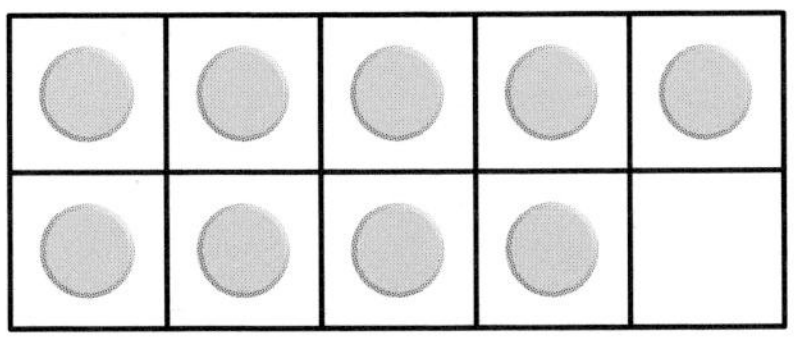

    9   10
  + 3   + 2

2

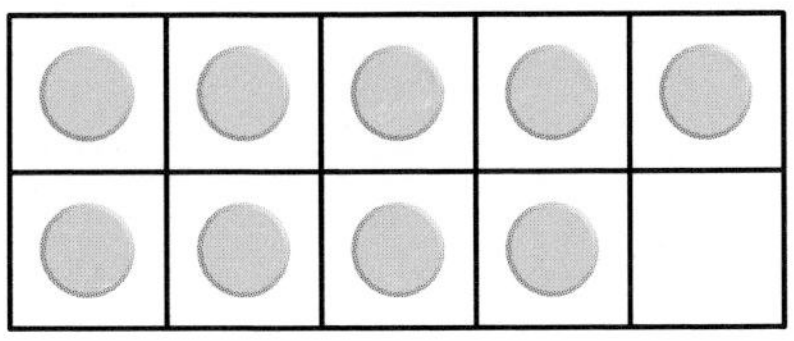

    9   10
  + 5   + 4

3

    8   10
  + 4   + 2

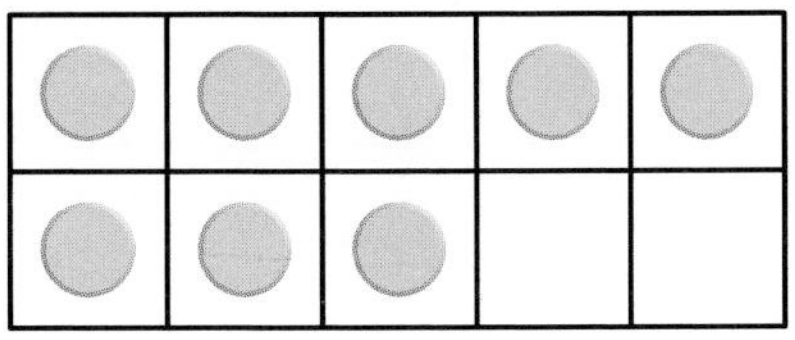

Think About It   Number Sense

How would you make a 10 to find the sum of 4 + 9?

Draw the counters. Then write the sums.
Use counters and Workmat 2 if you like.

It is easy to make a 10 to add!

4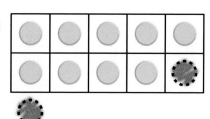

$$9 + 2$$ $$10 + 1$$

5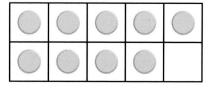

$$9 + 4$$ $$10 + 3$$

6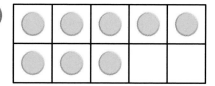

$$8 + 6$$ $$10 + 4$$

7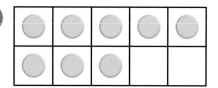

$$8 + 7$$ $$10 + 5$$

8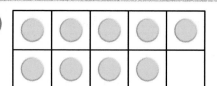

$$9 + 7$$ $$10 + 6$$

Problem Solving   Algebra

Complete the number sentence.

9 $9 + 8 = 10 + 7 = \boxed{}$

Home Connection Your child practiced making a 10 to add two numbers.
Home Activity Hold out 8 pennies in one hand and 5 in the other. Have your child move the pennies to show 10 in one hand and 3 in the other. Have your child explain why 8 + 5 is the same as 10 + 3. Repeat with other numbers.

© Pearson Education, Inc.

You can use different strategies to add.

I can make a 10!
8 + 7 is the same as
10 + 5. 10 + 5 = 15,
so 8 + 7 = 15.

I can use doubles!
8 + 8 = 16, so
8 + 7 = 15.

$$\begin{array}{r} 8 \\ + 7 \\ \hline 15 \end{array}$$

Check ✓

Add.

Then circle the strategy that you used.

1.
$$\begin{array}{r} 4 \\ + 8 \\ \hline \end{array}$$
make a 10

use doubles

2.
$$\begin{array}{r} 8 \\ + 8 \\ \hline \end{array}$$
make a 10

use doubles

3.
$$\begin{array}{r} 9 \\ + 5 \\ \hline \end{array}$$
make a 10

use doubles

4.
$$\begin{array}{r} 9 \\ + 8 \\ \hline \end{array}$$
make a 10

use doubles

5.
$$\begin{array}{r} 8 \\ + 6 \\ \hline \end{array}$$
make a 10

use doubles

6.
$$\begin{array}{r} 7 \\ + 5 \\ \hline \end{array}$$
make a 10

use doubles

Think About It   Reasoning

Does it matter which strategy you use to add? Explain.

Add.

7

9	8	7	9	5	6
+ 8	+ 7	+ 7	+ 4	+ 8	+ 7
17					

8

6	8	7	3	8	9
+ 9	+ 0	+ 6	+ 9	+ 5	+ 7

9

9	6	8	5	2	9
+ 5	+ 8	+ 8	+ 9	+ 5	+ 6

10

8	7	4	9	5	8
+ 6	+ 9	+ 9	+ 9	+ 7	+ 9

Problem Solving   Writing in Math

11 Write a story problem that can be solved using doubles. Then explain how to solve the problem.

_____

_____

_____

_____

Home Connection Your child chose a strategy and then used it to add two numbers. **Home Activity** Have your child explain how he or she solved the problems in Exercise 7.

Name_____

Learn! Algebra

You can add three numbers in any order.

③+⑥+ 4 = $\underline{13}$

□ 9

3 + 6 = 9
9 + 4 = 13

6 + 4 = 10
3 + 10 = 13

3 +⑥+④= $\underline{13}$

□ 10

Check ✓

Find each sum.

1 ②+⑦+ 3 = ___

□

2 +⑦+③= ___

□

---

2 ⑤+⑤+ 4 = ___

□

5 +⑤+④= ___

□

---

3 ③+⑥+ 2 = ___

□

3 +⑥+②= ___

□

Think About It   Reasoning

Explain why both problems in
Exercise 3 have the same answer.

Chapter 11 ★ Lesson 6

Practice

Circle the two numbers you choose to add first.
Then find each sum.

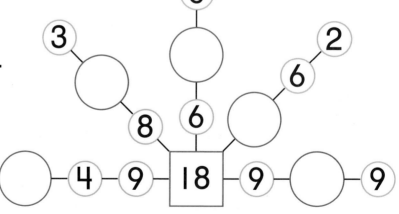

First add 6 + 4 = 10.
Then add 10 + 5 = 15.

4
```
  ⑥
  5      [10]
+ ④
─────
 15
```

5
```
  7
  9      [ ]
+ 1
─────
```

```
  5
  2      [ ]
+ 8
─────
```

```
  6
  6      [ ]
+ 3
─────
```

6
```
  3
  7      [ ]
+ 6
─────
```

```
  8
  2      [ ]
+ 2
─────
```

```
  7
  3      [ ]
+ 7
─────
```

Problem Solving **Algebra**

Find the missing numbers.

7 The three numbers on
each branch add up to 18.

6 — 3 — 2 — 6 — 8 — 6 — 4 — 9 — 18 — 9 — 9

428 four hundred twenty-eight

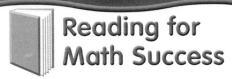
Name_____

Understand Graphic Sources: Tables

1 Read this story problem.

Mia has dolls and teddy bears.
Each toy box will hold 2 toys.
Mia thought about all the ways to
put the toys in the toy boxes.

Way 1	Way 2	Way 3

She made a table to show the different ways.

Dolls	Teddy Bears
2	0
1	1
0	2

2 Which way does the first row of the table show?

_____

3 Which way does the second row show? The third row?

_____   _____

Think About It   Reasoning

Should there be another row in the table? Explain.

4 Read this story problem.

Mick has 2 kinds of stickers to put on envelopes. Each envelope will have 2 stickers on it. How many different ways can Mick put the stickers on the envelopes?

5 Draw the ways that Mick could put the stickers on the envelopes.

Way 1	Way 2	Way 3
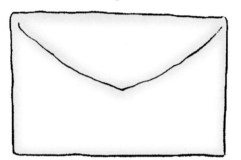	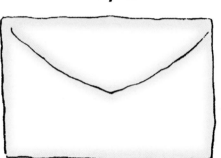	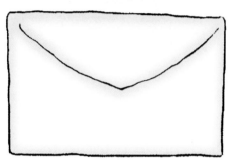

6 Complete the table to show the different ways.

Stars ⭐	Smiley faces 🙂

7 How many different ways can Mick put 2 stickers on each envelope?

_____ ways

 Home Connection Your child completed a table to help solve a story problem. **Home Activity** Think of problems similar to those on these pages, such as finding different ways to put two kinds of objects in a bag. Have your child fill a bag with two objects in three different ways and ask him or her to complete a table like the one above to show all of the possible solutions.

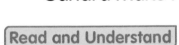

1. Sandra is making fruit baskets.
   She has pears, apples, and plums.
   Each basket holds 3 pieces of fruit.
   How many different baskets can
   Sandra make?

Read and Understand

You need to find how many
different ways Sandra can fill
a basket with 3 pieces of fruit.

Plan and Solve

You can make a table. Then
you can count the ways.

There are _____ different ways.

Look Back and Check

Did you find all of the ways?
How do you know?

Pears	Apples	Plums
3	0	0
0	3	0
0	0	3
2	1	0
2	0	1
1	2	0
0	2	1
1	0	2
0	1	2
1	1	1

Think About It Reasoning

How did the table help you answer the question?

Make a table to solve the problem.

2 Dad is making gift bags. He has yo-yos, kazoos, and rings. Each bag holds 3 toys. How many different bags can Dad make?

Dad can make _____ different bags.

Yo-Yos	Kazoos	Rings
3	0	0

Reasoning

3 What do you notice about each row of the table?

_____

_____

Home Connection Your child made tables to help solve problems.
Home Activity Ask your child to explain how he or she filled in the table at the top of the page and to tell how the table helped solve the problem.

Name_____

Add the doubles.

Then use the doubles to help you add.

1 Think $7 + 7 = $ _____   so $7 + 8 = $ _____

and $7 + 6 = $ _____

Draw the counters.

Then write the sums.

2

$$\begin{array}{r} 8 \\ + 6 \\ \hline \end{array}$$
$$\begin{array}{r} 10 \\ + 4 \\ \hline \end{array}$$

Add.

3
$$\begin{array}{r} 9 \\ + 5 \\ \hline \end{array}$$
$$\begin{array}{r} 10 \\ + 7 \\ \hline \end{array}$$
$$\begin{array}{r} 5 \\ + 8 \\ \hline \end{array}$$
$$\begin{array}{r} 9 \\ + 9 \\ \hline \end{array}$$
$$\begin{array}{r} 7 \\ 4 \\ + 3 \\ \hline \end{array}$$
$$\begin{array}{r} 5 \\ 4 \\ + 5 \\ \hline \end{array}$$

Complete the table to answer the question.

4 A clown has orange balloons
and purple balloons.
How many different ways
can the clown hold 2 balloons at a time?

There are _____ different ways.

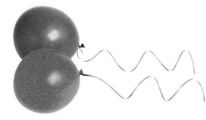

Orange	Purple

Name _____

Use the spinner and tally chart for Exercises 1 and 2.

1 Sam spun the spinner 18 times. He made a tally mark in the chart for each spin. How many times did the spinner land on green?

| Green | ЖЖ ЖЖ II |
| Red | ЖЖ I |

6   11   12   14
Ⓐ   Ⓑ   Ⓒ   Ⓓ

2 If Sam spins the spinner again, on which color is the spinner more likely to land?

green   red   yellow   blue
Ⓐ   Ⓑ   Ⓒ   Ⓓ

3 What is the temperature?

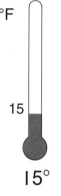
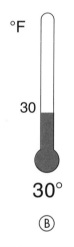
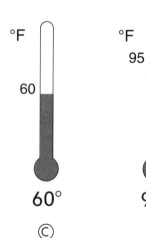

15°   30°   60°   95°
Ⓐ   Ⓑ   Ⓒ   Ⓓ

Writing in Math

4 If February 5 is a Thursday, what day will February 9 be? Tell how you found your answer.

_____

_____

Name_____

Learn! Algebra

Related facts are addition and subtraction facts that have the same numbers.

6 + 8 = 14

14 − 8 = 6

14 − 6 = 8 is another related subtraction fact.

Word Bank

related facts

Check ✓

Add. Then write a related subtraction fact.

1

8 + 3 = ___

___ − ___ = ___

2

6 + 6 = ___

___ − ___ = ___

3

9 + 5 = ___

___ − ___ = ___

4

7 + 9 = ___

___ − ___ = ___

Think About It   Reasoning

How are these two facts alike?

How are they different?

9 + 8 = 17
17 − 9 = 8

Write related addition and subtraction
facts for each picture.

5

___4___ + ___8___ = ___12___

___12___ − ___8___ = ___4___

6

___ + ___ = ___

___ − ___ = ___

7

___ + ___ = ___

___ − ___ = ___

8

___ + ___ = ___

___ − ___ = ___

9

___ + ___ = ___

___ − ___ = ___

10

___ + ___ = ___

___ − ___ = ___

Problem Solving Number Sense

Write two related facts to answer the questions.

11 8 boys and 6 girls are marching in a band.
How many children are there in all?
If 6 of the children go home,
how many children will be left?

___ + ___ = ___

___ − ___ = ___

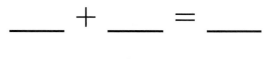

Home Connection Your child wrote related addition and subtraction facts.
Home Activity Ask your child to use pennies or other small objects to
show 8 + 7 = 15 and 15 − 7 = 8 and other pairs of related facts.

Name_____

Algebra

These related addition and subtraction facts make a **fact family**.

They all use the same three numbers: 7, 9, and 16.

$$9 + 7 = \underline{16}$$
$$\underline{7} + \underline{9} = \underline{16}$$
$$16 - 9 = \underline{7}$$
$$\underline{16} - \underline{7} = \underline{9}$$

Word Bank

fact family

Check ✔

Complete the fact family.

1

$$5 + 8 = \underline{}$$
$$\underline{} + \underline{} = \underline{}$$
$$13 - 8 = \underline{}$$
$$\underline{} - \underline{} = \underline{}$$

Think About It   Reasoning

Which fact families have only two facts? Explain.

Use the numbers on each hat to write a fact family.

2

$\underline{} + \underline{} = \underline{15}$

$\underline{} + \underline{} = \underline{}$

$\underline{} - \underline{} = \underline{}$

$\underline{} - \underline{} = \underline{}$

3

$\underline{} + \underline{} = \underline{}$

$\underline{} + \underline{} = \underline{}$

$\underline{} - \underline{} = \underline{}$

$\underline{} - \underline{} = \underline{}$

4

$\underline{} + \underline{} = \underline{}$

$\underline{} + \underline{} = \underline{}$

$\underline{} - \underline{} = \underline{}$

$\underline{} - \underline{} = \underline{}$

Problem Solving Algebra

Write the missing number for each fact family.

5  6 12

6  4 9

 Home Connection Your child wrote the related facts in a fact family.
Home Activity Remove the face cards from a deck of cards. Have your child pick 2 cards and write an addition fact, such as 7 + 8 = 15, using the numbers. Then ask your child to complete the fact family.

Learn! Algebra

You can use addition to help you subtract.

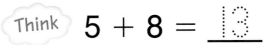

If $5 + 8 = 13$, then $13 - 8 = 5$.

Think $5 + 8 = \underline{13}$

so $13 - 8 = \underline{5}$

Check ✔

Add.

Then use the addition fact to help you subtract.

1

Think $5 + 9 = \underline{\hspace{1cm}}$

so $14 - 9 = \underline{\hspace{1cm}}$

2

Think $7 + 6 = \underline{\hspace{1cm}}$

so $13 - 6 = \underline{\hspace{1cm}}$

3

Think $9 + 6 = \underline{\hspace{1cm}}$

so $15 - 6 = \underline{\hspace{1cm}}$

4

Think $8 + 8 = \underline{\hspace{1cm}}$

so $16 - 8 = \underline{\hspace{1cm}}$

Think About It   Reasoning

If △ + ■ = ⬤ , then ⬤ − ■ = ?

Explain.

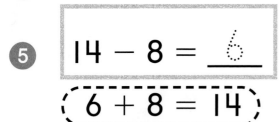

Circle the addition fact that will help you subtract.
Then subtract.

⑤ 14 − 8 = __6__

~~(6 + 8 = 14)~~

9 + 6 = 15

⑥ 12 − 3 = ___

9 + 7 = 16

9 + 3 = 12

⑦ 13 − 6 = ___

7 + 6 = 13

9 + 4 = 13

⑧ 15 − 8 = ___

8 + 7 = 15

5 + 8 = 13

⑨ 11 − 9 = ___

9 + 5 = 14

2 + 9 = 11

⑩ 16 − 7 = ___

7 + 7 = 14

9 + 7 = 16

⑪ 17 − 8 = ___

9 + 8 = 17

8 + 3 = 11

⑫ 18 − 9 = ___

9 + 9 = 18

9 + 7 = 16

Problem Solving Mental Math

Solve.

⑬ The chipmunk stored 9 of its 17 acorns.
How many acorns does it still need to store?   _____ acorns

Home Connection Your child used addition facts to help with subtraction.
Home Activity Write 15 − 6 on a piece of paper. Ask your child to write a
related addition fact and then solve the subtraction problem. Continue with
other subtraction problems.

Name_____

 **Learn!**

You can use a ten-frame to subtract.

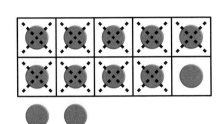

$$\begin{array}{r} 12 \\ -\ 10 \\ \hline 2 \end{array}$$ so $$\begin{array}{r} 12 \\ -\ 9 \\ \hline 3 \end{array}$$

Check ✓

Cross out to subtract.

Use a ten-frame and counters if you like.

1 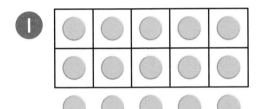 $$\begin{array}{r} 15 \\ -\ 8 \\ \hline \end{array}$$

2 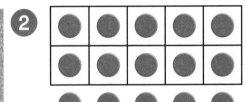 $$\begin{array}{r} 17 \\ -\ 9 \\ \hline \end{array}$$

3 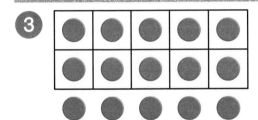 $$\begin{array}{r} 16 \\ -\ 9 \\ \hline \end{array}$$

4 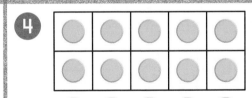 $$\begin{array}{r} 18 \\ -\ 9 \\ \hline \end{array}$$

5 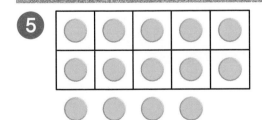 $$\begin{array}{r} 14 \\ -\ 8 \\ \hline \end{array}$$

6 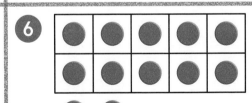 $$\begin{array}{r} 12 \\ -\ 8 \\ \hline \end{array}$$

Think About It **Number Sense**

Which difference do you think will be greater, $15 - 10$ or $15 - 8$? Explain.

Chapter 11 ★ Lesson 11 four hundred forty-one **441**

Cross out to subtract.

Use a ten-frame and counters if you like.

7 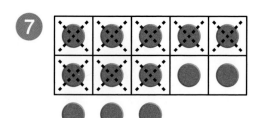 $\begin{array}{r} 13 \\ -\ \ 8 \\ \hline 5 \end{array}$

8 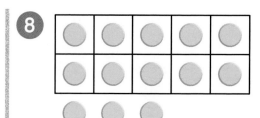 $\begin{array}{r} 13 \\ -\ \ 9 \\ \hline \end{array}$

9 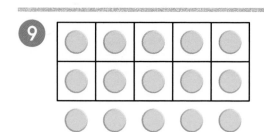 $\begin{array}{r} 15 \\ -\ \ 9 \\ \hline \end{array}$

10 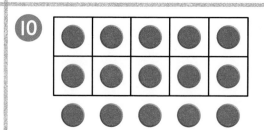 $\begin{array}{r} 16 \\ -\ \ 8 \\ \hline \end{array}$

11 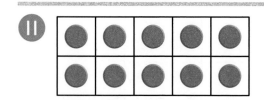 $\begin{array}{r} 17 \\ -\ \ 8 \\ \hline \end{array}$

12 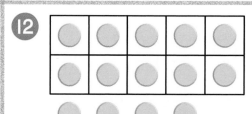 $\begin{array}{r} 14 \\ -\ \ 9 \\ \hline \end{array}$

13 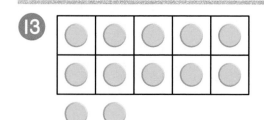 $\begin{array}{r} 12 \\ -\ \ 9 \\ \hline \end{array}$

14  $\begin{array}{r} 11 \\ -\ \ 8 \\ \hline \end{array}$

Problem Solving   Estimation

Circle your answer.

15 You bought a toy. You gave the clerk a dime and a few pennies. How much did the toy probably cost?

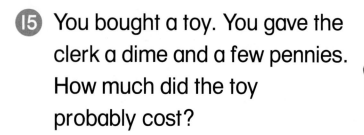

3¢   13¢   30¢

442   four hundred forty-two

Home Connection Your child used a ten-frame to subtract. **Home Activity** For Exercises 7 and 10 on this page, ask your child to write a subtraction sentence that takes away one more. (13 − 9 = 4; 16 − 9 = 7)

Name_____

You can use different strategies to subtract.

14 − 10 = 4, so
14 − 8 = 6.

$$\begin{array}{r} 14 \\ -8 \\ \hline 6 \end{array}$$

I can use a
related fact!
6 + 8 = 14, so
14 − 8 = 6.

Check ✓

Subtract.

Then circle the strategy that you used.

1
$$\begin{array}{r} 15 \\ -9 \\ \hline \end{array}$$
use a related fact

use 10

2
$$\begin{array}{r} 11 \\ -5 \\ \hline \end{array}$$
use a related fact

use 10

3
$$\begin{array}{r} 12 \\ -8 \\ \hline \end{array}$$
use a related fact

use 10

4
$$\begin{array}{r} 14 \\ -6 \\ \hline \end{array}$$
use a related fact

use 10

5
$$\begin{array}{r} 13 \\ -7 \\ \hline \end{array}$$
use a related fact

use 10

6
$$\begin{array}{r} 16 \\ -9 \\ \hline \end{array}$$
use a related fact

use 10

Think About It   Reasoning

Which strategy do you use more often?
Explain why.

Subtract.

7
13	14	17	15
− 9	− 7	− 8	− 6
4			

8
16	13	14	17	9	15
− 8	− 8	− 8	− 9	− 9	− 9

9
13	15	12	16	14	13
− 4	− 8	− 3	− 9	− 6	− 7

10
15	14	13	10	18	14
− 7	− 9	− 6	− 7	− 9	− 5

11
12	7	11	8	10	12
− 4	− 0	− 5	− 8	− 4	− 6

Problem Solving Reasonableness

Circle your answer.

12 If Jay has 12 − 8 ribbons and May has
12 − 5 ribbons, then which sentence is true?

Jay has more ribbons than May.

May has more ribbons than Jay.

Home Connection Your child chose a strategy and used it to subtract.
Home Activity Have your child explain how he or she solved the problems in Exercise 7.

Name_____

Learn! Algebra

Clifton has 7 bones. He gets 5 more bones. How many bones does Clifton have in all?

__7__ $\oplus$ __5__ = __12__ bones

If Clifton buries 6 of the bones, how many bones are not buried?

__12__ $\ominus$ __6__ = __6__ bones

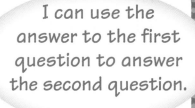

I can use the answer to the first question to answer the second question.

Check ✓

Solve each problem.

1   Kitty has 4 cat toys. She gets 3 more toys. How many toys does Kitty have in all?

___ ◯ ___ = ____ toys

If Kitty gets 8 more cat toys, how many toys will she have then?

___ ◯ ___ = ____ toys

Think About It   Reasoning

Can you answer the second question before you answer the first question? Explain.

Solve each problem.

2 There are 13 bunnies in the yard.
7 bunnies are brown. The rest are white.
How many bunnies are white?

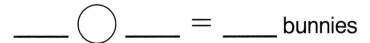

____ ◯ ____ = ____ bunnies

If 4 more white bunnies come into the yard,
how many white bunnies will there be in all?

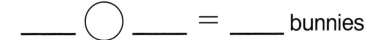

____ ◯ ____ = ____ bunnies

3 In a cage are 7 yellow birds and 7 orange birds.
How many birds are there in all?

____ ◯ ____ = ____ birds

Pam takes 5 birds from the cage.
How many birds are left in the cage?

____ ◯ ____ = ____ birds

4 The pet store has 9 hamsters.
The store gets 7 more hamsters.
How many hamsters does the store have now?

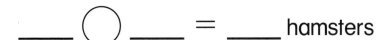

____ ◯ ____ = ____ hamsters

If the store sells 8 hamsters,
how many hamsters will be left?

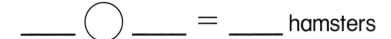

____ ◯ ____ = ____ hamsters

Home Connection Your child solved two-step story problems.
Home Activity Use spoons or forks to show an addition problem. Then
continue the problem by taking some away. Together with your child, write
the addition sentence and the subtraction sentence that solve the problem.

Name_____

Dorling Kindersley

1 One hen is hatching 7 eggs.
Another hen is hatching 7 eggs.
How many eggs are hatching in all?

____ ◯ ____ = ____

Do You Know...
an adult male chicken is called a rooster and an adult female chicken is called a hen?

2 There are 13 chicks
in the henhouse.
Only 4 of the chicks are noisy.
How many chicks are quiet?

____ ◯ ____ = ____

Circle the addition fact you used
to solve the problem.

6 + 7 = 13   7 + 7 = 14   4 + 9 = 13

Fun Fact!
Cows have four stomachs to digest the grass, corn, and hay that they eat.

3 There are 10 calves on the farm.
Only 4 of the calves are in the barn.
How many calves are not in the barn?

____ ◯ ____ = ____ calves

3 calves come back into the barn.
How many calves are in the barn now?

____ ◯ ____ = ____ calves

4 There are 6 pink pigs.
There are 4 spotted pigs.
There are 4 brown pigs.
How many pigs are there in all?

$$\begin{array}{r} 6 \\ 4 \\ +\ 4 \\ \hline \end{array}$$

There are _____ pigs in all.

5 If 1 pig is pink and 2 pigs are gray, what fraction of the pigs is pink?

$\dfrac{1}{2}$ $\dfrac{1}{3}$ $\dfrac{1}{4}$

6 A farmer bought 45 bags of feed.
Now he has 10 fewer than 45 bags.
How many bags does he have now?

_____ bags

7 Writing in Math

Draw a picture of 18 piglets.
Write a subtraction story about your picture.
Then write a number sentence to go with your story.

_____ ◯ _____ = _____

Name_____

Write an addition sentence and a subtraction sentence to go with the picture.

1

___ + ___ = ___

___ − ___ = ___

Use the numbers to write a fact family.

2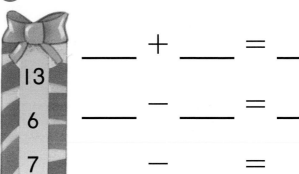

___ + ___ = ___

___ + ___ = ___

___ − ___ = ___

___ − ___ = ___

Add. Then use the addition fact to help you subtract.

3

9 + 6 = ___

so 15 − 6 = ___

Cross out to subtract.

4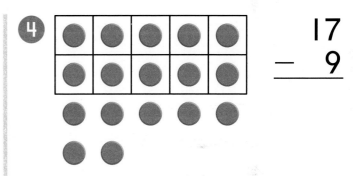

17
− 9
____

Solve each problem.

5 Ann put 9 red cars on the track. Then she put on 7 yellow cars. How many cars were on the track?

___ ◯ ___ = ___ cars

If Ann takes away 8 cars, how many cars will be left on the track?

___ ◯ ___ = ___ cars

Name_____

Add.

1
$$\begin{array}{r} 8 \\ + 8 \\ \hline \end{array}$$

14   15   16   17
Ⓐ   Ⓑ   Ⓒ   Ⓓ

2
$$\begin{array}{r} 2 \\ 7 \\ + 3 \\ \hline \end{array}$$

10   11   12   13
Ⓐ   Ⓑ   Ⓒ   Ⓓ

3 Which group of counters will help you find 8 + 4?

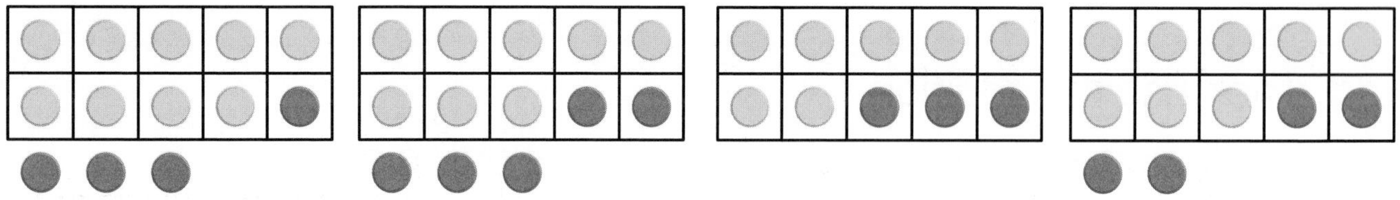

Ⓐ   Ⓑ   Ⓒ   Ⓓ

4 About how tall is a desk?

Ⓐ about 1 foot

Ⓑ about 2 feet

Ⓒ about 5 feet

Ⓓ about 8 feet

5 What is the missing number?

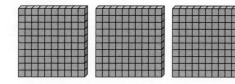

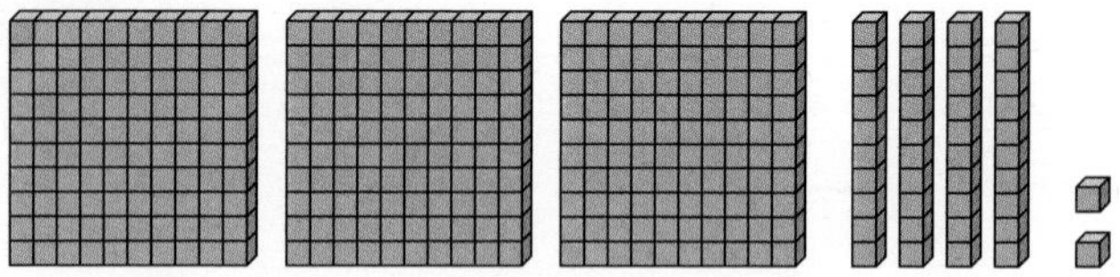

3 hundreds 4 tens 2 ones = _____

423   324   234   342
Ⓐ   Ⓑ   Ⓒ   Ⓓ

Chapter 11 ★ Section B

Multiplication as Repeated Addition

Sonia made this picture with more than 50 stickers.

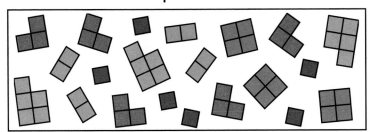

Can you find the three 5s?

Complete the table.

How many stickers are in each shape?	How many stickers are there in all?
① __5__	$5 + 5 + 5$ = __15__
② ____	= ____
③ ____	= ____
④ ____	= ____
⑤ ____	= ____

Writing in Math

⑥ If three 5s are 15, then how many are four 5s?

Explain how you got your answer.

_____

_____

Home Connection Your child encountered the idea of multiplication by doing repeated addition. **Home Activity** Ask your child to use addition to tell what four 3s equal and what five 2s equal. *(3 + 3 + 3 + 3 = 12; 2 + 2 + 2 + 2 + 2 = 10)*

Learning with Technology

Make Fact Families Using a Calculator

You can use a calculator to make a fact family.
Write the numbers you press for each fact.
Write the number in the display for each fact.
Press [ON/C] each time you begin.

1 Make a fact family.

2 Make another fact family.

3 Make a doubles fact family.

4 Make your own doubles fact family.

Think About It   Reasoning

How could you use a calculator to make a bigger doubles fact family?

Home Connection Your child used a calculator to make fact families (groups of related facts). **Home Activity** Ask your child to explain how he or she would make a fact family for 11 on a calculator. *(Sample answer: I would press 6 + 5 =, 5 + 6 =, 11 − 5 =, and 11 − 6 =.)*

Name _____

Make Smart Choices

What if you solve a problem, but your answer is not one of the choices? Try again!

Test-Taking Strategies

Understand the Question

Get Information for the Answer

Plan How to Find the Answer

Make Smart Choices

Use Writing in Math

1 Find the sum. Fill in the answer bubble.

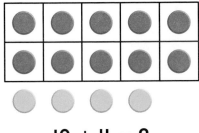

10 + 4 = ?

Ⓐ 10 Ⓑ 13 Ⓒ 14 Ⓓ 16

Your Turn

2 Find the sum. Fill in the answer bubble.

$$
\begin{array}{r}
7 \\
7 \\
+\ 3 \\
\hline
? \\
\end{array}
$$

Ⓐ 10 Ⓑ 14 Ⓒ 16 Ⓓ 17

You can do it!

Home Connection Your child prepared for standardized tests by learning that, if his or her answer is not one of the answer choices, he or she should try to solve the problem a second time. **Home Activity** Ask your child to explain how he or she solved the problem in Exercise 2. *(Some children will choose to add the doubles [7 + 7] first; other children will choose to make ten [7 + 3] first.)*

Name _____

 Read Together

Discover Math in Your World

DISCOVERY CHANNEL SCHOOL

Board Games

People have been playing board games for thousands of years. Pretend that you are playing a game with a friend.

Game Facts

Solve each problem. Watch out: The last one is tricky!

1 Your card says: Move 5 spaces. Your friend's card says: Move 5 spaces and then move 6 spaces. How many spaces will your friend move?

_____

2 Your next card says: Stay where you are. Your friend's card says: Go back 6 spaces. What space will your friend land on?

_____

3 Who is ahead now? Explain.

_____

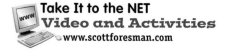
Take It to the NET
Video and Activities
www.scottforesman.com

Home Connection Your child solved problems about playing a game with a friend. **Home Activity** Ask your child to write a number sentence about playing a board game. For example, say to your child: "I moved 3 spaces on my first turn and 8 spaces on my second turn. How many spaces did I move altogether on those two turns?" (3 + 8 = 11 spaces)

Chapter 11

© Pearson Education, Inc.

Name_____

Add.

1
$$\begin{array}{r} 9 \\ + 6 \\ \hline \end{array}$$
$$\begin{array}{r} 5 \\ + 6 \\ \hline \end{array}$$
$$\begin{array}{r} 4 \\ + 9 \\ \hline \end{array}$$
$$\begin{array}{r} 7 \\ + 7 \\ \hline \end{array}$$
$$\begin{array}{r} 8 \\ 3 \\ + 2 \\ \hline \end{array}$$
$$\begin{array}{r} 5 \\ 6 \\ + 6 \\ \hline \end{array}$$

Subtract.

 2
$$\begin{array}{r} 16 \\ - 9 \\ \hline \end{array}$$
$$\begin{array}{r} 13 \\ - 8 \\ \hline \end{array}$$
$$\begin{array}{r} 12 \\ - 4 \\ \hline \end{array}$$
$$\begin{array}{r} 15 \\ - 7 \\ \hline \end{array}$$
$$\begin{array}{r} 16 \\ - 8 \\ \hline \end{array}$$
$$\begin{array}{r} 11 \\ - 5 \\ \hline \end{array}$$

Add the doubles.
Then use the doubles to help you add.

 3 *Think* $7 + 7 = $ _____   so $7 + 8 = $ _____

and $7 + 6 = $ _____

Draw the counters. Then write the sums.

4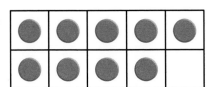

$$\begin{array}{r} 9 \\ + 6 \\ \hline \end{array}$$
$$\begin{array}{r} 10 \\ + 5 \\ \hline \end{array}$$

Write related addition and subtraction facts
to go with the picture.

____ + ____ = ____   ____ − ____ = ____

Add.

Then use the addition fact to help you subtract.

6

$6 + 8 =$ ___

so $14 - 8 =$ ___

Use the numbers to write a fact family.

7

___ $+$ ___ $=$ ___

___ $+$ ___ $=$ ___

___ $-$ ___ $=$ ___

___ $-$ ___ $=$ ___

Make a table to answer the question.

8 Eli has daisies and tulips.
The vase holds 2 flowers.
How many different ways can
Eli fill the vase?

There are ___ different ways.

Daisies	Tulips

Solve each problem.

9 Mrs. Green has 5 large pumpkins and 9 small
pumpkins. How many pumpkins does she have in all?

___ $\bigcirc$ ___ $=$ ___ pumpkins

Mrs. Green sells 7 pumpkins.
How many pumpkins does she have left?

___ $\bigcirc$ ___ $=$ ___ pumpkins

Paco and His Flying Saucer

Written by Howard Workman

Illustrated by Jackie Snider

This Math Storybook belongs to

_____

When Paco went shopping,
he saw exactly what he wanted.
A brand-new, bright red flying saucer!
The price tag read, "only **85** cents."
But Paco's piggy bank was empty.

How could he earn the money he needed?
"I guess I'll have to do some chores,"
he moaned and groaned.

12B

Paco's mom gave him **30** cents to water the plants.
Then she gave him another **30** cents
to feed the hamster.

And then she gave him another **30** cents
to take out the garbage.

"You should have enough money now," she said.

The woman behind the counter counted Paco's coins.
"You gave me too much money," she said. "I owe you some change."

"You do?" said Paco.

"I sure do," said the woman. "You gave me **90** cents, but your flying saucer costs only **85** cents. Here's your change."

Just then, Paco saw a shiny purple boomerang. The price tag read, "only **75** cents."

"WOW!" said Paco as the woman handed him his nickel in change.

"I'll be back as soon as I earn enough money for that boomerang!"

ONLY 85¢

ONLY 75¢

12F

Dear Family,

Today my class started Chapter 12, **Two-Digit Addition and Subtraction.** I will learn to add two-digit numbers and regroup when there are 10 or more ones. I will learn to subtract one two-digit number from another and regroup when there are not enough ones. Here are some of the math words I will be learning and some things we can do to help me with my math.

Love,

_____

Math Activity to Do at Home

Set out 10 dimes. Count the dimes by 10s with your child. Then pose addition problems for your child to solve using the dimes. For example, "How much are 3 tens and 3 tens?" Do the same with subtraction problems.

Books to Read Together

Reading math stories reinforces concepts. Look for these titles in your local library:

100 Days of School
By Trudy Harris
(Millbrook Press, 1999)

Shark Swimathon
By Stuart J. Murphy
(HarperCollins, 2001)

Take It to the NET
More Activities
www.scottforesman.com

My New Math Words

regrouping in addition You *make a ten* when the sum of the ones is 10 or more.

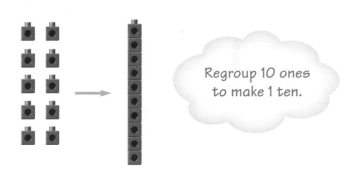

Regroup 10 ones to make 1 ten.

regrouping in subtraction You *break apart a ten* when there are not enough ones to subtract.

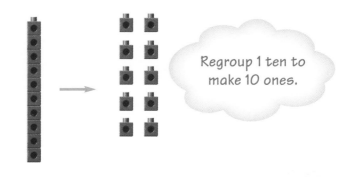

Regroup 1 ten to make 10 ones.

Money in the Bank

What You Need

I small game marker ●

How to Play

1. Toss your marker at the bank.
2. Add the amount the marker lands on to Paco's nickel.
3. Write a number sentence on a separate sheet of paper.
4. Keep playing until you have the 75¢ Paco needs to buy that boomerang!

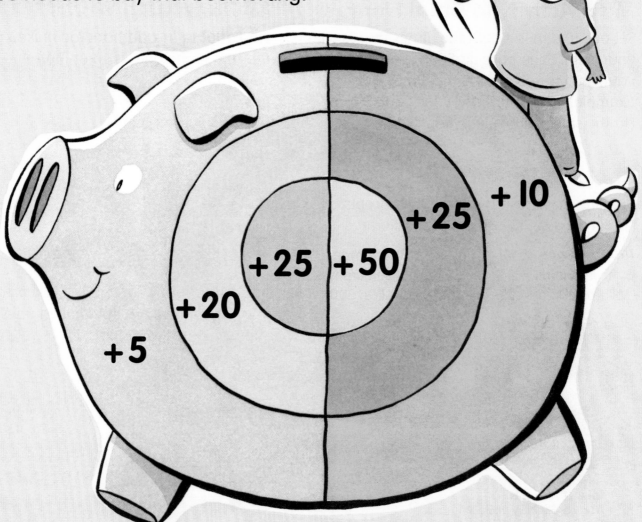

Name_____

Adding groups of 10 is like adding numbers less than 10.

3 groups of 10 plus 5 groups of 10 equals 8 groups of 10.

30 plus 50 equals 80.

30 + 50 = 80

Check ✓

Write each number sentence.

1

___ + ___ = ___

2

___ + ___ = ___

3

___ + ___ = ___

4

___ + ___ = ___

Think About It Reasoning

How is adding tens like adding numbers less than 10?

How is it different?

Write each sum.

5

40 + 10 = 50

6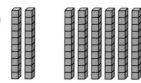

20 + 60 = ___

7

30 + 30 = ___   70 + 20 = ___   20 + 50 = ___

8

60 + 40 = ___   50 + 10 = ___   40 + 40 = ___

9

80 + 10 = ___   40 + 30 = ___   20 + 10 = ___

10

30 + 60 = ___   50 + 40 = ___   10 + 30 = ___

Problem Solving   Number Sense

Circle the two groups that answer the question.

11   Maria has two groups of stickers.
She has more than 70 stickers in all.
Which are Maria's stickers?

Name_____

How can you find the sum of 36 and 40?

Start at 36. Then count on by 10s: 46, 56, 66, 76.

36 + 40 = 76

Check ✓

Write each number sentence.

1

___ + ___ = ___

2

___ + ___ = ___

3

___ + ___ = ___

4

___ + ___ = ___

5

___ + ___ = ___

6

___ + ___ = ___

Think About It   Reasoning

When you add tens to a number, which digit changes? Which digit stays the same? Explain.

Write each number sentence.

7

$\underline{29} + \underline{50} = \underline{79}$

8

___ + ___ = ___

9

___ + ___ = ___

10

___ + ___ = ___

11

___ + ___ = ___

12

___ + ___ = ___

Problem Solving   Algebra

Write the missing numbers.

Then write the next addition problem in the pattern.

13

```
  24        34        44       [  ]      [  ]
+ 10      + [ ]     + 10      + 10     + [ ]
[  ]        44       [  ]       64      [  ]
```

Find the sum of 21 and 18.

First add the ones.　　　Then add the tens.

Check ✓

Write each sum.

Remember to add the ones first.

1

Tens	Ones
4	3
+ 5	6

Tens	Ones
3	5
+ 1	1

Tens	Ones
6	2
+ 2	4

Tens	Ones
3	1
+ 4	7

2

Tens	Ones
7	4
+ 1	4

Tens	Ones
2	7
+ 5	2

Tens	Ones
1	3
+ 4	6

Tens	Ones
6	1
+ 3	7

Think About It　Number Sense

Which two-digit numbers can you add to get a sum of 57?

Write each sum.

3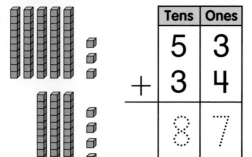

Tens	Ones
5	3
+ 3	4
8	7

4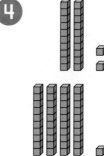

Tens	Ones
2	2
+ 4	1

5

Tens	Ones
1	5
+ 6	4

Tens	Ones
5	1
+ 3	1

Tens	Ones
2	3
+ 7	2

Tens	Ones
4	3
+ 1	6

6

Tens	Ones
2	5
+ 3	3

Tens	Ones
7	6
+ 2	1

Tens	Ones
5	4
+ 3	2

Tens	Ones
1	6
+ 1	2

Problem Solving   Reasoning

Circle the number that solves each riddle.

7 I am greater than 26 + 10.
I have more tens than ones.
Which number am I?

36   47   84

8 I am less than 12 + 25.
I have more ones than tens.
Which number am I?

31   26   52

Home Connection Your child learned how to add two-digit numbers without regrouping. **Home Activity** Ask your child to explain how to find the sum of 45 and 52. *(First add the ones and then add the tens; 97.)*

 **Learn!**

When there are 10 or more ones, you can regroup.

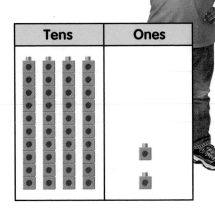

How do you add 4 to 38?

Show 38.
Add 4.

Regroup 10 ones as
1 ten to find the sum.

Tens	Ones

Tens	Ones

Tens	Ones

10 ones = 1 ten

$38 + 4 = \underline{42}$

Word Bank

regroup

Check ✓

Use cubes and Workmat 4. Do you need to regroup?
Circle **yes** or **no.** Then write the sum.

Show.	Add.	Do you need to regroup?	Find the sum.
1 15	8	(yes) no	$15 + 8 = \underline{}$
2 34	3	yes no	$34 + 3 = \underline{}$
3 65	5	yes no	$65 + 5 = \underline{}$
4 77	6	yes no	$77 + 6 = \underline{}$

Think About It   Reasoning

How do you know when you need to regroup?

Use cubes and Workmat 4. Do you need to regroup?
Circle **yes** or **no.** Then write the sum.

Show.	Add.	Do you need to regroup?	Find the sum.
5 47	5	(yes) no	$47 + 5 = 52$
6 62	8	yes no	$62 + 8 = \underline{}$
7 54	4	yes no	$54 + 4 = \underline{}$
8 23	6	yes no	$23 + 6 = \underline{}$
9 35	7	yes no	$35 + 7 = \underline{}$
10 16	9	yes no	$16 + 9 = \underline{}$
11 81	2	yes no	$81 + 2 = \underline{}$
12 78	3	yes no	$78 + 3 = \underline{}$

Problem Solving   Number Sense

Use the number line to add.

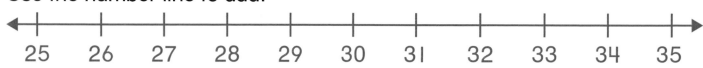

13 $26 + 5 = \underline{}$ | **14** $32 + 3 = \underline{}$

15 $29 + 1 = \underline{}$ | **16** $27 + 6 = \underline{}$

Home Connection Your child learned to add numbers with regrouping.
Home Activity Have your child explain how to find the sum of 13 and 8.
(21)

 **Learn!**

When can you estimate to solve a problem?

1 Yukiko has 2 packages of muffins.
Each package contains 9 muffins.
There are 20 children in her class.
Are there enough muffins for all of the children?

Read and Understand

We need to know if 2 packages of muffins are enough for 20 children. Do we need an exact answer or an estimate?

Plan and Solve

9 is less than 10, so $9 + 9$ is less than $10 + 10$. We can estimate that 2 packages contain fewer than 20 muffins.

exact answer 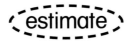 estimate

Look Back and Check

Does your answer make sense?

Think About It Reasoning

How did you decide whether you needed an exact answer or an estimate?

Circle **exact answer** or **estimate**.

2 Mrs. Cruz wants to put math books on her shelf.
The shelf is 40 inches wide.
Each math book is 2 inches thick.
How many books will fit on her shelf?

Do we need an exact answer or an estimate?

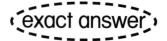 **exact answer**   estimate

---

3 Lidie wants to buy 5 apples.
They cost 12¢ each. She has 50¢.
Does she have enough money?

Do we need an exact answer or an estimate?

exact answer   estimate

---

4 Sandy wants to buy 9 bananas.
They cost 8¢ each. She has 90¢.
Does she have enough money?

Do we need an exact answer or an estimate?

exact answer   estimate

Problem Solving Estimation

Circle the better estimate.

5 About how many
can you hold in one hand?

about 10   about 100

6 About how many 🪙
can you hold in one hand?

about 5   about 50

Home Connection Your child determined whether an estimate or an exact answer was needed to solve a problem. **Home Activity** Ask your child to choose a problem on this page and to explain how he or she decided the answer.

Name_____

Write each number sentence.

 1

___ + ___ = ___

2 51

___ + ___ = ___

Write each sum.

3

Tens	Ones
1	5
+ 2	4

Tens	Ones
3	3
+ 3	2

Tens	Ones
4	7
+ 5	2

Tens	Ones
6	1
+ 1	7

Use cubes and Workmat 4. Do you need to regroup?
Circle **yes** or **no.** Then write the sum.

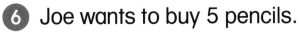

Show.	Add.	Do you need to regroup?	Find the sum.
4 35	5	yes no	35 + 5 = ___
5 43	6	yes no	43 + 6 = ___

Circle **exact answer** or **estimate.**

6 Joe wants to buy 5 pencils.
They cost 11¢ each. He has 50¢.
Does he have enough money?

Do we need an exact answer or an estimate?

exact answer   estimate

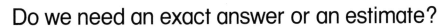

How much money in all?

31¢	36¢	41¢	51¢		37¢	42¢	50¢	52¢
Ⓐ	Ⓑ	Ⓒ	Ⓓ		Ⓐ	Ⓑ	Ⓒ	Ⓓ

3 Which fact is a related subtraction fact?

$$6 + 9 = 15$$

    Ⓐ $9 - 3 = 6$

    Ⓑ $15 - 9 = 6$

    Ⓒ $15 - 5 = 10$

    Ⓓ $9 - 6 = 3$

4 Which number sentence completes the fact family?

$$7 + 6 = 13$$

$$6 + 7 = 13$$

$$13 - 6 = 7$$

?

    Ⓐ $7 + 7 = 14$

    Ⓑ $6 + 6 = 12$

    Ⓒ $13 - 7 = 6$

    Ⓓ $13 - 3 = 10$

Writing in Math

5 Do all of the months of the year start on the same day of the week? Explain.

_____

_____

Subtracting groups of 10 is like
subtracting numbers less than 10.

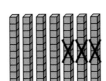

7 tens minus 3 tens
equals 4 tens.

70 – 30 = 40

Check ✓

Write each number sentence.

1

___ – ___ = ___

2

___ – ___ = ___

3

___ – ___ = ___

4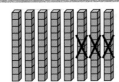

___ – ___ = ___

5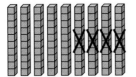

___ – ___ = ___

6

___ – ___ = ___

Think About It   Reasoning

How is subtracting tens like subtracting numbers
less than 10? How is it different?

Write each number sentence.

7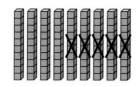

$$\underline{90} - \underline{50} = \underline{40}$$

8

$$\underline{} - \underline{} = \underline{}$$

9

$$\underline{} - \underline{} = \underline{}$$

10

$$\underline{} - \underline{} = \underline{}$$

11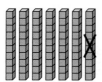

$$\underline{} - \underline{} = \underline{}$$

12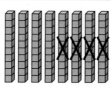

$$\underline{} - \underline{} = \underline{}$$

13

$$\underline{} - \underline{} = \underline{}$$

14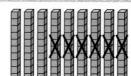

$$\underline{} - \underline{} = \underline{}$$

Problem Solving Mental Math

Solve.

15 A toy horse and a toy dog cost 60¢ altogether.
If the toy horse costs 40¢,
how much does the toy dog cost?

_____¢

40¢

?

Home Connection Your child subtracted groups of 10. **Home Activity** Ask your child to draw a picture of models like those shown above to show 80 − 30 and then find the difference. *(50)*

Name _____

 **Learn!**

How can you subtract 30 from 53?

$$53 - 30 = 23$$

Start at 53. Count back by 10s: 43, 33, 23.

Check ✓

Write each number sentence.

1

___ − ___ = ___

2

___ − ___ = ___

3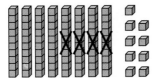

___ − ___ = ___

4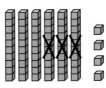

___ − ___ = ___

5

___ − ___ = ___

6

___ − ___ = ___

Think About It   Reasoning

When you subtract tens from any number, which
digit stays the same? Which digit changes? Explain.

Write each number sentence.

7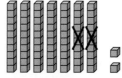

$$72 - 20 = 52$$

8

___ − ___ = ___

9

___ − ___ = ___

10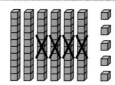

___ − ___ = ___

11

___ − ___ = ___

12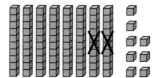

___ − ___ = ___

13

___ − ___ = ___

14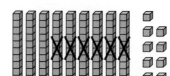

___ − ___ = ___

Problem Solving   Reasonableness

Answer the question.

15 Sara says that $45 - 30 = 75$.
Is she correct? Explain.

_____

_____

© Pearson Education, Inc.

Home Connection Your child subtracted tens from two-digit numbers.
Home Activity Ask your child to explain how to find the difference for
the problem 47 − 20. *(Start at 47 and then count back by 10s: 37, 27.)*

Learn!

Find the difference for the problem 27 − 14.

Tens	Ones
2	7
− 1	4
	3

Tens	Ones
2	7
− 1	4
1	3

First subtract the ones. | Then subtract the tens.

Check ✓

Write each difference.

Remember to subtract the ones first.

1

Tens	Ones
9	6
− 5	4

Tens	Ones
6	8
− 3	1

Tens	Ones
8	9
− 7	2

Tens	Ones
5	5
− 4	4

2

Tens	Ones
3	7
− 2	3

Tens	Ones
7	4
− 4	1

Tens	Ones
4	8
− 2	7

Tens	Ones
6	5
− 4	5

Think About It   Number Sense

Which number goes in the ones place when you
subtract all of the ones? Explain.

Practice

Write each difference.

3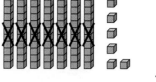

Tens	Ones
7	6
− 7	0
	6

4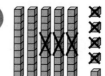

Tens	Ones
5	5
− 3	4

5

Tens	Ones
3	9
− 2	4

Tens	Ones
9	8
− 6	4

Tens	Ones
6	7
− 2	1

Tens	Ones
4	3
− 1	3

6

Tens	Ones
8	5
− 5	3

Tens	Ones
2	4
− 1	2

Tens	Ones
1	9
− 1	9

Tens	Ones
9	2
− 4	1

Problem Solving Algebra

Write the missing numbers.
Then write the next subtraction problem in the pattern.

7

```
  64      54      44      □       □
− 10    − □    − 10    − 10    − □
  □       44      □       24      □
```

Home Connection Your child learned to subtract two-digit numbers without regrouping. **Home Activity** Ask your child to explain how to find the difference for the problem 29 − 13. (*Subtract the ones and then subtract the tens; 16.*)

476 four hundred seventy-six

© Pearson Education, Inc.

If you need more ones, you can regroup.

Find the difference for the problem 43 − 8.

Show 43.
Are there enough ones to subtract?

Tens	Ones

Regroup
1 ten as 10 ones.

Tens	Ones

Subtract 8 to find the difference.

Tens	Ones

1 ten = 10 ones

43 − 8 = 35

Check ✓

Use cubes and Workmat 4. Do you need to regroup?
Circle **yes** or **no.** Then write the difference.

Show.	Subtract.	Do you need to regroup?	Find the difference.
❶ 32	5	(yes) no	32 − 5 = ___
❷ 56	4	yes no	56 − 4 = ___
❸ 75	9	yes no	75 − 9 = ___

Think About It   Reasoning

How do you know when you need to regroup?

Use cubes and Workmat 4. Do you need to regroup?
Circle **yes** or **no.** Then write the difference.

Show.	Subtract.	Do you need to regroup?		Find the difference.
④ 47	8	(yes)	no	47 − 8 = 39
⑤ 28	6	yes	no	28 − 6 = ___
⑥ 86	9	yes	no	86 − 9 = ___
⑦ 12	5	yes	no	12 − 5 = ___
⑧ 34	3	yes	no	34 − 3 = ___
⑨ 95	8	yes	no	95 − 8 = ___
⑩ 53	7	yes	no	53 − 7 = ___

Problem Solving Visual Thinking

Use the number line to subtract.

47   48   49   50   51   52   53   54   55   56   57

⑪ 57 − 6 = ___   ⑫ 51 − 4 = ___

⑬ 49 − 2 = ___   ⑭ 55 − 8 = ___

Home Connection Your child learned how to subtract numbers with regrouping. **Home Activity** Have your child explain how to find the difference for the problem 31 − 5. *(26)*

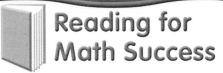

Reading for Math Success

Understand Graphic Sources: Graphs

1 Read this math problem.

Two first-grade classes collected soup labels to raise money for their school. The chart shows how many soup labels each class collected. Which class collected more?

Soup Labels Collected			
	Month 1	Month 2	Month 3
Room A	15	10	20
Room B	20	5	15

Then the classes made a graph to find out.

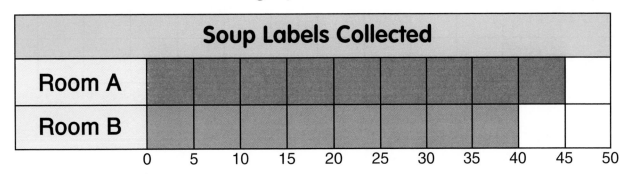

2 How many soup labels did Room A collect? _____ soup labels

3 How many soup labels did Room B collect? _____ soup labels

Think About It Reasoning

Which class collected more?

How can you use the graph to tell?

4 Read another math problem.

The first-grade classes also collected box tops to raise money for their school. The chart shows how many box tops each class collected. Which class collected more box tops?

Box Tops Collected			
	Month I	Month 2	Month 3
Room A	20	10	50
Room B	30	40	20

5 Complete the graph below to show how many box tops each class collected.

Box Tops Collected										
Room A										
Room B										

0   10   20   30   40   50   60   70   80   90   100

6 How many box tops did each class collect?

Room A: _____ box tops

Room B: _____ box tops

7 Which class collected more box tops?

_____

Home Connection Your child completed a graph to help solve a word problem. **Home Activity** Ask your child to explain how he or she used the graph on this page to determine how many box tops each class collected and which class collected more.

Name _____

You can make a graph to solve this problem.

1 Amy's class collected cans for recycling. Which team collected more cans?

Cans Collected				
	Week 1	Week 2	Week 3	Week 4
Blue Team	5	15	10	5
Green Team	20	10	5	15

Read and Understand

The chart shows how many cans each team collected. We want to find which team collected the greater number of cans.

Plan and Solve

Use the information in the chart to make a graph. Color one box for every 5 cans.

Cans Collected										
Blue Team	▨	▨	▨	▨	▨	▨	▨			
Green Team										

0   5   10   15   20   25   30   35   40   45   50

The _____ Team collected more cans.

Look Back and Check

How can you be sure your answer is correct?

Think About It   Reasoning

How could you show the same information using a tally chart or a picture graph?

Make a graph to solve the problem.

2 Miguel's class collected paper for recycling. The chart shows how many pounds of paper each team collected. Which team collected the most paper? **Color one box for every 10 pounds of paper.**

Paper Collected (in Pounds)				
	Week 1	Week 2	Week 3	Week 4
Yellow Team	10	20	20	30
Orange Team	20	30	30	20
Purple Team	20	20	10	30

Paper Collected										
Yellow Team										
Orange Team										
Purple Team										

0   10   20   30   40   50   60   70   80   90   100

The _____ Team collected the most paper.

Writing in Math

3 Write another question that could be answered using the bar graph above.

_____

_____

Home Connection Your child made graphs to solve problems. **Home Activity** Ask your child to explain how he or she made and used the graph on this page to solve the problem above.

Name_____

Dorling Kindersley

Do You Know...
that kittens should have regular checkups at the vet to help them stay healthy?

1 Haruo fed his kitten 33 fish bits in the morning and 20 fish bits in the evening. How many fish bits did Haruo feed his kitten altogether?

____ ◯ ____ = ____ fish bits

2 The next day Haruo gave his kitten 44 fish bits. His kitten ate only 20 of them. How many fish bits were left?

____ ◯ ____ = ____ fish bits

Fun Fact!

House cats belong to the same family as lions, tigers, and jaguars. They are all felines.

3 The animal shelter had 8 tabby kittens and 5 ragdoll kittens. How many kittens did the shelter have in all?

____ ◯ ____ = ____ kittens

6 kittens were adopted. How many kittens were left?

____ ◯ ____ = ____ kittens

4 The pet store had 58 cat brushes.
The store sold 14 of them.
How many brushes were left?

Tens	Ones
5	8
− 1	4

_____ brushes

5 There were 21 kittens at the pet store.
The Morris family bought 2 kittens.
How many kittens were left?

$21 - 2 =$ _____ kittens

6 Luz has

     .

She buys a toy for 42¢. Will she get change? _____

7 **Writing in Math**

Luz wants to buy a cat toy
for 48¢ and a cat snack
for 8¢. Does Luz need
to regroup to find how much
it will cost in all? Explain.

Home Connection Your child learned to solve problems by applying
his or her math skills. **Home Activity** Talk to your child about how he
or she solved the problems on these two pages.

Name _____

Write each number sentence.

 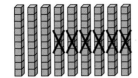

____ − ____ = ____

2

____ − ____ = ____

3

____ − ____ = ____

4

____ − ____ = ____

Write each difference.

Tens	Ones
4	8
− 2	4

Tens	Ones
5	6
− 4	1

Tens	Ones
7	5
− 3	2

Tens	Ones
8	9
− 5	3

Use cubes and Workmat 4. Do you need to regroup?
Circle **yes** or **no.** Then write the difference.

Show.	Subtract.	Do you need to regroup?	Find the difference.
6 61	5	yes no	61 − 5 = ____
7 47	6	yes no	47 − 6 = ____

Name_____

1 How many eyes are there? Count by twos.

   Ⓐ 6

   Ⓑ 10

   Ⓒ 12

   Ⓓ 14

---

2 Which fact will help you subtract?

$12 - 4 =$ ___

   Ⓐ $8 + 4 = 12$

   Ⓑ $4 + 4 = 8$

   Ⓒ $12 - 1 = 11$

   Ⓓ $10 + 4 = 14$

---

3 Which number sentence matches the picture?

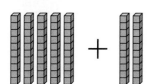

   Ⓐ $40 + 10 = 50$

   Ⓑ $40 + 20 = 60$

   Ⓒ $50 - 10 = 60$

   Ⓓ $50 + 20 = 70$

What is the sum?

4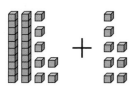

$27 + 8 =$ ___

24	25	34	35
Ⓐ	Ⓑ	Ⓒ	Ⓓ

5

Tens	Ones
3	2
+ 4	6

14	42	78	88
Ⓐ	Ⓑ	Ⓒ	Ⓓ

Name_____

Adding and Subtracting Three-Digit Numbers

First add the ones.
Then add the tens
and then the hundreds.

Add

Hundreds	Tens	Ones
1	5	7
+ 4	2	1
5	7	8

First subtract the ones.
Then subtract the tens
and then the hundreds.

Subtract

Hundreds	Tens	Ones
6	3	9
− 2	2	8
4	1	1

Add. Use models if you like.

1

Hundreds	Tens	Ones
2	1	0
+ 7	5	9

Hundreds	Tens	Ones
6	3	8
+ 3	4	1

Hundreds	Tens	Ones
5	6	2
+ 4	2	7

Subtract. Use models if you like.

2

Hundreds	Tens	Ones
7	7	5
− 4	6	2

Hundreds	Tens	Ones
9	9	9
− 3	5	1

Hundreds	Tens	Ones
8	6	3
− 1	4	0

 Home Connection Your child added and subtracted three-digit numbers without regrouping. **Home Activity** Ask your child to explain how he or she did the first problem in each exercise.

Name _____

Add and Subtract Using a Calculator

You can use a calculator to add and subtract.

Draw a path from **Start** to **Target.**
Use your calculator to help you.

1 Add.
Find the **Target Sum.**

Start		
12	15	80
91	33	14
27	42	1

Target Sum: 75

2 Subtract.
Find the **Target Difference.**

Start		
92	58	76
25	37	11
14	10	9

Target Difference: 11

Add and subtract in Exercises 3 and 4.
Find the **Target** number.

3

Start		
25	+ 5	+10
−10	+20	− 5
+ 5	−10	+10

Target: 40

4

Start		
0	+25	−20
−50	+35	+30
+5	−15	+45

Target: 100

Think About It   Number Sense

In Exercise 2, how did you use a calculator to figure
out that you were close to the Target Difference?

Home Connection Your child used a calculator to add and
subtract two-digit numbers. **Home Activity** Ask your child to
explain how to find the sum of 23 and 48 on a calculator.

Name_____

 Read Together

Use Writing in Math

When you write an answer to a math question, your answer should be **short** but **complete.**

1 There were 43 cans in the recycling bin. Sharon put 20 more cans in the bin. How many cans are in the bin now?

Now there are 63 cans in the recycling bin.

Here is how a boy named Tony solved this problem. He added the number of cans: 43 cans + 20 cans = 63 cans in all. Then he used words from the question to help him write his answer.

Which words did Tony use?
Raise your hand if you can find some of them.

Your Turn

Read the problem. Then write a **short** but **complete** answer to the question.

2 In May, Mr. Murphy's class collected 59 cans. Ms. Nelson's class collected 38 cans. How many more cans did Mr. Murphy's class collect?

_____

_____

 Home Connection Your child prepared for standardized tests by writing a complete answer to a math question. **Home Activity** Have your child explain how he or she solved the problem in Exercise 2. Then ask your child which words from the question he or she used in the answer.

four hundred eighty-nine   **489**

Discover Math in Your World

Discovery CHANNEL
SCHOOL

Read Together

All Aboard!

Have you ever been on a train? It is fun to travel by train. The first trains in the United States were built many years ago. Today's trains can go much faster than the first ones could. Use subtraction to find out how much faster.

Tracking Train Speeds

1 The first trains could travel 20 miles in one hour. Stagecoaches could travel only 7 miles in one hour. How many more miles could the first trains travel in one hour?

_____ miles

2 Today, most passenger trains in the United States travel 79 miles in one hour. How many more miles can they travel in one hour than the first trains?

_____ miles

3 The fastest trains in Japan and France can travel 186 miles in one hour. The fastest train in the United States can travel 150 miles in one hour. How many more miles can the trains in Japan and France travel in one hour?

_____ miles

Take It to the NET
Video and Activities
www.scottforesman.com

Home Connection Your child solved problems that compared the speeds of different trains and a stagecoach. **Home Activity** Discuss the distance 20 miles in relation to your home and another location. Then ask your child to tell you how many more miles a passenger train in the United States can travel in one hour than a stagecoach could travel decades ago. *(143 miles)*

© Pearson Education, Inc.

Chapter Test

Write each number sentence.

___ + ___ = ___

②

___ − ___ = ___

③

___ + ___ = ___

④

___ − ___ = ___

⑤

___ + ___ = ___

⑥

___ − ___ = ___

Write each sum.

⑦

Tens	Ones
4	2
+ 5	6

Tens	Ones
1	6
+ 7	1

Tens	Ones
2	4
+ 3	2

Tens	Ones
3	3
+ 6	2

Write each difference.

⑧

Tens	Ones
9	8
− 7	6

Tens	Ones
6	5
− 4	2

Tens	Ones
8	7
− 5	3

Tens	Ones
7	9
− 2	6

Use cubes and Workmat 4. Do you need to regroup?
Circle **yes** or **no**. Then write the sum.

Show.	Add.	Do you need to regroup?	Find the sum.
⑨ 55	8	yes no	55 + 8 = ___
⑩ 34	5	yes no	34 + 5 = ___
⑪ 47	6	yes no	47 + 6 = ___

Use cubes and Workmat 4. Do you need to regroup?
Circle **yes** or **no**. Then write the difference.

Show.	Subtract.	Do you need to regroup?	Find the difference.
⑫ 52	8	yes no	52 − 8 = ___
⑬ 29	7	yes no	29 − 7 = ___
⑭ 35	9	yes no	35 − 9 = ___

Circle **exact answer** or **estimate**.

⑮ Julio has 2 baskets of apples.
Each basket has 12 apples.
There are 20 children in his class.
Are there enough apples for all of the children?

Do we need an exact answer or an estimate?

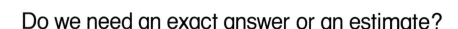

exact answer   estimate

Name_____

Subtract.

1
$$
\begin{array}{r}
70 \\
-\ 20 \\
\hline
\end{array}
$$

40	50	60	70
Ⓐ	Ⓑ	Ⓒ	Ⓓ

2
$$
\begin{array}{r}
83 \\
-\ 50 \\
\hline
\end{array}
$$

13	30	33	43
Ⓐ	Ⓑ	Ⓒ	Ⓓ

3 Which shape is divided into equal parts?

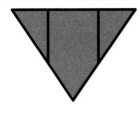         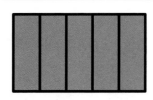

  Ⓐ   Ⓑ   Ⓒ   Ⓓ

4 Which would you use to find how long the bug is?

  Ⓐ   Ⓑ   Ⓒ   Ⓓ

5 Which fact completes the fact family?

$$
\begin{array}{c}
9 + 4 = 13 \\
4 + 9 = 13 \\
13 - 9 = 4 \\
? \\
\end{array}
$$

Ⓐ $13 - 4 = 9$

Ⓑ $13 - 7 = 6$

Ⓒ $4 + 5 = 9$

Ⓓ $9 - 4 = 5$

Add.

$$50 + 30$$ $$22 + 20$$ $$23 + 65$$ $$58 + 7$$ $$43 + 7$$

Circle the shape that shows a flip of the first boot.

Add. Then use the addition fact to help you.

$$4 + 9 = \underline{\hphantom{00}}$$

so $$13 - 4 = \underline{\hphantom{00}}$$

Write how much money in all.

In All
_____ ¢

Writing in Math

10 Explain how the facts in this fact family are related.

$$8 + 9 = 17 \qquad 17 - 8 = 9$$
$$9 + 8 = 17 \qquad 17 - 9 = 8$$

_____

_____

492B

Picture Glossary

add

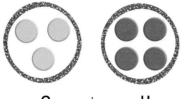

$$3 + 4 = 7$$

---

addition sentence

$$3 + 2 = 5$$

addends

---

after

5 comes **after** 4.

---

bar graph

Favorite Pets

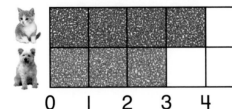

0   1   2   3   4   5

---

before

2 comes **before** 3.

---

between

3 comes **between** 2 and 4.

---

calendar

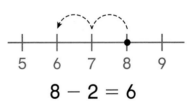

← month
← days
← date

← week

---

cent (¢)

A penny is 1 **cent** (1¢).

---

centimeter

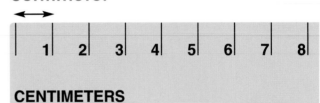

CENTIMETERS

---

circle

---

cone

---

count back

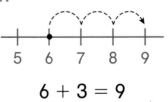

$$8 - 2 = 6$$

---

count on

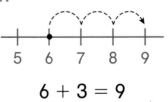

$$6 + 3 = 9$$

---

cube

cup

cylinder

difference

$$8 - 3 = 5$$

$$\begin{array}{r} 8 \\ -3 \\ \hline 5 \end{array}$$

difference

dime

10¢ or 10 cents

dollar

$1.00 or 100¢

doubles fact

$$3 \quad + \quad 3 \quad = \quad 6$$

equal parts

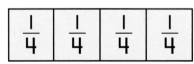

4 equal parts

equals (=)

$$2 + 3 = 5 \qquad 5 = 3 + 2$$

equals

estimate

about 10 strawberries

even numbers

2, 4, 6, 8, 10, ...

fact family

$$7 + 2 = 9 \qquad 9 - 7 = 2$$
$$2 + 7 = 9 \qquad 9 - 2 = 7$$

foot

A **foot** is 12 inches.

fraction

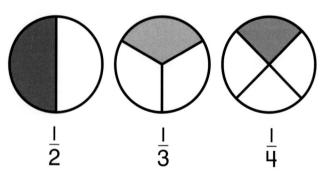

$$\frac{1}{2} \qquad \frac{1}{3} \qquad \frac{1}{4}$$

greater than (>)

4 is **greater than** 2.

$$4 > 2$$

half-dollar

50¢ or 50 cents

half hour

A **half hour** is 30 minutes.

hour

hour hand

An **hour** is 60 minutes.

inch

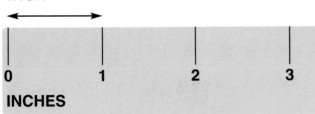

| 0 | 1 | 2 | 3 |

INCHES

kilogram

The book measures about 1 **kilogram**.

less than (<)

2 is **less than** 3.

2 < 3

line of symmetry

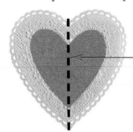

line of symmetry

liter

minus (−)

7 − 4 = 3

minus

minute

minutes   **minute hand**

There are 60 **minutes** in 1 hour.

nickel

5¢ or 5 cents

number line

number sentence

$$1 + 4 = 5$$

o'clock

It is 8 **o'clock**.

odd numbers

1, 3, 5, 7, 9, ...

ordinal numbers

fifth shelf

fourth shelf

third shelf

second shelf

first shelf

pattern unit

A B B A B B A B B

penny

1¢ or 1 cent

picture graph

Favorite Toys					
Balls	⚾	⚾	⚾	⚾	⚾
Skates	🛼	🛼	🛼	🛼	

pint

place value

hundreds   **tens**   **ones**

1   2   4

There are 1 hundred, 2 tens, and 4 ones in 124.

plus (+)

$$6 + 2 = 8$$

plus

pound

The bread weighs about 1 **pound**.

probability

It is **certain** to pick a .

It is **impossible** to pick a .

quart

quarter

25¢ or 25 cents

rectangle

rectangular prism

related facts

$$5 + 4 = 9$$
$$9 - 5 = 4$$

sphere

square

subtract

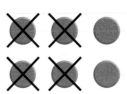

$$6 - 4 = 2$$

subtraction sentence

$$8 - 3 = 5$$

sum

$$2 + 3 = 5 \qquad \begin{array}{r} 2 \\ + 3 \\ \hline 5 \end{array}$$

⎿___ **sum** ___⏌

tally marks

temperature

°F

78

thermometer ⟶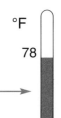

triangle

Credits